CONFLICT MINERALS

/ AFRICAN
/ ARGUMENTS

African Arguments is a series of short books about contemporary Africa and the critical issues and debates surrounding the continent. The books are scholarly and engaged, substantive and topical. They focus on questions of justice, rights and citizenship; politics, protests and revolutions; the environment, land, oil and other resources; health and disease; economy: growth, aid, taxation, debt and capital flight; and both Africa's international relations and country case studies.

Managing Editor, Stephanie Kitchen

Series editors

Adam Branch
Alex de Waal
Alcinda Honwana
Ebenezer Obadare
Carlos Oya
Nicholas Westcott

CHRISTOPH N. VOGEL

Conflict Minerals Inc.

War, Profit and White Saviourism in
Eastern Congo

HURST & COMPANY, LONDON

IAI International African Institute

Published in collaboration with the International African Institute.
First published in the United Kingdom in 2022 by
C. Hurst & Co. (Publishers) Ltd.,
New Wing, Somerset House, Strand, London, WC2R 1LA
Copyright © Christoph N. Vogel, 2022
All rights reserved.

Printed in Great Britain by Bell and Bain Ltd, Glasgow

The right of Christoph N. Vogel to be identified as the author
of this publication is asserted by him in accordance with the
Copyright, Designs and Patents Act, 1988.
Maps and Graphics: Giovanni Salvaggio

A Cataloguing-in-Publication data record for this book
is available from the British Library.

ISBN: 9781787387065

This book is printed using paper from registered sustainable
and managed sources.

www.hurstpublishers.com

Figures © Giovanni Salvaggio, 2022
Cover picture © Christoph N. Vogel, 2014

CONTENTS

LIST OF FIGURES AND TABLES

Figures

Tables

ACKNOWLEDGEMENTS

This book benefitted enormously from a huge number of friends and the generous support from different institutions, in particular the Swiss National Science Foundation, the Mercator Foundation, DAAD, the Rift Valley Institute, Congo Research Group and the FWO in Belgium. Moreover, I am grateful to five journals—*Review of African Political Economy*, *Antipode*, *Political Geography*, *Journal of Modern African Studies*, and *Extractive Industries and Society*—as well as the Governance in Conflict network at Ghent University for permission to draw from articles I have published with them.

I am deeply grateful to Stephanie Kitchen at the International African Institute, and Alice Clarke, Michael Eckhardt and the entire Hurst Publishers and Oxford University Press teams managing the African Arguments series. Without their steadfast support and wise guidance, this book surely would not exist. Moreover, very special thanks go to Giovanni Salvaggio, partner in crime and best mapmaker in the world, as well as to the International Peace Information Service and the Kivu Security Tracker for allowing me to use their geographical datasets on mine sites and violent incidents, respectively.

The first timid steps towards this book happened over a decade ago. Finalising a piece of work that has taken so long inevitably requires giving thanks to a huge number of colleagues, friends and companions. I have been blessed to work

ACKNOWLEDGEMENTS

with tremendous humans at Cologne University, Makerere University, the University of Zurich, New York University, ISP–Bukavu, Ghent University and elsewhere. If the roles of Timothy Raeymaekers, Koen Vlassenroot, Jason Stearns, Godefroid Muzalia, Benedikt Korf, Judith Verweijen, Kasper Hoffmann, Louisa Lombard and Christian Lund (who urged me to write this book) are not always sufficiently reflected, they were crucial in shaping my intellectual curiosity.

Walking the thorny paths of academia, I was lucky to find like-minded, supportive and inspiring mentors and peers, in particular Michel Thill, Ben Radley, Aymar Bisoka, Peer Schouten, David Mwambari, Stephan Hochleithner, Thiruni Kelegama, Rony Emmenegger, Esther Marijnen, Rachel Niehuus, Samuel Graf, Jasmine Truong, Maarten Hendriks, Muriel Côte, Karen Büscher, Marielle Debos, Kristof Titeca, Jeroen Cuvelier and Jean-Paul Kimonyo. Alongside those I forgot, they taught me to learn, understand and always remain critical towards both myself and the world around me.

I would not have had the chance to engage Congo, its history and its people if it were not for innumerable encounters, interviews and moments since 2008 with friends and guardian angels like Lievin Mbarushimana, Blaise Karege, Willy Mikenye, Gentil Kombi, Chrispin Mvano, Loochi Muzaliwa, Paulin Bishakabalya, Safanto Bulongo, Nissé Mughendi, Gérard Kikwaya, Oscar Dunia, Juvénal Twaibu, Wolf Sinzahera, David Ngoy, Claude Iguma, Kapeta Benda-Benda, Jimmy Matumona, Nickson Kambale, Bienvenu Matumo, Jean-Mobert Nsenga, Fred Bauma, Luc Nkulula, Zacharie Bulakali, Lebon Mulimbi, Jolino Malukisa, Christian Dolo, Sekombi Katondolo, Ganza Buroko, Christophe Hakizimana, Emile Gandika, Emmanuel Ndimubanzi, Bruno Kindu, Ley Uwera, Tembo Kashauri, Freddy Tsimba, Patient Ligodi, the entire *Baraza La Nchi*, *Cercle de Concertation* and *Kinshasa Masolo* crowds, GEC-SH and the Bukavu team, and

ACKNOWLEDGEMENTS

all the others who welcomed me and shared so much kindness and knowledge.

In and outside Congo, I was blessed to stand on the shoulders of giants such as Sonia Rolley, Richard Zink, Oliver Meisenberg, Emmanuel Lampaert, Jenö Staehelin, Warner ten Kate, Jean Baillaud, Cedric Turlan, Michelle Dörlemann, Trésor Kibangula, Pierre Boisselet, Ken Matthysen, Willet Weeks, Michel Kassa, Andreas Spaeth, Greg Mthembu-Salter, Michael Kavanagh, Justine Brabant, Chloé Lewis, Juvénal Munubo, Tristan terryn, Yangu Kiakwama, Dino Mahtani, Simone Schlindwein, Mélanie Gouby, Teddy Mazina, Filipe Ribeiro, Tatiana Carayannis, Christof Ruhmich, Manu Ngueyanouba, Bertrand Perrochet, Carlos Schuler, Nestor Bidadanure, Willy Nindorera, Rosebell Kagumire, Sean Jacobs, Philippe Beauverd, Tariq Riebl, Emilie Serralta, Zobel Behalal, Daniel Fahey, Alexis Huguet, Rachel Sweet, Diane Bihannic and Hanne Michiel.

Some people were and are a constant refuge, in particular Larissa Fuhrmann and Husam Suliman, Dirk Gillebert and Assia Barry, Joschka Havenith and Sara Blasco, Dominique Vidale-Plaza, Nadine Lusi, Nico Nassenstein, Ole Feltes, Yves Makwambala and Annabelle Giudice. I thank my family, Michèle, Oskar and Olivier, and the entire 'Clan Kitenge (and Mbuyu)'—Papa Louis, Maman Marcelline, André, Jean, Moridja, Honoré, Bobo, Ginette, Christian, Françoise, Kyungu, Kabange, Pascal and their families.

It goes without saying that I owe big thanks to Josaphat, husband to Elisée and proud daddy of Christoph and Nuru, with whom I conducted so many months of field research. Doing ethnography and investigations in violent environments carries important safety but also political and ethical caveats.[1] Moreover, criticising Orientalist, imperial and colonial practice also requires revisiting one's own positionality.[2] Despite being beyond the scope of this book, I have reflected, with others, on these challenges elsewhere.[3] Hence, while this book and some of my other works

ACKNOWLEDGEMENTS

that inspired it are, problematically, single-authored, a range of other publications reflect the crucial relevance of collaborative work to learn and produce situated knowledge together.[4] *Asante.*

Engaging and embracing Congo inevitably comes with gains and losses. MJ, my brother from another mother, and Zaida were murdered in 2017 while we worked together for the UN Security Council. Ever since, we mourn them and hold their memory high. MJ called Congo 'a paradise', surprising UN workers and his own parents alike. But I believe many Congolese may understand what he meant. Kevin Dunn wrote a very good paragraph on what MJ and I saw when we travelled eastern Congo together for work:

> Kivu is located on the very boundary between the more centralised kingdoms of Rwanda and Uganda and the more fluid political systems of Central Africa's forest regions. It is a place of mighty mountains, active volcanoes, dense forests, fertile soil, excellent grazing land and mineral riches, but also of immense population pressures. It is a meeting place and a melting pot, but also an area that repeatedly has tasted the bitter fruit of conflict, most often between groups claiming the status of autochthony and those defined as 'strangers.'[5]

One of the most basic challenges in writing about and researching a place like eastern Congo is to give space to violence and despair without essentialising it. Alongside the wealth of Congolese friends and companions, whom I failed to name exhaustively due to either confidentiality or gaps in my memory, both MJ and Kevin Dunn's words taught me a bit more in that regard. Finally, many years before working with MJ, in 2008, I first met Valériane, who has been a dear friend ever since, and became much more than that much later. If my doctoral dissertation was dedicated to MJ and Zaida, this book is for you, Valériane.

PROLOGUE

Congo is grand, it requires grandeur from us too.

(Luc Nkulula in reference to Patrice Emery Lumumba)[1]

This book deals with transnational issues. It is a product of transnational writing and of living in Zurich, Brussels, Paris, Goma, Bukavu, Bujumbura, Kinshasa, Kampala, Bangui, Havana and Cologne. Nonetheless, everything begins and ends in Congo.[2] If some call it the heart of darkness, I have my reasons to also call it the heart of brightness.[3] Having spent a few months working there in 2008 and 2009, I returned in 2010 to do research: on 15 October, I was at Kinshasa's N'Djili Airport, boarding a Goma-bound United Nations aircraft. After previous trips to the western and northern parts of the second-largest African country, this was my first time in eastern Congo. After the doors had closed and the cross-checks were complete, the pilots announced the flight would be rerouted to Bukavu, South Kivu, Goma's sister city at the other end of Lake Kivu. I was slightly irritated as I did not know anybody there. Before take-off, I managed to message friends asking for help. Landing at Kavumu Airport, 20 kilometres outside Bukavu, my phone buzzed with suggestions and I was able to connect with two humanitarians in town. Due to fighting earlier that day, the UN mission—freshly renamed MONUSCO (United Nations Organization Stabilization Mission in the Democratic Republic of the Congo)—offered a bus liaison, escorting us with armoured vehicles and a batch of Pakistani peacekeepers. Welcome to Kivu, *maisha ni nguvu apa*.[4]

Back then, I did field research for my master's thesis on the interplay between humanitarian action and armed groups.[5] Incidentally, three months earlier, in July 2010, then US President Barack Obama had signed one of the broadest packages of law in recent American history. Sponsored by lawmakers Chris Dodd and Barney Frank, and thus known as the Dodd–Frank Act, the Wall Street Reform and Consumer Protection Act of 2010 primarily aimed to re-regulate American financial markets after the 2008 subprime and mortgage crisis. Having failed to pass as a standalone law before then, section 1502 became part of the 'miscellaneous provisions'. Hidden there, the *loi Obama*—as Congolese call it—is one of the most impactful foreign laws on Congo: it stipulates that companies listed on US stock markets must disclose whether or not their supply chains contain gold or any of the so-called 3T minerals,[6] known as 'conflict minerals', sourced from Congo or its neighbouring countries. While my curiosity about everything else in Central Africa has continued, analysing the impact of Obama's law would—between 2013 and 2018—be a key objective of my PhD.

Why Conflict Minerals Inc.?

In 2014, Jean Bofane, a friend and one of the most gifted contemporary Congolese fiction writers, called his second novel *Congo Inc.* Much like that novel (which is albeit written in far better prose), this book is a story about Congo's transnational connections, in both social and technological terms. While I cannot claim to read Jean Bofane's mind, the idea of 'Inc.' (as in 'incorporated') hints at a host of things that speak evenly to this book. First of all, Congo, in its tragic *grandezza*, incorporates hope and despair at the same time. Beyond that, however, it also incorporates the world, its politics and its economy through the ways in which it has traversed modern history. More specifically, like *Congo Inc.*'s protagonist Isookanga, Congolese miners have become entangled in a transnational frenzy, pushing them to seek quick fortunes. Also, like Isookanga, mining entrepreneurs in eastern Congo have become—literally—incorporated in a destiny that is marked by external interference and internal quagmire.

If most writers, columnists and observers often fall into Manichean traps of Orientalism when narrating Congo, we know more than ever that there is little to gain in understanding the country without giving space to situated knowledge and the ambiguity that reigns beyond the white gaze. This requires us to perform an epistemic surrender in which we abandon our own worldviews and replace them with alternative angles, to research places beyond our lifeworlds, and to reconcile existing preconceptions with new knowledge and different ways of producing it. This book tries to contribute a small part to that, acknowledging that against all essentialist odds, Congo is an incorporating entity for those engaging with it. In so many ways, just as Luc Nkulula put it in the above quotation, it is exigent, demanding and pluriversal.

INTRODUCTION

Imagine consumers could shape industry and policy for the better. Children would leave sweatshops for schools, critical drugs and vaccines would be available based on need rather than purchase power, and mobile phones would be made of rare earths sourced from peaceful places. Occasionally, we tend to believe this is but a question of relentless campaigning and subsequent laws and policies. Videos going viral, online petitions, hashtags and clicks, billboards on college campuses—introduce new legislation on the floor of the US House and change happens. Nevertheless, some of that hope is grounded in a tragic illusion of a truly transnational humanity.

In a globalised world, digital connections are so ubiquitous that we take them for granted. In our digital frenzy, Facebook brings us closer to the other end of the globe than to our own neighbours. Outside of pandemic times, air travel frequency is unprecedented. Where once we were fully aware of that which we didn't know, now we are more than ever convinced that we know everything and act upon our imagined knowledge, rooted in norms we consider universal and our belief in knowing what is good for others. Like millions of imperial micro-entrepreneurs, Western consumers become 'white saviours', ideologically colonising the most remote places and galvanising into armchair human rights movements promoting a better world.[1]

In the United States and Europe, consumers have come to internalise a wet citizenship dream in which they hold governments and warlords, smugglers and corporations to account and steer their actions along the trope of universal values in a globalised era. These values are rooted in a diffuse set of codified and common-sense norms and ideas: human rights and humanitarian laws, Christian values, liberal tradition and vaguer feelings of compassion and disgust over wrongdoing and impunity. On the path from idea to action, these values often get condensed into a white saviour complex that produces alterity, using Orientalism as a 'political doctrine' to project flat, simplistic assumptions onto the Other.[2]

Echoing Edward Said, Mbembe noted that there is 'no description of Africa that does not involve destructive and mendacious functions'.[3] Clichés of backwardness, underdevelopment and violence in Africa thus inspire Manichean storyboards of campaigners, advocates and politicians alike. Assuming moral superiority and refuting 'situated knowledge', these storyboards sanitise colonial frames of intervention and dominate 'the space of politics' with neoliberal punchlines promoting a more just, equitable world.[4] In denying the receiving end a 'permission to narrate', such interventions reinforce state weakness, monopolise profit and perpetuate the status quo of global economic relations and violent politics.[5] The contested relation between violent conflict and natural resources is a case in point. In previous decades, this nexus has become a major subject of scrutiny in media, research and policy debates at a global scale.

The puzzle: (No) blood in my mobile

Popular framings of far-flung conflict areas have entrenched a consensus that natural resources cause civil wars. If the notion of 'blood diamonds' emerged in the West African wars of the 1990s (and inspired a homonymous Hollywood blockbuster), the 'conflict minerals' paradigm did much the same in the 2000s, yet more dramatically affected public opinion on war, violence and transnational intervention. These 'conflict minerals' are the artisanally mined tin, tantalum (coltan), tungsten (otherwise known as '3T') and gold suspected to originate from war zones in eastern Congo (yet not cobalt, as some would claim).[6] Also known as 'digital minerals' due to their use in high-end tech products, these minerals are alleged to fuel violence in the region.

This book tells a more comprehensive story: while minerals played a role in recent wars, eastern Congo's 'intractable security conundrum' is rooted in a broader set of exogenous and endogenous factors.[7] In the past three decades, a bundle of interlocking wars—interspersed with colonial backwash, regional politics, domestic crises, contestation around land and identity, weak governance and zero-sum politics—have led to unprecedented violence and mobilisation. This was once Eurocentrically dubbed 'Africa's World War' even if it is actually a set of multiple, nested conflicts that have melted into the wider story.[8] Against this backdrop, regular armies, rebel groups and power brokers of all kinds—politicians, customary leaders and businesspeople—keep operating on the back of civilians from one cycle of conflict to another.

In a mix of necessity to pay for the wars and exploiting opportunities for gain, certain actors have, as part of a more copious list of revenue-generating strategies, resorted to the trade of 'conflict minerals'. However, while this phenomenon emerged relatively recently when dozens of militias and government armies fought the 'Second Congo War' (1998–2003), the involvement of armed forces in mining in Congo can be traced back to colonial occupation. During the wars, many belligerents turned to minerals, with violent competition over ore deposits and trading routes becoming a lynchpin in the financing of war efforts. Since 2001, this has pushed non-governmental organisations (NGOs) and UN investigations to turn a spotlight towards the illegal exploitation and trade of minerals, portraying the wars in a manner that was in line with the then dominant scholarly hypotheses of 'resource wars'.

Based on the idea that greed drives violent conflict, eastern Congo emerged as a paradigm case of a brutal war over resources, that—according to a former senior UN official cited in the *New York Times*—imprisoned Congolese women in the 'rape capital of the world'.[9] Objectively untrue, this also conveyed deeply Orientalist imagery similar to other generalisations and tropes (for instance, considering Hamas 'uniquely interested in killing Jewish children').[10] Hence, while it is beyond doubt that natural resources play a role in Congo's turmoil, they are not the foundational cause, as some influential economists have tried to imply.[11] The causal relation, if any, between violent resource exploitation and rape is unclear. And although there are known cases of rape as a weapon of war in eastern Congo, other factors are legion—including colonial trajectories of sexual violence, violence in the context of sex work in mining areas, or plain misogyny.[12]

Nonetheless, prominent Western studies of civil wars in Africa maintain that conflict is caused by 'greed' for natural resources.[13] Many of these works thrive on ahistorical epistemics, arbitrary proxies and tinkered econometric regression.[14] Some also draw inspiration from racist or Malthusian assumptions, such as the number of young men in a society—alluding to an imagery of violent Black bodies—as a proxy to model the likelihood of violence. Yet, as anthropologist James Ferguson notes, 'accounts that cast Africa as a land of failed states, uncontrollable violence, horrific disease, and unending poverty simply recycle old clichés of Western presence and eternal African absence.'[15] While numerous works have debunked the greed thesis—suggesting minerals serve as a means to an end rather than the end itself—the tropes depicting Congo's wars as resource-driven stubbornly persist. In a bid to explain the world's deadliest conflict since the Second World War, the 'conflict minerals' paradigm was no less than a revolution in transnational advocacy.[16] Campaigns have used the paradigm to paint a neat, palpable picture of intractable war, while Western advocates linked images of raped women to the skyrocketing use of mobile gadgets. Driven by the Washington-based Enough Project, this simplistic pitch relied on the dizzying rise in global demand for tantalum that pushed Congolese workers, conflict actors and transnational traders into the mines around 2000.[17] Although the coltan peak was mostly caused by speculation, policymakers and advocates saw in it a blueprint suggesting that, in Congo and elsewhere, 'conflicts are more likely to be caused by economic opportunities than by grievance'.[18]

In line with orthodox economics and amplified by campaigns, the global outcry pressed policymakers to act. Governments and international institutions such as the Organisation for Economic Cooperation and Development (OECD) enacted a series of soft and hard laws to satisfy growing consumer demand for gadgets supposedly free from rape and war crimes. In the United States, a failed 'conflict minerals' draft law project got recycled into the miscellaneous provisions of the 2010 Wall Street Reform and Consumer Protection Act sponsored by Senator Chris Dodd and Representative Barney Frank.[19] The European Union (EU) and others followed suit with their own legislation. Section 1502 of the Dodd–Frank Act obliges companies listed on US stock markets to report on 'conflict minerals' in their supply chains. Its pending implementation led Congo's then President Joseph Kabila to declare a six-month ban on artisanal mining in eastern Congo. While the OECD worked out its due diligence guidance for responsible sourcing,[20] eastern Congo's mining communities—where Dodd–Frank came to fame as 'Obama's law'[21]—groaned under the ban.

What the different laws, guidelines, policies and projects share is the assumption of causal effects between 'conflict minerals' and war as such. However, this equation not only eclipsed the multiple drivers of conflict, but also dismissed historical context, as well as the fact that minerals played a minor role when the wars began in the early 1990s, or when they were compounded after the 1994 genocide in Rwanda. Little of this sentiment remains in the campaigns targeting international policymakers, even though chief advocates like the Enough Project's co-founder John Prendergast muster long-standing expertise on Central Africa on paper. As with similar campaigns (e.g. Kony2012), the Enough Project invested more time convincing American college students of the 'conflict minerals' story than investigating actual conflict dynamics. And whenever it did conduct research, its Washington-based leadership went to great lengths to remind their field consultants (via track changes in draft reports) that a too nuanced picture of conflict in eastern Congo 'will not help [in] transporting our talking points to policymakers in the Capitol', as a former Enough Project consultant once showed me.[22]

Meanwhile, since around 2010, international industries have ramped up efforts aimed at novel supply chain oversight systems to conform to the letter, if not the spirit, of section 1502 of Dodd–Frank. Alongside public initiatives by bilateral cooperation agencies and the International Conference on the Great Lakes Region (ICGLR), a regional body comprising Congo and its neighbours, the International Tin Association (ITA, formerly ITRI), an international lobby organisation for tin-using industries, developed a private sector-driven programme to formalise artisanal mining and trace mineral shipments 'from mines to markets'.[23] Known by its acronym iTSCi, the International Tin Supply Chain Initiative is a joint venture of ITA and its non-profit NGO partner Pact, in collaboration with Congolese government agencies. Arriving first in the new frontier market of 'ethical minerals', iTSCi applied a blueprint private sector model—first come, first served—to reorder supply chains by sealing them off from competitors and placing local producers in a stranglehold. It relies on contradictory Orientalist projections both imagining eastern Congo as an empty slate in terms of Western regulation and pinpointing savagery as the organising principle of politics and business. In neat 'white saviour' fashion, iTSCi positioned itself as a solution, offering 'conflict-free sourcing' to clean up 'fraudulent' mining economies. However, as this book demonstrates, it got embroiled in pre-existing struggles over authority, fostered unemployment and school dropouts, reduced local revenue, and helped perpetuate violent taxation and corruption amidst ongoing insecurity.

The uncritical equation of artisanal mining with criminality and state fragility not only ignored motivations and interests of local stakeholders, but also generated effects opposed to the stated aims of development actors—namely more violence, as empirical data demonstrates.[24] Readings of Congolese conflicts usually emphasise the decay of state institutions and the destruction of livelihoods and the social fabric, but fail to recognise how conflicts reshape social relations and produce new politics.[25] Instead of conducting a deeper analysis of the underlying causes of violence and instability in Congo, the struggle against 'conflict minerals' was and is flat in essence but exuberant in consequence. Four dynamics underpin this: first, associating protagonists of the 'conflict minerals' era with ethical sourcing resulted in 'façade institutions'[26] marred by fraud; secondly, iTSCi roamed into the negotiation of authority, in certain cases even legitimising armed groups; thirdly, a proliferation of cooperatives to formalise the sector—a sound idea in theory—entrenched patronage around customary, political and business leaders;[27]

and fourthly, to promote due diligence, the OECD holds annual stakeholder forums involving *incontournables* (indispensables) that morphed from rebel leaders to politicians, entrepreneurs or state officials. Like rebels turned generals in UN security sector reform workshops, they are embraced by co-optation while maintaining networks of patronage. The term *'incontournables'* is abundantly used in Congo to refer to big men-style actors. As Chapter 6 illustrates for the context of 'conflict minerals', the *incontournables* are Congo's wartime power brokers and entrepreneurs that remain indispensable, unavoidable and impossible to sideline—even as transnational mineral reform attempted to relegate wartime networks of mineral exploitation.

The argument: War, profit and white saviourism

Conflict Minerals, Inc. is the first book-length and field-based critique of transnational efforts to regulate 'conflict minerals' in eastern Congo. The book explains why these efforts had effects opposite to their stated aims, yet still triggered radical change for local political economies and, more broadly, the contours of conflict in eastern Congo. Juxtaposing the 'conflict minerals' narrative with decolonial theoretical reflections and long-term ethnography, including hundreds of interviews and participant observation, the book demonstrates how transnational advocacy and intervention can produce harmful outcomes when it is driven by Orientalist clichés. Orientalism, according to Said, is a discursive strategy that 'enables the political, economic, cultural and social domination of the West, not just in colonial times, but also in the present'.[28] Through this prism, the book shows how white saviourism-infused narratives about far-flung conflict zones, although well-intended, mobilised a mercantilist strategy—mixing colonial and neoliberal patterns—to forcefully incorporate, embed and streamline extractive reservoirs and expendable bodies.

INTRODUCTION

This book argues that although Congo's wars were not initially triggered by minerals, 'conflict minerals' advocacy was highly efficient in promoting policies focusing on profit rather than reliable assurance for conflict-free sourcing, socio-economic development or peace in the larger sense. This argument can be further conjugated in terms of how war, profit and white saviourism are interspersed in the imaginations and practices linking eastern Congo with the wider world. Popular—partly colonial and racist—framings of far-flung conflict entrenched a policy consensus that greed for resources is a cause and corollary of civil war. Nevertheless, the Congolese case shows that if minerals have played a role throughout the wars, violent conflict does not have its origin in minerals.

While digital advocacy in the twenty-first century increasingly contributes to awareness and policy change, it relies on simple logics, usually disconnected from empirical complexity.[29] Despite the fact such phenomena predate the digital age, technological progress heightens their impact. Transnational attempts to regulate 'conflict minerals' have thus been dropped into spaces paradoxically imagined as both unruly and 'empty' when in fact they are highly organised—engendering friction and rendering these very efforts incomplete at best and counterproductive at worst. Hence, although the struggle against 'conflict minerals' has reorganised mineral markets in eastern Congo by creating 'conflict-free' supply chains, it has failed to reduce violence, instead entrenching the exclusion and marginalisation of mining communities that became trapped in markets monopolised by powerful end users. Geared at Western consumers rather than Congolese citizens, transnational mineral reforms presumed a flat geography and a Weberian ideal state. This is a common framing of contemporary policy challenges that juxtapose North–South relations, including in campaigns and initiatives aimed at addressing the climate crisis.

'Conflict minerals' advocates proposed traceability and formalisation as a 'civilising' counterpoint to an artisanal mining sector pictured as profoundly violent, criminal and illegal. These frames of Othering justified making Congolese mines legible and transparent through their 'adverse incorporation' into global capitalist supply chains.[30] Throughout this, the push against 'conflict minerals' ignored the historical and political root causes of conflict. Rather than neutralising violent networks of mineral trade, the reforms co-opted them into new, 'conflict-free' supply chains. Combined with iTSCi's financial weight on local producers and its bid to establish a quasi-sovereign 'conflict-free' territory, this paradoxically reinforced dynamics of state weakness, privatised governance and fragmented authority which had allowed clandestine and violent trade to flourish in the first place.[31]

The imposition of foreign templates on fragmented political and economic orders has given the struggle against 'conflict minerals' the shape of a *mission civilisatrice* (civilising mission)—even if it happens to be in a more neoliberal fashion than its colonial blueprint. It is rooted in a reading of the Congolese conflicts as savage, mindless violence driven by greed and an implicit justification to impose ideologies of marketisation, progress and development. If concession-based and colonially inspired industrial mining ventures have been aimed at imposing order through spatial governance logics, the difference with conflict-free 3T mining is that these spatial logics are less visible in the artisanal sector; paraphrasing Ferguson, iTSCi is thus a 'thin' operation for it follows a more virtual (neo-)colonial territorialising logic in which it does not legally own concessions.[32]

Hailed as a silver bullet by Western advocates and policymakers, the impact of 'conflict-free' mining is ambiguous at best: while the only fully operational traceability programme has not lessened violence, it has created a monopoly and endangered the livelihoods of Congolese mining communities. Transnational efforts to clean up eastern Congo's mining sector thus highlight the problematic interplay of Western consumer ethics, digital technology and global trade with protracted violence and contested political orders at the margins of the postcolonial state in Africa. Disguised as an ethical and humanist pitch, a closer look at 'conflict-free' sourcing in eastern Congo reveals a colonial impetus, the most tangible result of which is the adverse incorporation of resource markets. If this reassertion of market control through monopoly of transnational industries resembles a neoliberally painted version of colonial concession and plantation economies, the concomitant dispossession of local labour has evolved from the tangible violent domination of the colonial era into more subtle but no less violent forms of domination and exploitation.

In that sense, this book shows how contemporary struggles over resources are framed by war, profit and white saviourism alongside flexible strategies to secure resource access via intermediaries as diverse as smugglers, warlords, advocates or peacebuilders. Different in style, the objectives remain the same: if the heydays of uncontrolled, violent mineral trade helped produce the Orientalist imagery feeding myopic advocacy on 'conflict minerals', the resulting policies have traded progress for profit and substituted upwards with downwards accountability, prioritising profit at the expense of development. The story of 'conflict minerals' serves both as a cautionary tale and a powerful call to decolonise transnational governance and peacebuilding practice. It highlights the lack of 'situated knowledge'[33] and critically interrogates the white saviourism that emanates from an unholy alliance that brings together (neo-)colonial frames, digital capitalism, neoliberal interventionism and humanitarianism.[34]

Against this backdrop, the book fundamentally questions the assumptions underpinning the 'conflict minerals' agenda.[35] It suggests that—whether intentionally or coincidentally—misreading of root causes formed a core obstacle to reform's enactment of positive change. 'Conflict-free sourcing' had ambiguous consequences, including new modes of corruption, resistance to external regulation, the recycling of wartime elites and a rise in unemployment and socio-economic precarity that has benefitted armed group recruitment. While 'conflict-free sourcing' undermined socio-economic development, it was occasionally complicit in perpetuating violence.[36] In that sense, the 'conflict minerals' paradigm has amplified an existing fragmentation of authority, as illustrated in an increasingly networked competition over access and, to speak with Said, the 'permission to narrate' when it comes to regulation and order in contexts of legal pluralism. This raises important questions on the interplay of public authority, colonial afterlives, violent conflict and transnational governance in late-modern capitalism, which this book explores from different angles.

The theory: Spaces of networked authority

This book seeks to tell the story of 'conflict minerals' for a wide audience. However, its argument derives from a series of theoretical premises around authority and networks, which I briefly introduce for interested readers. This requires a careful approach to certain concepts and terms considered as orthodox theory on political patronage and criminal networks risks 'flattening the African political and economic landscape', and disregards the mutually constitutive 'two publics' that are driving networked politics.[37] The section thus ends with a discussion of white saviourism as a broader angle of observation and a frame through which specific theories are applied in this book.

Authority

Authority is a polyvalent concept widely used in science and policy. It has countless definitions, but I take Max Weber's foundational work as a starting point to discuss what authority means in the context of this book. Weber conceptualised authority as legitimate domination, a form of power reciprocally structured by its giving and receiving ends.[38] This requires voluntary compliance, a grammar 'to which the powerful and their critics both subscribe at least to a certain degree', through a socialisation process that creates legitimacy.[39] States develop such grammars in their quest to perform 'stateness' through a systemic, institutional and bureaucratic structure, and an idea transported in symbolism, performance and imagery, aimed at giving meaning and creating identity and belonging.[40] However, it is misleading to think only Westphalian states do this. Inspired by the 'territorial trap', many scholars caution against a 'taken-for-granted spatial and scalar image of a state that both sits above and contains its localities, regions, and communities'.[41]

How then, can we understand authority in the context of 'conflict minerals'? Looking at most places in the world, 'efforts by states to establish their superior spatial claims to authority do not go uncontested'.[42] In postcolonial contexts, Dunn and Lund agree: a variety of 'institutions compete over territorial governance, over different forms of rent from resources, and over the grand narrative of history'.[43] Facing pressure on different scales, John Allen observes that states suffer from a displacement and renegotiation of authority, leading to what Anna Tsing called the friction of 'heterogeneous and unequal encounters [that] lead to new arrangements of culture and power'.[44] Accounting for contestation and fragmentation, Allen pinpoints the limits of Weber's ideal-type monopoly of violence, contending that authority is 'now shared with non-governmental organisations, multinational enterprises and other supranational as well as interstate organisations'.[45] The story of 'conflict minerals' is a case in point, featuring a continuous and iterative '"re-embedding" of new forms of private authority, where diverse forms of institutional regulation and rule-setting are folded into the here and now'.[46] This echoes Mbembe's concept of 'private indirect government' where authority is the capacity to decide in the type and reach of access to resources—whether that is for subsistence or surplus. As Mbembe wrote in parallel to Tilly's work on state-building, this highlights the 'political significance of taxation' as a normalised extractive practice by states (or other entities) that relies on their consideration as legitimate authorities.[47] Taxation, in turn, is linked to access, defined as an 'ability to derive benefits from things' (e.g. minerals).[48] Access to resources, or the taxes imposed on their extraction and trade, can be organised in many ways along the fluid binary of (in-)formality.[49] The multiplicity of actors and strategies to gain access to minerals (or tax them) is thus reflective of what Allen called the diverse 'playing field' of competing and contested claims to authority.[50]

Networks

The empirical fragmentation of authority requires a more spatial reflection, looking at networks rather than only analysing institutions. Given its transnational setting, the story of 'conflict minerals' features a wealth of competing 'glocal' claims to authority operating at different scales.[51] While transnational efforts of 'clean sourcing' seek to impose their brand of formalising artisanal mining, miners and traders also defend their own practices and regimes. Others—state actors, armed groups or cooperatives—straddle the spectrum, shopping among options and employing crisis-proof strategies of 'making do', including brokerage, patronage, navigation and practical norms. These strategies are enacted in networks with fluid, flexible boundaries that permeate state or institutional order, relying on individual skill and the 'strength of weak ties'.[52] These networks cut through statutory and visible institutions, policies and linkages, and, in the context of mineral reform, connect highly diverse sets of actors—from international development workers or state officials to commercial brokers and violent entrepreneurs.

How then can we understand the networks of mineral trade in eastern Congo without succumbing to sombre, Orientalist tropes of smugglers and warlords? This book foregrounds emic theorisation, which requires conceptualising from terms used by Congolese themselves to understand the lifeworlds of participants in mineral markets. Chapters 6 and 7, for instance, analyse the networked logics of taxation and access in the context of transnational reform by drawing on emic concepts. More broadly, the book picks up the ubiquitous everyday notion of *la crise* to look at eastern Congo as a 'crisis economy', in which *négociants* (traders) and *incontournables* function as nodes, benefitting 'from being the broker between otherwise unconnected nodes'.[53] They use social capital to straddle risk and opportunity, and use different skills to operate a volatile but ultimately socially embedded economic environment.[54] These are activated in the multiple social, political and economic ties that form dynamic, versatile networks of power, profit and protection. They are adaptable, transform quickly, and feature cooperation and conflict that affects their stability and efficiency in relation to contextual factors. Shaping different individual and collective rationalities, the functional mechanics and ideological foundations of networks allow for case-by-case analysis that more precisely embraces the politics of resources beyond formulaic clichés of methodological individualism. This conceptualisation also rebukes some of the tautological ideas imbued in Weberian ideal-types and Eurocentric patronage theories, allowing us to understand networks as more than mere exchange networks by embracing context and historicity, as well as the fluidity and flexibility of boundaries that are constantly renegotiated in settings of political contestation.[55]

White saviourism

The colonial epistemics of the struggle against 'conflict minerals' complicate our understanding of networked struggles over contested authority. This is frequent in Western advocacy, and led Teju Cole to coin the term 'white-saviour industrial complex' in his critique of Invisible Children's Kony2012 campaign. Using this prism, the book situates its theoretical approach in the context of (neo-)colonialism, Orientalism and racism that justifies a transnational reform which ultimately seeks to monopolise both the permission to narrate 'conflict minerals' and the extraction of these very minerals. White saviourism 'is about having a big emotional experience that validates privilege'; it foregrounds morality but downplays 'that those who are being helped ought to be consulted over the matters that concern them.'[56] This is often embodied by White narrators, not seldom celebrities, paired with non-White sidekicks.[57] The Kony2012 movie, for instance, featured Invisible Children's Jason Russell with his son Gavin, and Jacob Acaye, a former child soldier in the Lord's Resistance Army.[58] Adding to simplistic, factually wrong messages, the racialised iconography led to sharp rebuttals by African intellectuals.[59] Notable conflict minerals advocates are Ryan Gosling, Nicole Richie and Robin Wright, usually appearing with Enough Project's John Prendergast or on short trips to Congo where they preferably get filmed in hospitals alongside Congolese victims.[60]

Most often found in the form of transnational digital advocacy, white saviourism is obsessed with violence, poverty and despair in Africa. As cultural studies scholar Shringarpure noted, it uses imagery that 'can be traced back to colonial civilising mission ideologies' that buoyed unprecedented brutality and extraction.[61] These imageries borrow from classic and often contradictory colonial and Orientalist themes of Otherness and alterity. In its justification, white saviourism commonly depicts Africa both as a continent governed by savage rulers and an empty blank slate void of any history at the same time. Such misperceptions are partly rooted in a lack of knowledge about the politics that precede Western interventions—both during colonial times and today. However, they are in equal part conditioned by a pressure to appeal to an audience with limited will and time to engage in faraway complexity but with an appetite for (often scandalous) bites of information to which they can directly relate. This, as decolonial theorists highlight, can be traced back to constructions of the Other as an imagined opposite of the Self.[62] The discursive and conceptual basis of white saviourism is colonial and imperialist on several fronts, for it denies agency and voice as much on the basis of gender and class as of race writ small.[63] This is important to understand how Western advocacy simultaneously reified colonial epistemics and sponsored a neoliberal intervention thriving on extractable reservoirs and expendable subjects. However, it raises a set of fundamental questions about transnational solidarity: namely, what if the feedback links between the subaltern and those with a voice are broken despite the mobile technologies that emboldened it in the first place? Like a 2.0 version of *Tintin in the Congo*—a 1931 Belgian comic now widely acknowledged as racist—genuinely concerned Americans and Europeans became the noble protagonists in a binary tale of Black subjects whose agency is relegated to being either victims or villains.[64] Like the colonial figure of Tintin, the story of 'conflict minerals' therefore says more about Western consumers than Congolese citizens. In a broader perspective, it showcases how transnational advocacy contributes to awareness and change, but remains fundamentally caught in flat, Western epistemic frames. While human rights rightly feature on the agenda of advocates, they are considered universalist and indisputable. In consequence, the privileged and dominant frames of thought represented by white saviourism become lost in an epistemic misunderstanding, and erasure, of the Other.[65]

The method: Writing political ethnography

As Clifford and Marcus wrote, 'ethnography is actively situated between powerful systems of meaning. It poses its questions at the boundaries of civilizations, cultures, classes, races, and genders. Ethnography decodes and recodes.'[66] In this sense, this book follows a constructivist and interpretivist approach to bridge the gap between research and politics, emphasising the political in itself—here, the question of networked struggles over authority with regards to transnational mineral reform.[67] It is as political as the evolutions it investigates, and seeks to reconcile constant intellectual friction between remaining impartial and taking sides against injustice.[68] Paradoxically, Western campaigners and consumers—despite good intentions to sever what they saw as a causal link between resources and violence—became complicit in reifying colonial frames. In the name of human rights, the struggle against 'conflict minerals' singled out snapshots of a broader conundrum of violence, pitting raped women against child soldiers and miners at gunpoint. In so doing, international advocacy turned a blind eye to the *longue durée* of violent extraction that has shaped this part of the world. This allowed for subsequent policies and projects to use a purportedly humanist and ethical frame for tightening the grip on extractable reservoirs, the mines of eastern Congo and expendable subjects (i.e. those working these mines). Similar to the colonial-era management of resources and bodies, the protagonists of ethical mineral sourcing quickly understood that extractable reservoirs—as opposed to the neoclassic dictum of 'abundant resources'—are non-renewable and must therefore be monopolised as much as possible. Human bodies, in turn, are renewable and thus expendable subjects available for labour.

INTRODUCTION

The choice to foreground a story of Black villains and Black victims to justify tackling an economy seen as illegal and criminal—rather than advocating for structural changes in fighting the violence and inequality affecting Black lives in global supply chains—opened the doors for what this book investigates: the mismatch between the stated aims of the 'conflict minerals' campaign and its outcomes. Beyond the white saviour mentality that perpetuates the use of extractable reservoirs and expendable subjects, the (neo-)colonial undertone of Western campaigning is also driven by dynamics of Othering that marginalise non-Western agency and voice to create, in Derrida's terms, a translation problem between the *what* (is the problem), the *why* (is it a problem) and the *how* (to address the problem). While there might be universal agreement about *what* the problem is (in this case, 'conflict minerals'), things are less clear as to the *why* and *how*.

So, why are 'conflict minerals' a problem? American college students might deplore that their mobile phone may link them to the raping of women by warlords greedy for coltan. However, while the quick fix would be to refuse to buy every other new smartphone on the market, it would not really have an impact: the world's largest tantalum mines are not in Congo, but in Australia, and rape is not causally related to mining (it does, however, correlate with war and social breakdown, amongst other phenomena). A Congolese petty trader, in turn, might deplore how war has eroded non-mining livelihoods, and that violent exploitation of minerals has contributed to entrenching a climate of impunity. She might add that her business—and thus the schooling and health-care of her children—suffers from unpredictability due to illegal taxation and random extortion. She might also add that the preponderance of mining in eastern Congo's economy has unmade the equilibrium of agriculture, cattle-herding, timber, craft and trade, replacing subsistence with dependence.

How, then, should the problem be addressed? A Europe-based campaigner may suggest boycotts, sanctions and bans alongside initiatives to address fraud and informality and to 'restore state authority'. They may suggest adding projects that provide assistance to victims of sexual violence and efforts in nature conservation. Whether related to 'conflict minerals' or presumed secondary effects, such responses can perpetuate tropes and unearth the cognitive dissonances that prevail despite global digital and logistic connectivity. They also highlight how Western campaigns and governance interventions in the postcolony have struggled to account for 'situated knowledge'.[69] Congolese activists and miners, meanwhile, may have their own advice and recommendations. In the West, we tend to either forget, filter or disregard their voices. Dissecting transnational phenomena such as the evolution of the 'conflict minerals' paradigm therefore requires an engaged and politically sensitive approach to anthropology, a critical attitude towards the topic and one's own positionality, and a reflexive methodological toolkit. Seeking 'a fuller understanding of the interplay between transnational effects and domestic politics',[70] this book relies on multisited ethnography and thick description to analyse translocal connections and contentious politics using a critical, decolonial and situated approach.[71] This requires 'put[ting] the whole of politics back into political anthropology, albeit in a culturally aware manner, [to] go beyond "hope" and the Promethean illusion of "speaking truth to power."'[72] In a similar line of thought, Ferguson and Gupta remind us of the pitfalls of such exercises:

> [T]he ethnographic challenge facing us today with neoliberal globalization is to understand the spatiality of all forms of government, some of which may be embedded in the daily practices of nation-states while others may crosscut or superimpose themselves on the territorial jurisdiction.[73]

Transnational governance, neoliberal politics and dynamics of conflict, exclusion and marginalisation play out more violently in the margins and frontiers of state-building and transnational business.[74] Yet, despite unspeakable violence, the Congolese example also defies many classic policy assumptions: '[It] seems to be ruled by various "semi-autonomous subsystems of power", which means that political rule in this country is once again established among the existing powers, without, however, destroying them.'[75]

Understanding entanglements of transnational governance, remote wars and political authority requires strategies of investigation that reflect the very 'glocal' socio-spatial dynamics in the intellectual act and the bodily practice of research.[76] While such an approach is as imperfect as any other, it can help 'going into realms of the social that are not easily discernible within the more formal protocols used by many other disciplines.'[77] Rooted in these reflections, the following paragraphs present the concrete and practical methodological contours of the book.

The backbone of my data collection was gathered predominantly through collaborative fieldwork together with a number of Congolese colleagues and friends, semi-structured interviews and participant observation. During 13 months of fieldwork between 2014 and 2018, I conducted 210 interviews and over 150 informal discussions.[78] Beyond that, I performed participant observation in five mining areas (Nyabibwe, Lemera, Rubaya, Numbi and Nzibira; see Figure I.1), three urban hubs (Bukavu, Uvira and Goma) and relevant national capitals (Kinshasa, Bujumbura and Kigali). I also regularly observed everyday routines in government offices, mining shafts and the houses of local traders, among many others.[79] This involved 'follow the thing' exercises to capture the mobility of mineral trade between mines and urban trading hubs. Inherently multisited, this can reveal the 'powerful, important, disturbing connections between Western consumers and the distant strangers'.[80] A quantitative blob in a mostly qualitative approach, I carried out a survey with 250 participants in the field sites to triangulate ethnographic data.

Moreover, Congolese government, UN and NGO officials shared documents, statistics and maps, adding to a vast body of

Figure I.1: Fieldwork sites

scientific and policy writings, grey literature and tracts I have assembled in my personal archives over the years. To balance Eurocentric, colonial tropes, my fieldwork for and beyond this book pays particular attention to the ways in which Congolese friends and interlocutors narrate Congo, and I also spent significant time walking around, observing 'normal life' to increase my sensitivity to usual or unusual situations but also to decentre my own Western mindset and better situate the lenses through which I observe. In most of that, I worked with several research associates, with one of whom I have co-published a significant amount of work (see Prologue and Acknowledgements). Yet, despite this variety of methods, I too faced 'serious difficulty in acquiring information on violent, informal and "illegal" economic activities' spanning across multiple scales:[81]

> [C]lassic techniques of anthropological research, emphasizing community studies and lengthy immersion in local life to gain acceptance, have adapted to the changing interests of anthropologists as they move beyond their early focus on small-scale communities ... to investigate the regional, national and global context of local phenomena.[82]

Ellis and MacGaffey's claim holds true for eastern Congo too, where a roadblock economy creates de facto boundaries inside a national territory.[83] The lack of records and reliable figures more broadly—as well as uncertainty over classification—is typical for the space between areas of origin and *entrepôts* of transit.[84] Participants in such economies deal with a type of uncertainty similar to what is described in the concept of navigation that outlines how individuals develop a flexible behaviour—often enhanced by legal pluralism—with regards to uncertain, quickly changing surroundings.[85] While this may impact the validity of data, it also matters to the very logistics and security of field research, as noted in the observation that 'security constraints provide many actors with a perfect excuse to no longer invest in conflict research, thus reducing the knowledge about contemporary conflicts'.[86]

Perhaps it is precisely the fragmented character of authority that can sometimes increase one's chances of ending up 'never caught in the wrong place at the wrong time'.[87] While this research included passing frontlines between government troops and armed groups, the aftermath is as relevant as immediate safety: mere 'approval of and adherence to protocols is of course not sufficient to ensure adequate ethical judgment; [and] such protocols cannot anticipate the many dilemmas other than issues of informed consent and data security.'[88] I thus developed an approach prioritising the safety of myself, my colleagues and my interlocutors—before, during and after interviews. This led to frequent cancellations of trips or meetings. Ethnographies of contested issues are conditioned by positionality and politics, which raises multiple ethical questions.

> The Kivus ... are characterized by a burgeoning 'economy of truth-making' ... the engine of which is *radio trottoir* (pavement radio) or the rumors machine. As elsewhere, Kivutians manufacture meaning in order to make sense of, but also manipulate, events. In such a context, representations can become the paramount field of battle.[89]

There is a burgeoning debate between relativism and human rights in current anthropology, to the point that the former— otherwise long-standing—has been called the 'chameleon-like ambidexterity of the politically uncommitted'.[90] In places like eastern Congo, having hosted the world's most deadly conflict since the Second World War, 'neutrality and impartiality (including their rejection) constitute an immensely complex ethical minefield'.[91] However, this begs the question of how one ethically takes sides at all if the lines are blurred.[92] Without succumbing to Adam Kuper's scathing critique, I contend that Scheper-Hughes' plea for a politically engaged anthropology in contexts of violence and injustice is easier to fine-tune when working on contexts such as South African apartheid and Latin America than in eastern Congo, where over 120 non-state groups and army factions vie for power, violate human rights and also offer some protection.[93] Still, I do not pinpoint Congolese essentialism or exceptionalism—conflict zones are never Manichean and always ambiguous.[94]

Finally, the rarely addressed emotional and mental health aspects during and after fieldwork matter too.[95] If emotions such as hope, resignation, joy, fear, pity, anger, sadness or grief are eclipsed, it can lead to 'errors of judgement with potentially damaging consequences for the researcher herself and/or for informants'.[96] In extreme cases, researchers 'may suffer from "secondary trauma," the sustained effects on witnesses of observing gross human rights violations'.[97] It is therefore paramount to balance the seeming weakness of emotions against the feigned strength of adrenaline described as the 'Barbarian syndrome'.[98] Taking this back to the discussion on ethics and positionality, it also matters how we place ourselves between emotions and rationalising distance. Raeymaekers, in his attempts to navigate the 'spectral realities' that can emerge in the more sinister moments of fieldwork, reminds us of how easily the situatedness of ethnography in conflict zones leads our subconscious to succumb to imageries we elsewhere call out as colonial, racist tropes.[99] For these reasons, this book made a conscious political choice of marrying relativism with activism. While it is activist in challenging the privileged, it sticks to a more relativist assessment of those less privileged, in particular those targeted by frames of Othering.

The structure: Outline of the book

This book is a critical analysis of 'conflict minerals' conjugated with a long-term ethnography of eastern Congo's mining sector and its broader dynamics of conflict. It is organised into an introduction and seven further chapters, each with its own objective. This introductory chapter has introduced the overall topic and argument, and presented the book's theoretical, methodological and empirical approach. Chapter 1 offers a history of the violent changes and continuities in eastern Congo's modern history. Chapter 2 traces the genesis of the 'conflict minerals' paradigm, discusses its intellectual foundations, and juxtaposes them with a brief historical and sociological analysis of mining in Congo.

Based on that, Chapter 3 takes transnational advocacy on 'conflict minerals' as a starting grid to illustrate the evolution of the paradigm into laws, guidelines and practical policy. The following three chapters form the empirical and ethnographical backbone. Using qualitative research and survey data, Chapter 4 traces how the establishment of 'ethical monopolies' contributed to impoverishing Congolese mining communities. It demonstrates how reforms driven by good intentions fell prey to a mixture of detached analysis and profit-oriented policy. Chapter 5 takes a deep ethnographic dive to describe two key types of actors in eastern Congo's mining sector: the intermediary traders called *négociants* and the masterminds of political and economic life known as the *incontournables*. Looking at eastern Congo's supply chains from their perspective, the chapter assesses the evolution from 'conflicted' to 'conflict-free' mining. Chapter 6 uses critical geographical and anthropological theory to comparatively analyse supposedly clean and conflicted supply chains. Through a dialectic analysis, it illustrates the surprising parallels of mineral governance between 'white saviours' and armed groups. Finally, the concluding chapter returns to broader lessons and implications. Based on a few non-academic vignettes, it returns to the initial stereotypes that permitted the 'conflict minerals' paradigm to emerge and persist. It then summarises how the prospects of ethical sourcing turned into a broken promise, closing with a call for better analysis and better policy. This call centres on respect for the intricate, complicated character of politics and conflict in most parts of the world and, more importantly, the aspirations and rights of those grappling with policies made in the name of 'better lives'.

1

VIOLENT CONTINUITIES

To situate the problem of 'conflict minerals' in its historical, political and geographical context, it is imperative to sketch the changes and continuities of conflict in eastern Congo. Entering its fourth decade of cyclical wars, the region appears to be stuck in never-ending violence and insecurity—and attempts to make sense of it often end up being either flat and simplistic or obscure and incomprehensible. If the former would endorse a framing of eastern Congo along tired clichés, colonial ideologies and funky but erroneous shortcuts—as sketched in the introduction—the latter equally fail in offering bite-sized and accessible analysis. Beyond home-grown problems, the complex history of Congo and concomitant knowledge production are therefore also issues of representation and imagery. As Dunn noted,

> Western understandings of the Congo, even in the twenty-first century, rely heavily upon earlier representations generated by Westerners. This has led to an interesting paradox: While Westerners are generally uninformed about Congolese history and politics, they feel they know it well because of the powerful images of it encountered everyday.[1]

The following overview of the changes and continuities of violent politics and the *longue durée* of conflict in eastern Congo attempts to strike a balance between the depth and multiplicity of causes and consequences while sticking to parsimony and straightforward assessment. Setting out with a brief overview of the colonial era, this chapter then looks at the country's post-colonial turbulences and the era of Zaire to understand the path to breakdown in the 1990s, and the cycles of violence and war that frame Congo's recent history. Whether a 'geological scandal' or the 'heart of darkness', debates about Congo never lack semantic or metaphorical creativity.[2] If public discourse, Western media and pundits of all kinds regularly excel in simplifying over 150 years of rich, tragic and complex history, a closer look reveals a wealth of writing that explains the multiple ways in which Congo's 'imperial encounter' and subsequent colonial brutality planted the seeds for a turbulent modern history.[3] Postcolonial rulers received a blueprint from a crumbling colony that left just 16 university graduates whilst maintaining opportunities galore for what Bhabha called 'mimicry', helping to perpetuate arrogance and prejudice.[4] In that sense, (eastern) Congo's modern history is framed by continuities from a colonial past into a colonial present. These continuities form a field of tension between precolonial governance, fluid patterns of customary rule, regional competition and border-making, and the political manipulation and fixation of identity and belonging often used to boil down complexity into frames legible to invaders with scant contextual knowledge.[5] This setting has continuously emboldened imperialist as much as domestic ambitions to divide, rule and extract, even if the colonial and postcolonial state always remained imperfect and 'impotent' in this quest.[6]

Colonial Incorporation

The continuities of violence and intervention in what is the Democratic Republic of the Congo today are rooted in more than half a millennium of incorporation into Western politics and capitalism.[7] While a full history of precolonial Congo and its colonisation since the fifteenth century is beyond the scope of this book, it is crucial to remember the imperfect, diachronic momentum that evolved first from Western attempts to set foot in what was then a vast piece of land (wrongly) considered peripheral in an era of nascent international relations.[8] The logistic difficulties faced by colonisers gained the broader Great Lakes area epithets such as Conrad's 'Heart of Darkness', which have gone on to dominate the imagination and justify intervention, even though highly developed—even if seemingly rudimentary or acephalous—polities such as the Kongo or Kuba kingdoms in the west and south, or Rwanda and Burundi in the east, predate European intervention and played a key role in transatlantic and global history.[9] European colonial efforts from Cão to Stanley initially struggled to gain traction, relying on intermediaries and collusion with Arab East African colonialism in the context of the slave trade, before moving on to a more encompassing attempt at domination on the premises of alterity, extractive labour and sovereign violence.

If in the run-up to and during the Berlin Conference of 1885 colonial-national borders were negotiated between European rulers, colonial rule later 'domestically' replicated these practices by interfering in previously fluid dynamics of territory and identity.[10] In the interlacustrine area linking today's Kivu with neighbouring Rwanda, different forms of mobility shape social life, of which the recent, conflict-induced migration is but one form. Historically, belonging used to be relational rather than territorially fixed and, as is still the case today, conflict in the late nineteenth century was not limited to one place: scale always mattered.[11] Regional struggles, colonial terror and the regional slave trade were entangled with specific local tensions. Precolonial kingdoms in what today is North and South Kivu often resisted colonialism and even mounted their own expansionist projects. Examples include, but are not limited to, the clashes confronting several kingdoms as Mwami Buhini of the Nyanga launched raids into the Bashali area in 1880. In 1895, Rwandan King Kigeri IV Rwabugiri pushed to extend his territory into present-day Masisi, Rutshuru and Kalehe. In 1896, Afro-Arabic slave traders operated a raid along the Osso, Lowa and Mweso rivers in the Masisi area. Later, around 1910, the so-called *abaryoko* and their mystical leader, Prince Ngyiko, contested colonial imposition.

Over time and space, different rulers took turns in governing and fighting over control. Much of this resonates today as politicians and opinion leaders muse about the precolonial reach of 'their' respective entities, trading heated claims of legitimacy. The fixation of colonial borders put a halt to organic shifts in power, demarcating the then German colony of Ruanda-Urundi (later a Belgian protectorate) from the then Congo Free State, which became Belgian Congo in 1908 after two murderous decades where millions of Congolese were killed in spates of direct and indirect violence.[12] In 1910, a colonial decree 'created' so-called indigenous chieftaincies and sub-chieftaincies, reconferring some power to customary leaders—although not without meddling in appointments and hereditary lines, and forcing chiefs into schemes of hybrid taxation (while they had prerogatives to tax the population, this came with obligations to also levy taxes for the colonial power). Ruanda-Urundi became a Belgian protectorate in 1922, having been occupied by Belgium since 1916. This paved the way for somewhat more coordinated but no less exploitative and racist colonial rule on both sides of the colonial border until 1960, most notably in the shape of a forced migration project known as Mission d'immigration Banyarwanda (MIB) in the 1930s and 1940s. Aimed at using expendable subjects to access extractable resources, this and other disruptive policies have since helped amplify numerous conflicts around land, identity and citizenship.

In parallel to the tumultuous politics of the independence years, tensions erupted in the Kivus within and between so-called autochthonous populations and Banyarwanda. Owing to the 1959 arrival of Tutsi refugees fleeing pogroms in Rwanda, the status of Banyarwanda (Tutsi in particular) increasingly became a matter of suspicion among non-Rwandophone populations.[13] Although the newly established Congolese army was able to control the escalation, a mixture of political, economic and ethnic tensions would converge into the 1964–66 wave of violent conflicts known as the Kanyarwanda War in North Kivu.[14] During this war, different legal and historical readings clashed: on the side of the Hutu population, independence was considered a point zero at which all residents of the newly independent territory acquired citizenship, including themselves, a narrative strongly opposed by groups considering themselves autochthonous. Yet, the Kanyarwanda War combined a number of local conflicts, not all of which were driven by identity. As such, it is illustrative of the multiplicity of social dynamics and contestations that frame later conflicts as much as transcend the ethnic divisions imagined and reinforced by colonial and racial stereotyping.

Mobutu and Zaire

After turbulent years of independence in the Kivus and elsewhere, the early Mobutu years heralded a short-lived economic honeymoon wrapped in the new leader's 'counterhegemonic' discursive and political project that culminated in the making of Zaire.[15] While the country heeded an unprecedented economic boom between 1965 and 1973, the eastern region similarly experienced a largely peaceful era. However, a combination of corruption, zero-sum politics and 'tinderboxing' around land and citizenship changed things quickly.[16] In parallel to the post-Zairianisation economic crises since the mid-1970s, and ill-fated military adventures domestically and abroad, Mobutu issued a series of laws that 'switched on and off' citizenship of Kinyarwanda speakers, without disambiguating groups (Banyamulenge in South Kivu, Hutu and Tutsi Banyarwanda in North Kivu) or periods (precolonial residents, MIB descendants, refugees, etc.).[17] In consequence, land access became 'ethnic' in terms of (legal) ownership and (political) belonging. Trying to quell tensions, Mobutu instrumentalised divisions by redistributing concessions to his cronies favouring Banyarwanda and simultaneously gave in to 'autochthonous' demands, revoking citizenship rights of Banyarwanda.[18] While the 1966 Bakajika Law decreed all land belonged to the state, and thus nullified preceding colonial or customary ownership, the 1972 Citizenship Law granted Banyarwanda full rights again, reinvigorating the 1964 Constitution. It specified that persons having arrived from Ruanda-Urundi before 1 January 1950 had Zairian nationality as of 30 June 1960.[19] When, in 1977, Mobutu decreed Banyarwanda would re-obtain Zairian citizenship, protests erupted in the national assembly, with certain parliamentarians invoking a constitution provision that defined citizenship as being conferred individually.

Political and land conflicts led to the creation and entrenchment of ethnic *mutualités*. In 1980, Banyarwanda leaders would create the MAGRIVI (Mutuelle des agriculteurs de Virunga), a mix of socio-political self-help group and agricultural cooperative, in a bid to federate North Kivu's Hutu population and form a sizeable group. The Hunde organised into the long-standing Bushenge ('independence' in Kihunde) Hunde, the Nyanga into the Bunakima, the Tembo into the Buuma, the Nande into the Kyaghanda Yira, and the main Tutsi *mutualités* into Ubumwe, the Association cooperative des groupements d'éleveurs du Nord-Kivu (Cooperative Association of North Kivu Herder Groups) and UNAR. *Mutualités* exist widely across Congo, and some of them have roots in the independence struggles of the 1940s and

1950s.[20] The 1981 Nationality Law again revoked prerogatives of Kinyarwanda speakers in Zaire, illustrating Mobutu's divide-and-rule politics. Its fourth article outlined that citizenship now depended upon membership in a community established on Congolese soil for a long time, with 1885 being the cut-off date.[21] Mobutu further deprived Banyarwanda from citizenship by mounting a census excluding Hutu and Tutsi, unmaking previous decrees.[22] This stood in contrast to 'autochthonous' politics that had invoked the inseparability of the living and the ancestors as a *sine qua non* to amend customary and land governance. Land and soil thus again became 'ethnic' in two parallel ways: (1) as an arena of competition over (legal) ownership and (2) as the meaning of (political) belonging.[23]

When Zaire experienced the tumultuous dawn of Mobutu's single-party rule in the early 1990s—with riots in Kinshasa, mass inflation and the establishment of the Conference nationale souveraine (CNS)—political tension grew further in the east where demographic change and identity politics had eroded state legitimacy and relations between communities. Meanwhile, ethnopolitical tensions erupted into war in neighbouring Rwanda, where the Rwandan Patriotic Front (RPF) began launching attacks into the country from its exile in Uganda. Many young Tutsi from Masisi and Rutshuru left at the time to join the RPF. In March 1993, fighting broke out in Masisi and Walikale, with a series of attacks and massacres between 'ethnic' militia, known as the Ntoto War.[24] Hutu and Tutsi in MAGRIVI created patrols known as *irondo*, and clashed with Hunde, Tembo, Kano and Nande mobilising in the Katuko and Batiri.[25] Pillage of cattle and fields were common currency amongst belligerent forces.[26] Inter-community dialogues were organised in February 1994, yet these efforts would eventually be futile as provincial politics complicated local conflict and a looming regional crisis diverted attention. Eastern Zaire's security problems merged with violence in neighbouring states, as genocidal violence kicked off in Rwanda, and to a lesser extent Burundi.[27] From July 1994, the arrival of refugees, *interahamwe* militia and remnants of the Rwandan Armed Forces (Forces armées rwandaises [FAR]) heralded a decisive shift in regional security. While the arriving ex-FAR maintained their structure and weaponry inside the refugee camps, arms were sold cheaply and preferentially to Congolese Hutu, who were considered allies. Domestic breakdown and a set of regional conflicts contributed to unprecedented violence and mobilisation, leading to one of the deadliest series of wars since the defeat of Nazi Germany.[28]

The two Congo Wars

The arrival of the Alliance of Democratic Forces for the Liberation of Congo (Alliance des forces démocratiques pour la libération du Congo-Zaire [AFDL]) in 1996 added another layer of confrontation. Tutsi within the AFDL and their RPF allies went to forcefully dismantle Rwandan refugee camps in Goma, Bukavu and elsewhere, driving both genocidal forces and civilians deeper into the Zairian hinterlands. In the meantime, different Mai-Mai groups—some of which had been involved in the 1993 war—moved towards Goma and got involved in the AFDL's fight against Congolese and Rwandan Hutu, as well as Forces Armées Zaïroises (FAZ) troops.[29] Within a year, the AFDL and its allies took Kinshasa, while embedded RPF focused on tracking down ex-FAR and genocidal forces (committing massacres in certain places). By 1998, the new Congolese president, Laurent-Désiré Kabila, had already broken from his Rwandan sponsors, triggering the creation of the Congolese Rally for Democracy (Rassemblement congolais pour la démocratie [RCD]). On 2 August 1998, General Sylvain Buki announced the RCD as a breakaway faction of the AFDL. While the RCD played a key role in the Second Congo War overall, it also controlled large parts of Masisi and Rutshuru—chasing the genocidal Army for the Liberation of Rwanda (Armée de libération du Rwanda [ALiR]) and its successor group, the Democratic Forces for the Liberation of Rwanda (Forces démocratiques de libération du Rwanda [FDLR]), into Walikale, Lubero and Shabunda. Kabila in turn rallied FDLR, Congolese Hutu militia and Mai-Mai groups to weaken the RCD's grip over the Kivus.[30] What followed has (Eurocentrically) been dubbed 'Africa's World War', even if it was more a set of nested and multilayered conflicts melting into one wider conundrum. Born out of the Second Congo War, yet a complex of its own, the Ituri War developed parallel dynamics.[31] In a mix of logistic necessity to pay for war and opportunities to gain, certain actors resorted—in addition to cross-border trade and state capture—to minerals as a resource. Throughout the 'Second Congo War',[32] violent competition over mineral deposits and trading routes became a fulcrum, financing army units and armed groups alike. However, as generations of army factions, rebel groups, politicians, customary leaders and entrepreneurs kept on 'living by the gun' in cycles of 'no peace, no war', revenue generation has diversified in eastern Congo ever since.[33]

Meanwhile, a series of (inter-)national peace agreements were negotiated (in Lusaka, between Congo and other countries [1999]; in Pretoria, between Congo and Rwanda [2002]; and the Inter-Congolese Dialogue in Sun City, South Africa [2002]). The various accords aimed at the reunification of the country and culminated in the formation of a transitional 1+4 government in Kinshasa. However, given the unsolved grievances and the RCD's lack of representation in the transitional institutions, some Banyarwanda leaders grew sceptical towards Kinshasa. This created rifts within the RCD, preceding the Bukavu siege by Jules Mutebusi in 2004 and the creation of the National Congress for the Defence of the People (Congrès national pour la défense du

Figure 1.1: Armed groups in eastern Congo in 2013[34]

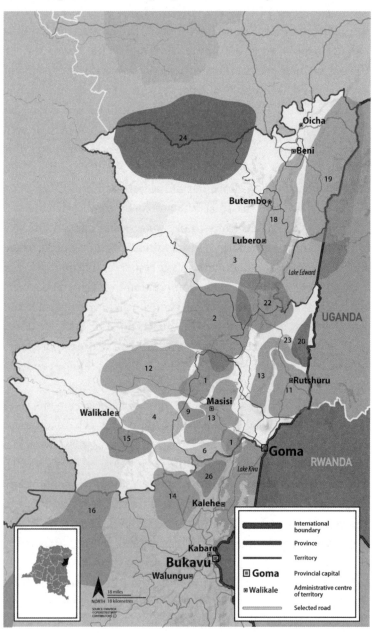

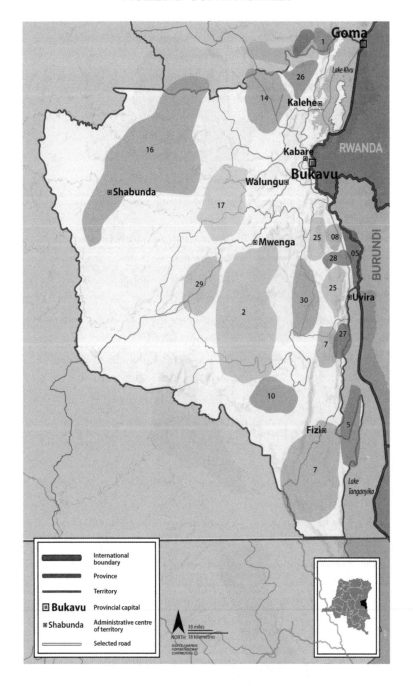

1	APCLS	(Alliance des patriotes pour un Congo libre et souverain)
2	FDLR	(Forces démocratiques de libération du Rwanda)
3	UPCP	(Union patriotique des congolais pour la paix, led by Kakule Sikuli)
4	FDC	(Forces de défense du Congo)
5	FNL	(Front national de libération)
6	Mai-Mai Kifuafua	(Mai-Mai group under Delphin Mbaenda)
7	Mai-Mai Yakotumba	(Mai-Mai group under Amuri Yakotumba)
8	MCC Bede	(Mouvement congolais pour le changement)
9	Guides-MAC	(Mouvement d'action pour le changement)
10	Mai-Mai Mulumba	(Mai-Mai coalition under Mulumba, Aochi and Shoshi)
11	M23	(Mouvement du 23 mars)
12	NDC	(Nduma Defence of Congo)
13	Nyatura	(Umbrella term for the Congolese Hutu militia)
14	Raia Mutomboki in Kalehe area	(Kalehe-based Raia Mutomboki groups)
15	Raia Mutomboki in Walikale area	(Walikale-based Raia Mutomboki groups)
16	Raia Mutomboki Kikuni	(Raia Mutomboki group under Juriste Kikuni)
17	Coalition Raia Mukombozi	(Raia Mutomboki group under Ngandu Lundimu and Donat Kengwa)
18	URDC	(Union pour la rehabilitation de la démocratie au Congo)

19	ADF	(Allied Democratic Forces)
20	Mai-Mai Shetani	(Mai-Mai group under Shetani)
21	FRPI	(Front de résistance patriotique de l'Ituri)
22	RUD-*Urunana*	(Rassemblement unité et démocratie)
23	FDLR-Soki	(FDLR splinter faction under Soki)
24	Mai-Mai Morgan	(Mai-Mai group under Morgan)
25	Local Defence	(Uvira-based local militia groups)
26	Mai-Mai Kirikicho	(Mai-Mai group under Kirikicho)
27	Mai-Mai FPDC-Mayele	(Mai-Mai Force populaire de défense du Congo)
28	Mai-Mai Fujo/ ex-Baleke	(Mai-Mai coalition under Fujo, formerly Baleke)
29	Mai-Mai N'yikiribha	(Mai-Mai group under N'yikiribha)
30	ALEC	(Alliance pour la libération de l'est du Congo)

peuple [CNDP]) by Laurent Nkunda in 2005, which inspired the emergence of the Resistant Congolese Patriots (Patriotes résistants congolais [PARECO]).[35] In South Kivu, where the CNDP never gained a foothold, the creation of the Republican Federalist Forces (Forces républicaines fédéralistes) by Banyamulenge leaders exemplified an emerging cleavage between former RCD comrades, and—as with the CNDP—also led to counter-mobilisation by Mai-Mai and other militia. Like the RCD, the CNDP established a parallel administration in its area, including appointing clerks and local authorities. Following a failed attempt in 2008, the 2009 Goma Conference assembled over 20 different armed groups, most of which reintegrated into the army. The result was heavy competition for military ranks.[36] Shortly after, Nkunda was arrested by Rwanda, and his rival Bosco Ntaganda led CNDP troops back into the Armed Forces of the Democratic Republic

Figure 1.2: Armed groups in eastern Congo in 2015[37]

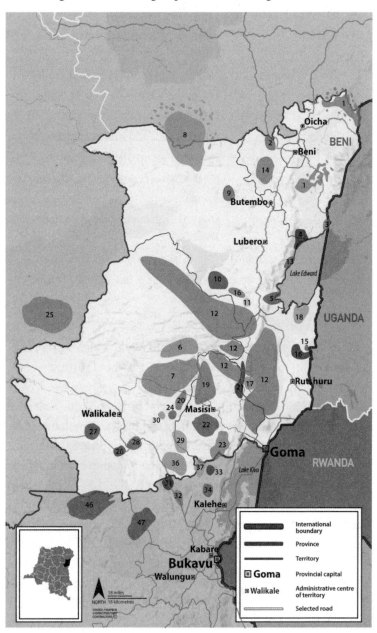

VIOLENT CONTINUITIES

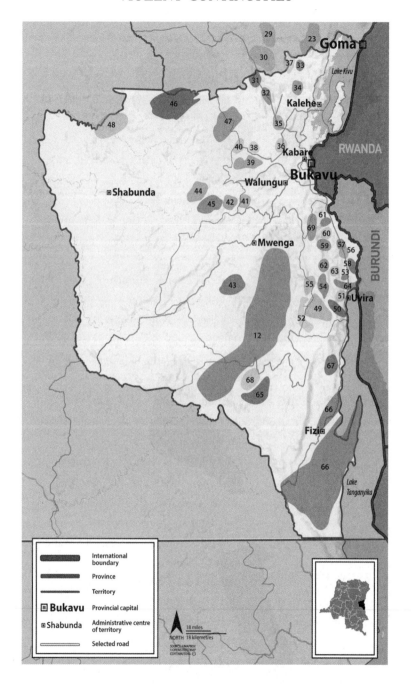

1	ADF	(Allied Democratic Forces)
2	FOLC	(Forces œcumeniques pour la libération du Congo)
3	Mai-Mai Kasindiens	(Mai-Mai group with roots in the 1990s mobilisation)
4	Mai-Mai Nguru	(Mai-Mai group under Nguru)
5	MPLC	(Mouvement populaire pour la libération du Congo)
6	NDC	(Nduma Defence of Congo)
7	NDC-Rénové	(Nduma Defence of Congo-Rénové)
8	Mai-Mai Manu	(Formerly Mai-Mai Morgan, under Manu)
9	FDK	(Force de défense du Kongo)
10	UPCP-Lafontaine	(Union patriotique des congolais pour la paix, led by Kakule Sikuli)
11	UPCP-Damaceni	(UPCP splinter group under Damaceni)
12	FDLR	(Forces démocratiques de libération du Rwanda)
13	Mai-Mai PAREM	(Patriotes résistants Mai-Mai)
14	Mai-Mai Vurondo	(Mai-Mai group with roots in the 1990s mobilisation)
15	Kambale group	(Former FDLR-Soki splinter group)
16	RUD-*Urunana*	(Rassemblement unité et démocratie)
17	Nyatura-Domi	(Nyatura group under Domi, formerly Muchoma and Bapfakururimi)
18	Mai-Mai Charles	(Mai-Mai group under Charles Bokande, formerly Shetani)
19	APCLS	(Alliance des patriotes pour un Congo libre et souverain)
20	FDC-Guides	(Forces de défense du Congo)
21	Nyatura-FDDH (Kasongo)	(Forces de défense des droits humains, led by Kasongo Kalamo)

22	Nyatura-Delta	(Nyatura group under Delta Gashamare)
23	Nyatura-Kalume	(Nyatura group under Matias Kalume)
24	Guides-MAC	(Mouvement d'action pour le changement)
25	Mai-Mai Simba	(Mai-Mai group under Mando Mazeri, with roots in the 1960s)
26	Raia Mutomboki Akilo	(Raia Mutomboki group under Akilo)
27	Raia Mutomboki Mirage	(Raia Mutomboki group under Mirage)
28	Raia Mutomboki Elenge	(Raia Mutomboki group under Elenge)
29	Mai-Mai Kifuafua Limenzi	(Kifuafua faction under Limenzi)
30	Mai-Mai Kifuafua Delphin	(Kifuafua faction under Delphin Mbaenda)
31	Raia Mutomboki Shukuru	(Raia Mutomboki group under Shukuru Kawaya)
32	Raia Mutomboki Hamakombo	(Raia Mutomboki group under Bwaale Hamakombo)
33	Raia Mutomboki Musole	(Raia Mutomboki group under Musole)
34	Raia Mutomboki Butachibera	(Raia Mutomboki group under Butachibera)
35	Raia Mutomboki Mweeke	(Raia Mutomboki group under Mweeke)
36	Raia Mutomboki Imani Bitaa	(Raia Mutomboki group under Imani Bitaa)
37	Mai-Mai Kirikicho	(Mai-Mai group under Kirikicho Mirimba)
38	Raia Mutomboki Blaise	(Raia Mutomboki group under Blaise)

39	Raia Mutomboki Lukoba	(Raia Mutomboki group under Lukoba)
40	Raia Mutomboki Kashungu	(Raia Mutomboki group under Kashungushungu)
41	Raia Mutomboki Maheshe	(Raia Mutomboki group under Maheshe)
42	Raia Mutomboki Ndarumanga	(Raia Mutomboki group under Ndarumanga)
43	Mai-Mai N'yikiribha	(Mai-Mai group under N'yikiribha)
44	Raia Mutomboki Mabala	(Raia Mutomboki group under Mabala Mese)
45	Raia Mutomboki Makombo	(Raia Mutomboki group under Makombo)
46	Raia Mutomboki Takulengwe	(Raia Mutomboki group under Takulengwe, ex-Kikuni)
47	Raia Mutomboki Donat/Ngandu	(Raia Mutomboki group under Donat Kengwa and Ngandu Lundimu)
48	Raia Mutomboki Kazimoto	(Raia Mutomboki group under Kazimoto, ex-Kikuni)
49	Gumino	(Banyamulenge groups led by Nyamusharaba, formerly Tawimbi)
50	Mai-Mai Toto	(Mai-Mai group under Toto)
51	Mai-Mai Fujo	(Mai-Mai group under Fujo Zabuloni)
52	Local Defence Hauts Plateaux	(Uvira-based local militia groups)
53	Mai-Mai Nyerere	(Mai-Mai group under Nyerere)
54	Mai-Mai Mushombe	(Mai-Mai group under Mushombe)
55	Mai-Mai Mahoro	(Mai-Mai group under Mahoro)
56	Mai-Mai Karakara	(Mai-Mai group under Karakara)

57	Mai-Mai Simusizi	(Mai-Mai group under Simusizi)
58	Mai-Mai Kilolo	(Mai-Mai group under Kilolo and Gere)
59	Local Defence Intervention	(Uvira-based local militia group led by 'Intervention')
60	Local Defence Molière	(Uvira-based local militia group led by Molière Mutulanyi)
61	Local Defence Mahinduzi	(Uvira-based local militia group led by Mahinduzi)
62	Local Defence Santos	(Uvira-based local militia group led by Santos)
63	Local Defence Kashumba	(Uvira-based local militia group led by Kashumba)
64	FNL-Nzabampema	(Nzabampema wing of the Front national de libération)
65	Mai-Mai Mulumba	(Mai-Mai group under Mulumba)
66	Mai-Mai Yakotumba	(Mai-Mai group under Amuri Yakotumba)
67	Mai-Mai Bwasakala/Réunion	(Mai-Mai group under Bwasakala and Réunion Warusasa)
68	Mai-Mai Chochi/ Yenga	(Mai-Mai group under Shoshi and Yenga)
69	Local Defence Rushombo	(Uvira-based local militia group with unknown leaders)

of the Congo (Forces armées de la république démocratique du Congo [FARDC]) to redeploy in North and South Kivu.

Kaleidoscopic conflicts

With Nkunda off the balance sheet and Ntaganda appointed FARDC general, Kinshasa and Kigali organised their military rapprochement through joint operations against the FDLR. The

Figure 1.3: Armed groups in eastern Congo in 2017[38]

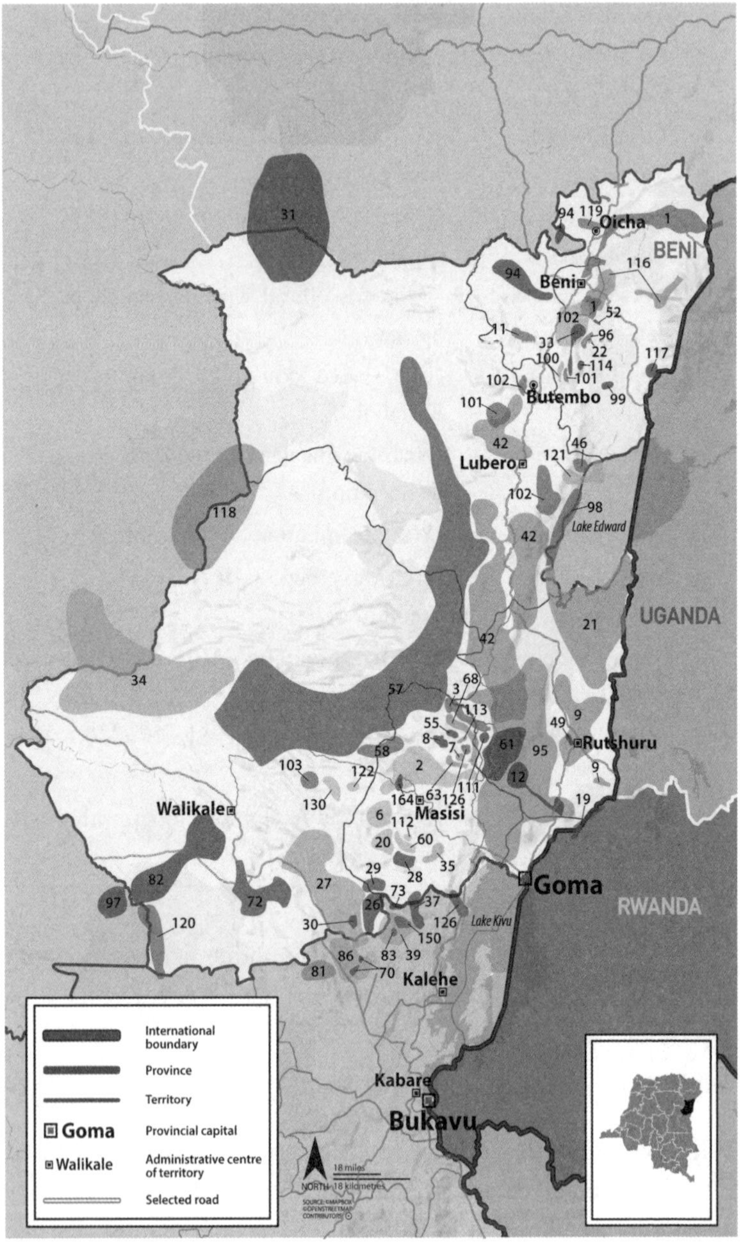

VIOLENT CONTINUITIES

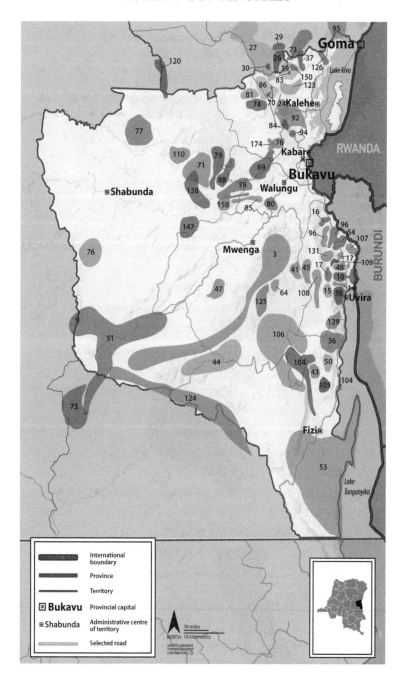

1	ADF	(Allied Democratic Forces)
2	APCLS	(Alliance des patriotes pour un Congo libre et souverain)
3	CNRD	(Conseil national pour le renouveau et la démocratie; FDLR split-off)
4	Nyatura Nzayi	(Nyatura group under Nzayimana)
5	Mai-Mai Muhima	(Mai-Mai group under Muhima)
6	FDC-Guides	(Forces de défense du Congo)
7	Local Defence Busumba	(Masisi-based militia led by ex-M23)
8	FDLR	(Forces démocratiques de libération du Rwanda)
9	RUD-*Urunana*	(Rassemblement unité et démocratie)
10	FNL-Nzabampema	(Nzabampema wing of the Front national de libération)
11	URDC Kombi	(Union pour la rehabilitation de la démocratie au Congo)
12	Nyatura-FDP	(Nyatura-Forces de défense du peuple)
13	Raia Mutomboki Shemakingi	(Raia Mutomboki group under Shemakingi)
14	Local Defence Zone	(Uvira-based local militia group led by 'Zone')
15	Local Defence Kashumba	(Uvira-based local militia group led by Kashumba)
16	Local Defence Mahinduzi	(Uvira-based local militia group led by Prosper Mahinduzi)
17	Mai-Mai Mbulu	(Mai-Mai group under Mbulu)
18	Mai-Mai Délégués	(Mai-Mai group with unclear leadership)
19	Former M23	(Former Mouvement du 23 mars)
20	Guides-MAC	(Mouvement d'action pour le changement)

21	Mai-Mai Charles	(Mai-Mai group under Charles Bokande, formerly Shetani)
22	Mai-Mai Corps du Christ	(Mai-Mai group under Baraka Lolwako and David Maranatha)
23	FRPI	(Front de résistance patriotique de l'Ituri)
24	Raia Mutomboki Kabanzi	(Raia Mutomboki group under Weteshi Kabanzi)
25	Raia Mutomboki Manyilisa	(Raia Mutomboki group under Manyilisa)
26	Mai-Mai Kifuafua Baeni/Limenzi	(Kifuafua faction under Limenzi and Baeni)
27	Mai-Mai Kifuafua Delphin	(Kifuafua faction under Delphin Mbaenda)
28	Nyatura Kigingi	(Nyatura group under Kigingi)
29	Mai-Mai Kifuafua Maachano	(Kifuafua faction under Maachano)
30	Mai-Mai Kifuafua Shalio	(Kifuafua faction under Shalio)
31	Mai-Mai Simba-Manu	(Mai-Mai group under Manu, formerly Morgan)
32	Mai-Mai Mwenyemali	(Mai-Mai group under Mwenyemali)
33	Mai-Mai Nzirunga	(Mai-Mai group under Nzirunga)
34	Mai-Mai Simba Forces Divines	(Mai-Mai group under Mando Mazeri, with roots in the 1960s)
35	Nyatura Mahanga	(Nyatura group under Mahanga)
36	Mai-Mai Réunion aka FPC	(Mai-Mai group under Réunion Warusasa, member of CNPSC)
37	Nyatura Bizagwira	(Nyatura group under Bizagwira)
38	Mai-Mai Makanaki	(Mai-Mai group under Makanaki)

39	Mai-Mai Kirikicho	(Mai-Mai group under Kirikicho Mirimba)
40	Raia Mutomboki Machite	(Raia Mutomboki group under Machite)
41	Mai-Mai Mahoro	(Mai-Mai group under Mahoro)
42	Mai-Mai Mazembe	(Umbrella term for Mai-Mai groups in Lubero, including UPDI)
43	Mai-Mai Mulumba	(Mai-Mai group under Mulumba, member of CNPSC)
44	Mai-Mai Mushombe	(Mai-Mai group under Mushombe)
45	Mai-Mai Nguru	(Mai-Mai group under Nguru)
46	Mai-Mai N'yikiribha	(Mai-Mai group under N'yikiribha)
47	Mai-Mai Nyerere	(Mai-Mai group under Nyerere)
48	Mai-Mai PAREM	(Patriotes résistants Mai-Mai)
49	Mai-Mai Echilo	(Mai-Mai group under Echilo, member of CNPSC)
50	Mai-Mai Malaika	(Mai-Mai group under She Assani, member of CNPSC)
51	Mai-Mai Vivuya	(Mai-Mai group under Vivuya)
52	Mai-Mai Yakotumba	(Mai-Mai group under Amuri Yakotumba, member of CNPSC)
53	Mai-Mai Karakara	(Mai-Mai group under Karakara)
54	Nyatura APRDC	(Alliance des patriotes pour la restauration de la démocratie au Congo)
55	Twirwaneho	(Banyamulenge self-defence groups)
56	NDC-Rénové	(Nduma Defence of Congo-Rénové)
57	NDC	(Nduma Defence of Congo)
58	Raia Mutomboki Mamba	(Raia Mutomboki group under Mamba)
59	Nyatura-Delta	(Nyatura group under Delta Gashamare)

60	Nyatura-Domi	(Nyatura group under Domi Ndaruhutse)
61	Mai-Mai Mupekenya	(Mai-Mai group under Mupekenya)
62	Nyatura Kavumbi	(Nyatura group under Kavumbi)
63	Nyatura-Kalume	(Nyatura group under Matias Kalume)
64	Nyatura-FDDH (Kasongo)	(Forces de défense des droits humains, led by Kasongo Kalamo)
65	Local Defence Ngengwe	(Uvira-based local militia group led by Ngengwe)
66	CNPSC	(Coalition nationale du peuple pour la souveraineté du Congo)
67	Raia Mutomboki Akilo	(Raia Mutomboki group under Akilo)
68	Raia Mutomboki Blaise	(Raia Mutomboki group under Blaise)
69	Raia Mutomboki Butachibera	(Raia Mutomboki group under Butachibera)
70	Raia Mutomboki Donat/Ngandu	(Raia Mutomboki group under Donat Kengwa and Ngandu Lundimu)
71	Raia Mutomboki Elenge	(Raia Mutomboki group under Elenge)
72	Mai-Mai Kiwis Kalume	(Mai-Mai group under Kiwis Kalume, member of CNPSC)
73	Raia Mutomboki Hamakombo	(Raia Mutomboki group under Bwaale Hamakombo)
74	Raia Mutomboki Imani Bitaa	(Raia Mutomboki group under Imani Bitaa)
75	Raia Mutomboki Kimba	(Raia Mutomboki group under Kimba)
76	Raia Mutomboki Kazimoto	(Raia Mutomboki group under Kazimoto, ex-Kikuni)

77	Raia Mutomboki Lukoba	(Raia Mutomboki group under Lukoba)
78	Raia Mutomboki Mabala	(Raia Mutomboki group under Mabala Mese)
79	Raia Mutomboki Maheshe	(Raia Mutomboki group under Maheshe)
80	Raia Mutomboki Mungoro	(Raia Mutomboki group under Mungoro)
81	Raia Mutomboki Mirage	(Raia Mutomboki group under Mirage)
82	Raia Mutomboki Musole	(Raia Mutomboki group under Musole)
83	Raia Mutomboki Safari	(Raia Mutomboki group under Safari)
84	Raia Mutomboki Ndarumanga	(Raia Mutomboki group under Ndarumanga)
85	Raia Mutomboki Shukuru	(Raia Mutomboki group under Shukuru Kawaya)
86	Raia Mutomboki Kikwama	(Raia Mutomboki group under Kikwama)
87	Raia Mutomboki Wemba	(Raia Mutomboki group under Wemba)
88	Mai-Mai Aigle	(Mai-Mai group under 'Aigle', member of CNPSC)
89	UPCP Lafontaine	(Union patriotique des congolais pour la paix, led by Kakule Sikuli)
90	Raia Mutomboki Shabani	(Raia Mutomboki group under Shabani)
91	Mai-Mai Réné	(Mai-Mai group under Réné, member of CNPSC)
92	Raia Mutomboki Bipompa	(Raia Mutomboki group under Bipompa)

93	MNLDK-Kyandenga	(Mouvement national pour la libération durable du Kongo)
94	Nyatura John Love	(Nyatura group under 'John Love')
95	Mai-Mai Mazimano	(Mai-Mai group under Mazimano)
96	Raia Mutomboki Kisekelwa	(Raia Mutomboki group under Kisekelwa)
97	Mai-Mai FMP	(Front des mouvements populaires, led by Jackson Muhukambuto)
98	Mai-Mai Dario	(Mai-Mai group under Dario)
99	Mai-Mai Léopards-Muthundo	(Mai-Mai group under Muthundo)
100	MRC-L	(Mouvement révolutionnaire du Congo-Lumumba)
101	UPLC	(Union des patriotes pour la libération du Congo)
102	Raia Mutomboki Shebitembe	(Raia Mutomboki group under Shebitembe)
103	Mai-Mai Ebu Ela	(Mai-Mai group under Ebu Ela, member of CNPSC)
104	RED-*Tabara*	(Résistance pour un état de droit-*Tabara*)
105	Gumino	(Banyamulenge groups led by Nyamusharaba, formerly Tawimbi)
106	Mai-Mai Bigaya	(Mai-Mai group under Bigaya)
107	FOREBU/FPB	(Forces républicaines du Burundi/Forces populaires du Burundi)
108	FNL-Nibizi	(Nibizi wing of the Front national de libération)
109	Raia Mutomboki Kabazimia	(Raia Mutomboki group under Kabazimia)

110	Nyatura Bagaruza	(Nyatura group with unknown leadership)
111	Nyatura JED	(Nyatura Justice Égalité Démocratie)
112	Nyatura Jean-Marie	(Nyatura group under Jean-Marie)
113	Mai-Mai Kithikyolo	(Raia Mutomboki group under Kithikyolo)
114	Mai-Mai Sibenda	(Raia Mutomboki group under Sibenda)
115	Pakombe militia	(Local militia involved in Beni violence)
116	Mai-Mai Lwanga	(Raia Mutomboki group under Lwanga)
117	Mai-Mai Simba	(Mai-Mai group under Luc Yabili, with roots in 1960s mobilisation)
118	M'vuba militia	(Local militia involved in Beni violence)

operations, coined Umoja Wetu (Swahili for 'Our Unity'), were a blow to the FDLR, but came at a heavy humanitarian cost that contributed to a fragmentation of conflict across the Kivu provinces. As the CNDP disbanded in 2009 to integrate the FARDC, PARECO also fell apart, with some troops joining the army and others evaporating around Masisi. As Umoja Wetu was replaced by joint FARDC–UN operations (Kimia II) in 2010, the Congolese army also embarked on a regimentation process, transforming its structure from brigades to regiments. However, this seemingly administrative process was highly political. Since the failed integration attempts known as *mixage* and *brassage* a few years before, discontent and parallel hierarchies had been a main feature of the FARDC. Nonetheless, instead of forcing coherence and discipline, the regimentation process focused on distributing senior posts to ex-CNDP commanders and recalibrating patronage networks in the army.

In several areas, especially Shabunda, Kalehe and Walikale, this has had disastrous outcomes. The recall of army units for reorganisation created a security void that allowed for a weakened Rwandan FDLR to reorganise in these areas. The subsequent deployment of new, mostly ex-CNDP-led regiments further fanned anti-Rwandophone fear and xenophobia. As a result, populations and hard-line politicians alike invested in rallying a new generation of militia. Known as the 'angry citizens', the Raia Mutomboki quickly developed into dozens of decentralised groups and began taking on the FDLR. If the movement was successful between 2010 and 2012, this was partly due to the strategy of trying to be even more violent towards the FDLR and its civilian dependents than the Rwandan group itself used to be. Later, the Raia Mutomboki's focus turned towards Rwandophone-led army units, a development mirrored by other South Kivu armed groups, such as the Mai-Mai outfit under Amuri Yakotumba.[39]

Driven by uncertainty over their fate, ex-CNDP leaders around Bosco Ntaganda and Sultani Makenga defected to create the M23 (Mouvement du 23 mars) in 2012. The group conquered Goma in November 2012 only to retreat again after 10 days and consolidate in Rutshuru, before suffering a split between the Ntaganda and the Makenga factions. Coupled with pressure on Uganda and Rwanda to withdraw support, this allowed for a decisive FARDC campaign, with backing from the UN, Nyatura and Mai-Mai troops. In sequence, the landscape of belligerents in eastern Congo fragmented. Many of the militia that helped fight the M23 surrendered and joined a new, third national demobilisation programme in 2013, which ultimately failed like its predecessors. The operations against the M23 were followed by large-scale operations against the Ugandan-originating Allied Democratic Forces (ADF), an inwards-oriented Muslim armed group with recruitment and supply networks around its bases in the Rwenzori area, in Uganda and the broader region.

Turning into a protracted crisis persisting into the 2020s, FARDC operations against the ADF led to a string of massacres

Figure 1.4: Armed groups in eastern Congo in 2020[40]

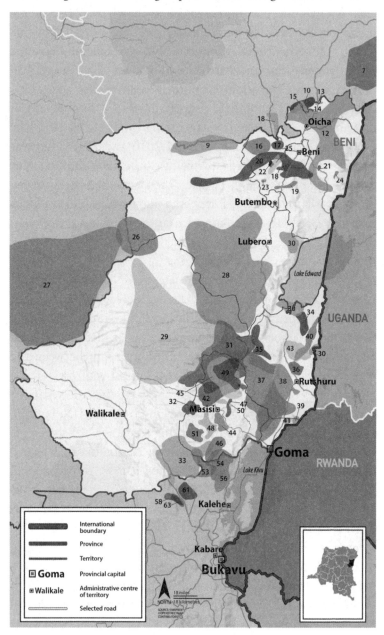

VIOLENT CONTINUITIES

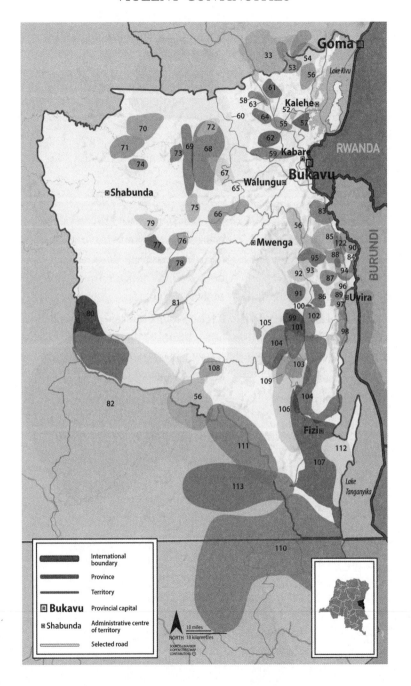

7	FRPI	(Front de résistance patriotique de l'Ituri)
9	Mai-Mai Simba Mangalibi	(Mai-Mai group under Mangalibi, ex-Manu/ex-Morgan)
10	MNLDK-Kyandenga	(Mouvement national pour la libération durable du Kongo)
11	Mai-Mai Barcelone	(Mai-Mai group under Baraka Lolwako)
12	ADF	(Allied Democratic Forces)
13	FLEC/NG	(Front de libération à l'Est du Congo/ Nouvelle génération)
14	Mai-Mai Ngolenge	(Mai-Mai group allied to UPLC, formerly under Jackson Muhukambuto)
15	Mai-Mai Uhuru OAPB	(Organisation d'autodéfense pour la paix à Beni)
16	Mai-Mai Shingo Pamba	(Mai-Mai group under Matabishi, MNLDK split-off)
17	Mai-Mai Mandefu	(Mai-Mai group with roots in the earlier Front de résistance populaire de Lubwe-Ruwenzori, led by Mandefu)
18	Mazembe-APASIKO	(Alliance des patriotes pour le salut intégral du Kongo)
19	Mai-Mai Léopards	(Mai-Mai group emerging from Léopards-Muthundo and Nzirunga groups)
20	UPLC	(Union des patriotes pour la libération du Congo)
21	APRC	(Armée du peuple pour la reconstruction du Congo)
22	Mai-Mai Ninja	(Splinter faction of the UPLC)
23	FAP	(Force d'autodéfense populaire)

24	APR	(Armée patriotique de Ruwenzori)
25	RNL	(Résistance nationale Lumumbiste, aka 'Mille tours par seconde')
26	Mai-Mai Simba UPLD	(Union des patriotes pour la libération et le développement)
27	Mai-Mai Simba Forces Divines	(Mai-Mai group led by Mando Mazeri, with roots in the 1960s)
28	FPP/AP	(Front populaire pour la paix/Armée du peuple, ex-Mazembe)
29	NDC-Rénové/Guidon	(Nduma Defence of Congo-Rénové/Guidon)
30	Mai-Mai FMP	(Front des mouvements populaires, led by Jackson Muhukambuto)
31	NDC-Rénové/Bwira	(Nduma Defence of Congo-Rénové/Bwira)
32	Guides-MAC	(Mouvement d'action pour le changement)
33	Mai-Mai Kifuafua	(Mai-Mai group under Delphin Mbaenda)
34	AFRC	(Alliance des forces de résistance congolaise, ex-Mai-Mai Charles)
35	Nyatura FPDH	(Force de défense du peuple hutu)
36	Amka Jeshi	(Urban militia in Kiwanja, led by Kasereka Celestin)
37	Nyatura CMC	(Collectif des mouvements pour le changement, ex-Nyatura Domi)
38	FDLR	(Forces démocratiques de libération du Rwanda)
39	Former M23	(Former Mouvement du 23 mars)
40	RUD-*Urunana*	(Rassemblement unité et démocratie)
41	Nyatura Turarambiwe	(Umbrella term for several small Nyatura factions)

42	APCLS	(Alliance des patriotes pour un Congo libre et souverain)
43	Nyatura FPPH	(Forces pour la protection du peuple hutu)
44	Nyatura GAV	(Groupe armé les volontaires)
45	Nyatura APRDC/ Abazungu	(Alliance des patriotes pour la restauration de la démocratie au Congo)
46	Mai-Mai Kifuafua Maachano	(Kifuafua faction under Maachano)
47	Nyatura Bagaruza	(Nyatura group with unknown leadership)
48	Nyatura Delta FDDH	(Forces de défense des droits humains, led by Delta Gashamare)
49	Nyatura Jean-Marie	(Nyatura group under Jean-Marie)
50	Nyatura Musheku	(Nyatura group under Musheku)
51	UPDC-Kapasi	(Union des patriotes pour la défense du Congo)
52	Raia Mutomboki Soleil	(Raia Mutomboki group under Soleil)
53	Mai-Mai Kirikicho	(Mai-Mai group under Kirikicho)
54	Nyatura-Kalume	(Nyatura group under Kalume)
55	Raia Mutomboki Shabani	(Raia Mutomboki group under Shabani)
56	CNRD	(Conseil national pour le renouveau et la démocratie)
57	Groupe JKK/CCCRD	(Coalition congolaise pour le change-ment radical et la démocratie)
58	Raia Mutomboki Mungoro	(Raia Mutomboki group under Mungoro)
59	Raia Mutomboki Blaise	(Raia Mutomboki group under Blaise)

60	Raia Mutomboki Bralima	(Raia Mutomboki group under 'Bralima')
61	Raia Mutomboki Butachibera	(Raia Mutomboki group under Butachibera)
62	Raia Mutomboki Bipompa	(Raia Mutomboki group under Bipompa)
63	Raia Mutomboki Hamakombo	(Raia Mutomboki group under Bwaale Hamakombo)
64	Raia Mutomboki Lance	(Raia Mutomboki group under Lance Muteya)
65	Raia Mutomboki Lukoba	(Raia Mutomboki group under Lukoba)
66	Raia Mutomboki Ndarumanga	(Raia Mutomboki group under Ndarumanga)
67	Raia Mutomboki Mabala	(Raia Mutomboki group under Mabala Mese)
68	Raia Mutomboki FPP	(Forces populaires pour la paix, under Donat Kengwa/Ngandu Lundimu)
69	Raia Mutomboki Walike	(Raia Mutomboki group under Walike)
70	Raia Mutomboki Kazimoto	(Raia Mutomboki group under Kazimoto, ex-Kikuni)
71	Raia Mutomboki Kabazimia	(Raia Mutomboki group under Kabazimia)
72	Raia Mutomboki Musolwa	(Raia Mutomboki group under Musolwa)
73	Raia Mutomboki Charles Quint	(Raia Mutomboki group under Charles Quint)
74	Raia Mutomboki Kabé	(Raia Mutomboki group under Kabé)
75	Raia Mutomboki 100kg	(Raia Mutomboki group under '100kg')

76	Raia Mutomboki Kimba	(Raia Mutomboki group under Kimba)
77	Raia Mutomboki Kampanga	(Raia Mutomboki group under Kampanga)
78	Raia Mutomboki Bozi	(Raia Mutomboki group under Bozi)
79	Raia Mutomboki LeFort	(Raia Mutomboki group under LeFort)
80	Raia Mutomboki Musumbu	(Raia Mutomboki group under Jean Musumbu)
81	Mai-Mai Makindu	(Mai-Mai group under Makindu)
82	Mai-Mai Malaika	(Mai-Mai group under She Assani)
83	Mai-Mai Rasta	(Mai-Mai group under Rasta)
84	FNL-Nzabampema	(Nzabampema wing of the Front national de libération)
85	Mai-Mai Buhirwa	(Mai-Mai group under Buhirwa, split-off from Mwenyemali)
86	Mai-Mai Ilunga	(Mai-Mai group under Ilunga, split-off from Mushombe)
87	Mai-Mai Kashumba	(Former Local Defence, led by Kashumba)
88	Mai-Mai Kijangala	(Mai-Mai group under Kijangala)
89	Mai-Mai Makanaki	(Mai-Mai group under Makanaki)
90	Mai-Mai Mbulu	(Mai-Mai group under Mbulu)
91	Mai-Mai Issa Mutoka	(Mai-Mai group under Issa Mutoka)
92	Mai-Mai Ruma	(Mai-Mai group under Ruma, formerly N'yikiribha)
93	Mai-Mai Mushombe	(Mai-Mai group under Mushombe)
94	Mai-Mai Nyerere	(Mai-Mai group under Nyerere)
95	RED-*Tabara*	(Résistance pour un état de droit-*Tabara*)
96	Mai-Mai Rushaba	(Mai-Mai group under Rushaba)
97	Mai-Mai Réné	(Mai-Mai group under Réné)

98	Mai-Mai Réunion FPLC	(Forces pour la libération du Congo)
99	Mai-Mai Ngalyabatu	(Mai-Mai group under Ngalyabatu)
100	Mai-Mai Mupekenya	(Mai-Mai group under Mupekenya)
101	Twirwaneho	(Banyamulenge self-defence groups)
102	AFP–Gutabara	(Alliances de fédéralistes patriotes, aka Android and Abakenya)
103	Gumino	(Banyamulenge group)
104	Mai-Mai Mutetezi FPDC	(Forces populaires pour la défense du Congo, led by Ebu Ela, ex-CNPSC)
105	Mai-Mai Bishake	(Mai-Mai group under Bishake)
106	Biloze Bishambuke	(Umbrella term for militia in Fizi)
107	Mai-Mai Yakotumba	(Mai-Mai group under Yakotumba)
108	Mai-Mai Aochi	(Mai-Mai group under Aochi, ex-CNPSC)
109	Mai-Mai Shoshi	(Mai-Mai group under Shoshi, ex-CNPSC)
110	Mai-Mai Apa na Pale	(Mai-Mai group under Mundusi)
111	Mai-Mai Mulumba	(Mai-Mai group under Mulumba, ex-CNPSC)
112	Mai-Mai Alida	(Mai-Mai group under Alida, ex-CNPSC)
113	Mai-Mai Brown	(Mai-Mai group under Brown)

Note: For operational reasons, our 2020 mapping included other provinces beyond the Kivus; as such, some numbers are missing here.

in 2014 and 2015, with the ADF, its satellite groups, army units and other militia involved in the killings.[41] At the same time, the decentralisation foreseen in the 2006 Constitution began to materialise between 2013 and 2016. Though North Kivu was not affected by this reorganisation of provincial boundaries from nine to 26 (the former Grand Kivu Province had been partitioned in

1986), new *communes rurales* were to be created.[42] While this process entrenched conflict over land and identity in many places in eastern Congo and beyond—as the 2018 Yumbi violence in Bandundu highlighted—it also contributed to a slow and steady deterioration of security in the highlands of Uvira and Fizi. There, local conflict and the fallout of the Burundian political crisis since 2015 contributed to new waves of armed mobilisation and violence. While not ethnic in essence, the resulting insecurity took on community-based dynamics rooted in longer trajectories of militarisation, insecurity, outside influence and political manipulation, not only in the highlands but—with different dynamics—in the lowland border areas as well.[43]

Between 2015 and 2016, a new cycle of conflict dynamics also began in Masisi, Walikale and Lubero, marking the decline of the FDLR. In June 2016, the Rwandan rebellion split into two groups, the FDLR and the National Council for Renewal and Democracy (Conseil national pour le renouveau et la démocratie [CNRD]), the latter comprising all South Kivu-based FDLR as well as parts of the North Kivu units. Two years earlier, the Walikale-based Nduma Defence of Congo (NDC), led by Sheka Ntabo Ntaberi, had split. Helped by connections with senior army officers, Sheka's deputy, Guidon Shimiray, established the NDC–Rénové and embarked on an unprecedented campaign of expansion and co-optation of smaller armed groups. Benefitting from support from the FARDC, the NDC–Rénové became the lynchpin of the military campaign against the FDLR. It was able to mount an efficient system of taxation, while its clashes with FDLR and Nyatura militia led to renewed displacement in Masisi, Walikale and Lubero.[44] Amidst the confrontation, the FDLR's long-standing commander Sylvestre Mudacumura was killed in September 2019, with scores of civilians killed in Bashali in January and February 2020. By then, the NDC–Rénové had become North Kivu's most important belligerent, with a remarkably efficient operational command and diverse sources of income. Their success was rooted in part in Shimiray's ruthless yet smart leadership, but also benefitted from FARDC supply in arms and ammunition as well as the wide-ranging impunity offered to them. Despite this, in June 2020, internal tensions that had cooked up around Shimiray over time triggered a division. With tacit support by senior army officials, Shimiray's co-commanders, Gilbert Bwira and Mapenzi Likuhe, formed their own branch—fomenting weeks of internecine fighting with a heavy humanitarian toll on civilians.

This led to a reordering of alliances and conflict dynamics stretching to the entire southern part of North Kivu. Meanwhile, the Beni violence started spreading increasingly into southern Ituri, whilst violence around the highlands of South Kivu saw an uptick in 2020 and 2021. Adding to ADF violence and FARDC military operations, areas around Beni and Butembo as well as southern Ituri came to face Congo's tenth and most deadly outbreak of the Ebola virus disease between 2018 and 2020. Compounded by both violent resistance against healthcare providers and a faulty international and national approach to the epidemic, the outbreak helped further delegitimise national and international intervention.[45] Moreover, Ituri Province itself has slipped back into open conflict since 2017, as a new assemblage of militia known as Cooperative for Development of the Congo (Coopérative pour le développement du Congo [CODECO]) began operating attacks against villages and military positions in and around Djugu. Throughout 2021, this conflict became increasingly deadly.[46]

The political transition from Joseph Kabila to Félix Tshisekedi has not yet altered eastern Congo's security predicament. Emerging from elections classified as fraudulent by many, the new president faced uneasy cohabitation with his predecessor's parliamentary bloc and numerous long-standing stalwarts in key political, judicial and security institutions. Coupling savvy tactics with patience, Tshisekedi and his Congolese and international allies embarked on a two-year journey to slowly loosen Kabila's grip over the country. If observers keep wondering to what extent these developments were framed by secretive accords between the two presidents, they align both in astonishment over how Tshisekedi imposed himself through a patchy but vast new coalition known as Sacred Union of the Nation (Union sacrée de la nation) and in the analysis that two years of quarrelling over de facto power left the entirety of Congo's social and security problems unsolved. It was only in mid-2021 that Kinshasa turned the spotlight to eastern Congo again. In an unprecedented move, Tshisekedi declared martial law for Ituri and North Kivu (but not South Kivu). If human rights violations and acts of violence had been peaking in the first months of 2021, the 'state of siege' and a pending new national demobilisation programme are—at the time of writing in late 2021—yet to prove their usefulness to trigger sustainable conflict resolution and herald a more peaceful future for eastern Congo. By the end of 2021, indicators of violence and displacement seemed to be on the rise again, with hotspots between Beni and Irumu, in Masisi, and in the highlands of southern South Kivu.

These developments highlight the volatility of coalitions and splits between armed groups, sometimes remote-controlled by FARDC and political elites. Many armed groups—like political and customary authorities—operate relatively close ties at the provincial, national and even regional levels. Most of these conflicts are not linked to minerals writ small; they have social, political and economic undertones in an environment of 'no war, no peace' that frames populations' struggles for subsistence and efforts at peacebuilding. This rich context notwithstanding, the 'conflict minerals' paradigm—as the next chapter will demonstrate—only cursorily accounts for the interlocking trajectories of violence and promotes a simplistic colonial view, promoting white saviourism as quick fix to all problems.

2

GENESIS OF A DIGITAL PARADIGM

Zooming in on the evolution of artisanal mining and armed conflict, this chapter gives an account of the converging factors that allowed minerals to play a role in the Congolese wars and, as importantly, in the collective imagination of these wars. After a short explainer on the social geology of 'conflict minerals' and a brief history of mining in Congo, the chapter traces how armed and unarmed stakeholders turned to artisanal mining in a bid for both subsistence and accumulation. It then demonstrates in what ways mining became inscribed into conflict dynamics, but also remained outside these at other times. Subsequently, the chapter analyses the scrutiny that stacked up from early UN and NGO reports in the early 2000s, when global tantalum prices experienced a steep rise that helped turn eastern Congo into a short-lived transnational El Dorado of violent trade. The chapter finally discusses how transnational advocacy on 'conflict minerals' has not only framed outsider imagery of violence and greed in Congo, but become amalgamated with sexual violence, gorilla extinction and other issues, leading to stubborn tropes.

CONFLICT MINERALS INC.

What are 'conflict minerals'?

Since the early 2000s, there has been broad agreement across science and policy that the term 'conflict minerals' essentially regroups four substances: gold, tantalum (coltan), tin and tungsten. While the importance of artisanal gold in eastern Congo's political economy of conflict is undisputed and well documented, notably in regular UN reports, this book focuses on the latter three, known as 3T, since they are the ones primarily affected by currently operating traceability, formalisation and certification programmes.

Tantalum ($_{73}$Ta) is a metal gained from tantalite ore. With a density of $17g/cm^3$, this blueish-black ore is one of the heaviest known metals. It has particular properties, such as high resistance to corrosion and oxidation, high conductivity and a melting point of over 3,000 degrees Celsius. These qualities contribute to coltan's quasi-mystical value and reputation in Congolese mining communities.[1] They also make it a sought-after commodity for industries in need of heat-resistant conductors—in particular high-end mobile electronics—or non-corrosive surfaces, as well as so-called superalloys. Tantalite ore can be found across the world, key reservoirs being located in Canada, Australia, Ethiopia, Egypt, Congo, China, Mozambique and Brazil. It often occurs together with niobium, cassiterite, manganese or iron. In eastern Congo, most tantalite is found in the shape of columbite-tantalite, colloquially known as 'coltan'. Congo harbours an estimated 5–10% of known world reserves and has, in recent decades, sourced an average of 10–20% of annual global production.[2] Congo's most important known coltan deposits sit on the edges of North Kivu's Masisi territory and South Kivu's Kalehe and Shabunda territories, as well as in Tanganyika Province. On average, pure tantalum is traded internationally at 100–150 USD/kg, with occasional boom and bust cycles and fluctuation related to supply and demand. As opposed to tin, tungsten and other ores, tantalum is usually bilaterally traded outside classic commodity stock markets.

Tin ($_{50}$Sn) is a metal derived from cassiterite ore and the tin dioxide (SnO_2) contained within it. Its colour ranges from light to dark grey, raw cassiterite often appearing sandy. It has a density of 6–7g/cm^3 and melts at 230 degrees Celsius. Its use by humans dates back at least five millennia, and it is one of the longest-known metals. China, Indonesia, Brazil and Peru are estimated to possess the largest global deposits. Tin is predominantly used in metal alloys—most famously bronze when melted with copper—and to coat other substances. In the past decade, international tin prices have held steady around 15–30 USD/kg. In eastern Congo, cassiterite is often sold between 2–5 USD/kg at the mining sites and 5–8 USD/kg in domestic trading. Hundreds of cassiterite mines are scattered in North and South Kivu, Maniema and Tanganyika Provinces. Tin is the most widespread of the 3T minerals in eastern Congo but the least valuable one.

Tungsten, or wolfram ($_{74}$W), is a greyish metal sourced from wolframite ore. A rare metal, it has a density of 19g/cm^3 and the highest melting point of all metals, at 3,400 degrees Celsius. While these values outdo tantalum, tungsten is brittle—making it less useable for certain products. It is used for light bulbs and superalloys and in armaments. China is the world's leading producer, followed by Russia, Canada, Bolivia and Vietnam. Wolframite is less prominent in eastern Congo's mineral markets and sourced mostly as a by-product from coltan and cassiterite mines. Recent tungsten prices have fluctuated around 30–50 USD/kg.

While in legal and regulatory terms all 3T minerals are treated equally in Congo, the role of coltan is particularly relevant for the 'conflict minerals' paradigm given its peculiar economics, providing it with a mystical aura. Today, the 2000 coltan boom continues to fascinate Congolese and others to the degree that the materialities and metaphysics of this 'digital mineral' are often explained with 'magics', and an entire book has been dedicated to it.[3] As with diamonds elsewhere, coltan inspired miners to 'draw a "rhizomatic" map ... they use to describe the operations of capitalism' and channel their aspirations.[4] Smith observes that coltan's 'value is not simply economic' but embedded into multiple, often metaphysical systems of meaning.[5] Often this relates to the ways in which Congolese miners see themselves as a neuralgic part of transnational supply chains, but also within the global resource economy and human society at large.

Some of this fascination is rooted in the fact that, until the mid-1990s, coltan was a mere by-product of cassiterite and other minerals. It was usually sold as random waste metal while more important stocks were often stored in parastatal warehouses. Long known by specialised industries, its use has skyrocketed since 1960; however, compared with tin, a majority of Western societies were not intimately familiar with it, and neither were Congolese until the Second Congo War closed in on the Kivus and a curious price peak occurred.[6] Mineral exploitation initially played a marginal (if any) role in the economics of conflict and focused largely on large-scale concessions as the object of negotiation between Laurent-Désiré Kabila's AFDL rebellion and international mining companies. This significantly changed with the onset of the subsequent Second Congo War and renewed Rwandan (and Ugandan) intervention. But before coming to that, a brief overview on the broader history of mining in Congo is helpful to set the stage.

A short history of mining in Congo

Congo is widely known for harbouring abundant mineral reservoirs that play a central role in its political economy. Despite scant literature, there is some evidence of precolonial mining within Congo's contemporary borders. Controlled by customary leaders in Katanga, most notably King Msiri in the nineteenth century, the previously decentralised dynamics of copper mining were concentrated in the hands of local smelters; they paid tributes in exchange for the right to buy and transform raw copper into bracelets and other artefacts used to trade with other areas in precolonial Congo. These practices survived into the era of the Congo Free State, which 'pioneered methods for securing economic extraction in the absence of modern state institutions'.[7] However, mining activities at that time did not play a significant role in the area that is now known as Kivu.[8]

Colonial mining operations began to gain pace in the latter days of the Congo Free State, when mining replaced the predominant rubber economy of Leopold II's private colony. From 1906 onwards, mining activities concentrated on Katanga and mostly focused on copper (which remains Congo's top export good in terms of volume today) and cobalt (for which Congo has become the world's top producer). Much of the business centred around the Union minière du Haut-Katanga—renamed Gécamines in 1966—which has remained the country's flagship mining company, with numerous joint ventures. In 1919, the Société minière du Beceka was created to exploit diamonds from the Kasai region. It transformed into the Société minière de Bakwanga (MIBA) in 1961. Even today, Gécamines and MIBA are the two foremost Congolese parastatal mining outfits, despite not operating in the two Kivus.

In eastern Congo, mining operations were initiated by the Chemins de fer du Congo supérieur aux Grand Lacs (CFL), which acquired a 4 million-hectare concession in return for building a railway to connect the Congo River with the Kivu area. Mining began in 1923, when CFL's owner—the Groupe Empain—set up the Compagnie minière des Grands Lacs

(MGL). Extraction mainly targeted gold, but soon branched out to tin and associated ores such as tungsten, tantalum, niobium and pyrochlore. During that era, pits were run by nine companies, including MGL, that merged into the Société minière du Kivu (SOMINKI) in 1976. SOMINKI was led by Belgian shareholders organised in COGEMIN, a subsidiary of Empain, with less than 30% Zairian participation. Until the 1980s, it was the largest concessionary and industrial mining operator in the former Grand Kivu Province (regrouping Maniema, North Kivu and South Kivu from 1966 to 1988).

While SOMINKI avoided nationalisation during Zairianisation, it did not escape economic decline in the 1980s. In 1997, it was liquidated and replaced by the Société aurifère Kivu-Maniema (SAKIMA), in which the Canadian Banro Corporation briefly operated a 93% stake. Having taken power from Mobutu, Laurent-Désiré Kabila created the Société minière du Congo and expropriated SAKIMA. Later, a 1998 US court ruling pressured the late Kabila's son and successor Joseph Kabila to settle the dispute with Banro. SAKIMA became a fully state-owned company, holding numerous mining concessions in the Kivus and Maniema, whilst not actually doing a lot of mining itself. Despite its own operations being halted around 2002, the company continues to formally exist and is currently involved in various joint ventures with Congolese and foreign firms. Meanwhile, from the 1990s, myriad medium-size private trading houses, called *comptoirs*, began to operate, sharing the market with industry heavyweights.[9]

Currently, most mining in Congo follows two grand ideal types of supply chains. One is industrial, sustained by heavy installations and machinery and usually organised as deep-shaft, but sometimes also open-pit, operations.[10] Virtually the entirety of copper and a good share of cobalt mining is done this way, as well as vast parts of Congo's diamond, gold and tin production. However, most industrial mining is done outside the Kivu region, most predominantly in former Katanga Province. The other type—artisanal mining (known also by its acronym ASM)—has sporadically existed since precolonial times, but grew significantly in popularity during the 1970s and 1980s when major miners suffered the fallout of global economic decline—compounding the dire socio-economic situation in the late, ailing Zairian state.

Numerous unemployed citizens took to the margins of decrepit industrial mines to make ends meet in the absence of other job opportunities.[11] Initially, Mobutu responded with repression—especially against artisanal diamond miners in Kasai[12]—but in 1983 a new law liberalised the sector, allowing artisanal miners and private trading houses to exist. Nevertheless, the idea that 'deregulation and privatization would prove a panacea for African economic stagnation was a dangerous and destructive illusion'.[13] While this move put legislation on a par with existing practice, it also meant a state-sponsored 'informalisation'. However, while industrial mining had been dominant since colonial times, these policies triggered a lasting boom of artisanal mining in Grand Kivu. Although there have been major industrial projects ever since, such operations have repeatedly come under strain, as seemingly suggested by the recent breakdown of Banro's gold operation in South Kivu and other examples in Ituri.[14]

When the country re-emerged as Democratic Republic of the Congo out of a crumbling Mobutist state, it took some years to build a new legal framework governing mineral exploitation. Until its replacement by a new law in March 2018 (kicking off a controversy over industrial mining taxation and royalties), the 2002 mining code formed this framework, alongside the government regulations specifying how the code was to be implemented. One of the most important innovations of the 2002 mining code was the introduction of a formal status for artisanal miners (also known as *creuseurs*) through ID cards and the creation of dedicated artisanal mining areas (known as *zones d'exploitation artisanale*, or ZEAs), even if many miners continue to operate entirely informally since few ZEAs exist in the Kivus.[15] Meanwhile, a broader 'informalisation'[16] of artisanal mining reigned in eastern mining areas as unrecorded trade and episodes of militarisation dominated 3T and gold mining and trade in the Kivus over the course of the following decade. Moreover, a wave of transnational initiatives to formalise artisanal mining would paradoxically reinforce so-called *para-fiscalité*, a Congolese euphemism for illicit taxation, red-tape fraud and clandestine trade. Amongst other factors, this is owing to the fact that ASM formalisation often remains a superficial and partial exercise, which depends on the same institutions rooted in the sector's very own dynamics of 'informalisation' and—in its 'conflict-free' version—follows an apolitical 'tick-box' mentality in tracking 3T trade, which ignores the social and political aspects of formalisation.[17]

Economies in *and* of *war*

The intellectual foundations of the 'conflict minerals' paradigm took their cues from the intersection of violence, war and natural resource exploitation from the late 1990s onwards. During these years, the correlation of artisanal 3T and gold mining with warfare and violent accumulation informed salient media pitches and collective imaginations, including stereotypes linking minerals and rape, with Eurocentric social science pinpointing corruption and political violence as key features of neopatrimonialism.[18] The resulting imageries were further reinforced by colloquial truisms, such as the emblematic *article quinze*, a fictitious Zairian constitutional provision illustrating the art of 'muddling through' in the absence of reliable state infrastructure. Yet, as opposed to Manichean international campaigns, the role of minerals is a story of both economies *of* war, akin to the propositions of greed theory, and economies *in* war, which paint a more nuanced picture. This section traces the emergence of the 'conflict minerals' paradigm in eastern Congo—both on the ground and as it was perceived globally—and explains the roots of transnational policy that would emerge in the form of hard and soft laws. While the push for 'conflict-free' sourcing of 3T minerals came with a 'do-gooder' white saviour mentality, this chapter explains how that benefitted—and became subordinated to—transnational extractive interests that were framed by a misguided analysis of eastern Congo's ASM sector and its conflict dynamics, rendering its impact incomplete and flawed.

In 1998, during the Second Congo War, RCD troops quickly started pillaging an ex-SOMINKI coltan warehouse as they entered Goma. Other armed groups followed suit and developed an interest in mining, as did neighbouring armies as they progressed across the Kivus.[19] The Rwandan and Ugandan armies chartered aircraft to evacuate shipments from Bisie to Goma or straight to Kigali and Kampala, from where they entered global markets.[20] When the frontline of fighting moved westwards in 1999, North Kivu was under firm control of the RCD rebellion that then split into a Kigali-backed and a Kampala-allied faction. The former, called RCD-Goma,[21] developed finely jointed military and civilian hierarchies, mimicking state institutions such as provincial ministries and their technical branches. This involved a mining department and, at the height of the coltan boom in November 2000, the creation of the rebels' very own mining company. Named Société minière des Grands Lacs (SOMIGL), it was bestowed with monopoly rights to export coltan from the territory controlled by the RCD-Goma. The creation of SOMIGL roughly coincided with the global coltan peak—a development not unbeknownst to the group and its Rwandan sponsors, but of short-lived nature despite its lasting impact in collective memory.

Box 1: A vertiginous price peak

Tantalum is subject to 'natural' market-related boom and bust cycles, although it is not publicly traded like other minerals. Prior to the 2000 price peak, these cycles had been kept in check by a small number of interlocking dynamics: the market was small, and stakeholders coordinated in a lobby structure called the Tantalum and Niobium International Study Centre (TIC). Most contracts were futures, allowing secure sales for producers and secure prices for buyers. However, although trade was concentrated in contracts among a narrow group of businesses, the looming digital revolution and subsequent demand exploded an established unimportant spot market. This market was mostly supplied by Central African coltan, the single most important source of tantalum outside the big industrial mines, whose production was tied in with the futures. The concomitant speculation had tantalum prices multiply in the second half of 2000, only to collapse again in 2001, making coltan an object of myth and bewilderment.

After half a year or so, SOMIGL brought in dizzying tax rents to the RCD-Goma, which compounded with the breakdown of international coltan prices in early 2001 and led the company to founder again by April 2001. Under the brief RCD-led monopoly, many traders also ventured into smuggling networks (paradoxically often also including RCD commanders or other armed groups) to export coltan through other routes. Certain trading houses halted operations in protest against the SOMIGL cartel. Nonetheless, the net rent of SOMIGL's operations is estimated to have been at least 2 million USD, and after its shutdown the RCD-Goma began levying taxes in the mining sector similar to those instituted by the 2002 mining code, with individuals close to the group invested in *comptoirs* operating at the time.[22]

The Rwandan army and the RCD-Goma offered a blueprint for other conflict parties in the Congolese wars. Regular army units and Mai-Mai and Raia Mutomboki factions also turned to controlling and taxing artisanal production, including at road-blocks.[23] Some of the resulting networks later had a second lease of life in the new market for 'conflict-free' minerals. Like the RCD-Goma, other armed actors also began to excel in creating stamps and mimicking state symbols in their quest for revenue generation, showing 'a remarkable level of official documentation and red tape, which, however, is mostly used to the disservice of ... citizens'.[24] While this extends beyond minerals, it once was all about coltan. The 2001 report of the UN Panel of Experts judged that Rwanda may have made up to 250 million USD or more during the 2000 coltan peak.[25] Beyond SOMIGL's short-lived grip on much of eastern Congo's coltan production, several other examples illustrate how different conflict parties have repeatedly managed to establish spatially and temporally limited, yet efficient, taxation and protection rackets geared towards the generation of mineral rent.

These examples speak to the idea that 'even in the most severe and anarchic instances of state collapse ... there is seldom a total governance void'.[26] Moreover, it highlights how militarised networks—in specific periods and areas and with varying degrees of efficiency—have run 'complexes of power, profit and protection'[27] in the 3T sector, as the following section illustrates. Such a reading casts doubts on the idea that greed leads to war economies uniquely geared towards the destruction of order and the creation of insecurity for the sake of plunder. While scholars pinpoint the analytical weaknesses of such concepts, it is important to understand the making of such orders, however tenuous they may be over time and space.[28] This requires investigating the repertoires and the full spectrum of governance techniques, which often appear to be literal 'governance experiments', in a mining sector framed by insecurity and low predictability. In that sense, militarised mining happened not only under the afore-mentioned RCD-Goma, SOMIGL and foreign patrons, but also under a variety of other armed groups.[29] While examples differ in style and degree, many of them were marked by replacing central state authority with privatised yet state-like arrangements, tying belligerents to business communities within and beyond Congo's borders.

Rather than a breakdown of order, those are examples of emerging, alternative systems of order, even if they are often wrapped in pretentious, superficial state officialdom. This has continued beyond the grand wars. However, the persistence of fraudulent networks of mineral exploitation and trade more recently can also be ascribed in part to a post-war settlement that prompted the government to reward loyalty of key individuals and militarised networks by distributing rents from Kinshasa to military elites, including former belligerents.[30] Since 2003, this has encouraged further insurgency and similar revenue-generating patterns.[31] The subsequent post-war settlement offered armed actors a chance to re-emerge as providers of authority, negotiating taxation and access against protection. However, 'the oligopolistic nature of these spaces does not necessarily have to mean that they are "lawless outposts"'[32]—more often than not they feature complex systems floating between extortion and a modicum of legitimate domination.[33]

This ambiguous interplay of authority, violence and extraction rarely features in Western advocacy. Instead, the imagery of raped women and child soldiers has been connected to the sky-rocketing global use of mobile devices to support a revolution in global scrutiny rooted in the idea that 'conflict minerals' alone dominate eastern Congo's wars. Campaigns banked on warning global consumers against unintended complicity, suggesting their hunger for high-end gadgets helped brutal belligerents recruit child soldiers and rape women.[34] The complexity of conflict notwithstanding, policymakers and advocates took 'coltan peak'[35] as a confirmation that 'conflicts are more likely to be caused by economic opportunities than by grievance'[36] and—in Congo and elsewhere—that minerals rents financed belligerents. This narrow reading of a bundle of nested wars added to a set of insular strategies for conflict resolution in the early 2000s: politically, there was a flat, teleological push for power-sharing, while the military strategy consisted of supporting hasty military integration.[37] Likewise, resource governance policy was ahistorical and apolitical: guided by unrepentant advocacy, soft and hard laws were tabled in Western capitals, aimed at curbing the trade in 'conflict minerals' to foster 'conflict-free' sourcing initiatives in Central Africa.

The uncritical equation of resource exploitation with neocolonial assumptions on criminality, corruption and state fragility not only ignored the motivations and interests of artisanal miners,[38] it also helped generate effects opposite to the stated aims of development actors, namely more violence, as suggested by longitudinal statistics on human rights violations. While readings of the Congolese conflicts emphasise the destruction of state institutions and economic livelihoods, it is often forgotten that violent conflict also reconfigures authority across all spheres of social and economic life. Hence, it is 'important to [also] examine the deeper social and political causes of destitution that lead to a shift in local livelihoods from agriculture to mineral extraction'.[39] Alternative arrangements (including coercion) between communities and elites—such as protection rackets trading security against taxation—heralded a new type of social contract.[40] The justification for transnational regulation, however, needed to overcome such nuance to be efficient in public discourse,[41] even though seasoned Congo scholars already warned in 2002 that

> ... if there is criminal gain from tantalum on the part of Congolese and foreign actors, tantalum mining has also become a critical mode of survival .... International action against the 'war economy' in the Congo must therefore be careful to punish the real villains.[42]

'Conflict-free' sourcing, then, relied on the assumption that technical reform can solve fundamentally political challenges. In other words, 'conflict minerals' were singled out as the ultimate explanation for war and conflict, and regulation as the core of peacebuilding and conflict resolution policy. Even so, the apolitical and contradictory description of eastern Congo as both an arena of violence and an empty space upon which a new order can seamlessly be implemented is both an illusion and a colonial trope. Transnational regulation of 'conflict minerals' dropped into spaces imagined as unruly or empty when in fact they were highly organised. As Ferguson argues from a *longue durée* view, 'Africa has proved remarkably resistant to a range of externally imposed projects that have aimed to bring it into conformity with Western or "global" models.'[43] This is proved true worldwide: from 'ungoverned spaces' in Iraq or Afghanistan to agrarian change in South Asia or gang violence in Latin America, resistance to outside domination is human and legion, taking multiple forms and shapes.[44] In other words, the 'transterritorial deployments' that form part of 'interventions, broadly conceived, [e.g.] the economic penetration of merchants and capitalist practices',[45] rarely occur in a void. The case of iTSCi's mineral traceability scheme is illustrative. In this case, it stepped into a field that was void of policy (i.e. responsible sourcing) and another one full of competing, contested orders (i.e. economic governance at large). It thus clashed with a contested arena of existing rules and politics where long-standing operators could re-brand themselves as immaculate social entrepreneurs and state bureau-crats could invent new taxes weighing on local producers. This brings us back to Anna Tsing's observation that 'the diversity of supply chains cannot be fully disciplined from inside the chain. This makes supply chains unpredictable and intriguing as frames for understanding capitalism.'[46]

In many ways, iTSCi became the centrepiece of a new trans-national governance complex that, like the World Bank's struc-tural adjustment, aimed at 'substituting upward for downward accountability'.[47] As a private sector effort to meet legal require-ments such as section 1502 of the Dodd–Frank Act and the ICGLR's certification mechanism, as well as to follow interna-tional guidance such as that of the OECD, iTSCi took the shape of 'private indirect government'.[48] From the outset, it operated so much in the shadows of public oversight that even the Congolese government once had to publicly ask for its statistics. Struggling alternatively with either monopoly or exclusion, many Congolese miners and small-scale intermediary traders did not think twice. One of the few who categorically refused to partake in fraud told me in 2014, overwhelmed by disillusion, 'selling to iTSCi is like flushing [minerals] down the toilet'.[49] In sum, and similarly to the kaleidoscope of belligerents that keep conflict alive in eastern Congo,[50] transnational reform to get rid of 'conflict minerals' became yet another 'semi-autonomous field' of authority.[51] In such a pressure cooker of overlapping claims, it therefore comes as no surprise that new regulation is fragmented and moulded into the existing political economy, which remains tenuous, and marked by collusion and contestation alike.

Establishing how systems of 'power, profit and protection'[52] are formulated, the constellations of contestation in which they oper-ate, and how they affect order and access to livelihoods requires an investigation of the spatial and fluid character of authority and networks. This includes understanding the diverse patterns of choice among miners, cooperatives and traders, and the interplay of exogenous and endogenous factors, of political dynamics and hidden registers of violence, power and patronage. This is important since—their role in financing the war notwithstanding—minerals are a key livelihood through which communities build sustainable social relationships in rapidly changing economies as they interact with 'rapid, and potentially depleting, forces and processes.'[53] While 'conflict-free sourcing' may appear sound on paper, it thus reflects the pitfalls of externally driven governance practice, and serves as a cautious reminder that correlation is not the same as causation. In true white saviour fashion, it reproduces different colonial frames, including the empty slate idea, that collide with fragmented authority and the supposedly criminal character of African trade, even though the 'legality of trade is no benchmark to measure the extent to which it fuels conflict'.[54]

Logics of violence and extraction

Out of a wealth of potential examples, the following three cases are snapshots demonstrating how the exploitation of minerals can intersect with temporary, tenuous deployments of authority in the shape of 'governance experiments' to negotiate protection against taxation. They are specific moments in space and time, but hint at wider connections of territory, population, resources and authority. While such arrangements are often short-lived, and the predatory nature of the associated rackets contingent upon a range of other factors (for example, external support, legitimation capacity and coherence, as well as the negotiation with other power brokers such as business or customary leaders), they highlight how the 'sovereign capabilities of non-state actors' can be stimulated in the context of war and post-war political settlements, rather than just being driven by natural resource wealth.[55] They also show how some of the repertoires—often relating in one form or another to the 'state-as-idea'—are used to bolster the deployment of authority.[56]

The first case—a look at the RCD-Kisangani/Mouvement de libération (K/ML)—illustrates that the clout of armed actors can be overstated. After the RCD's 1999 split, Mbusa Nyamwisi's K/ML branch quickly became the dominant military actor in the Grand Nord area around Butembo, Beni and parts of Ituri. From the 1970s onwards, top-down centralised governance faced limitations due to self-reliant, thriving cross-border businesses which had antagonised the Nande community, forming the broader Yira community together with the Konjo on the Ugandan side of the border, from the Kinshasa government. Networks of affluent Nande trading elites posed a formidable challenge to the RCD-K/ML's aspirations to establish its state-like administration. As opposed to orthodox understandings of conflict as economic breakdown, this situation enhanced cross-border trade as pre-existing networks converged with a new transnational militarised elite, thereby overcoming a deadlock that had marked the Mobutu era.[57] Between 2000 and 2003, the Grand Nord's business heavyweights—many of whom export gold and timber and import Asian retail consumer goods—had a deal with the RCD-K/ML administration and its armed wing, the Army of the Congolese People (Armée du peuple congolais [APC]). By developing fixed, pre-paid tax regimes, traders partly imposed their ideas of security governance. This *auto-prise-en-charge*[58] aimed at creating certainty and anticipation for traders, allowing them to do business while replacing their top source of uncertainty—unforeseen, random taxation and pillage—with predetermined rates. The RCD-K/ML administration, in turn, had to comply with certain demands of the entrepreneurs as it depended on stable revenue to re-finance its military operations.[59] With the RCD-K/ML rebellion dissolving into a political party and Mbusa joining the central government in Kinshasa in 2004, these networks were reproduced both within the ex-APC networks that were integrated into the national army and those remaining outside. In the post-war decade, many former RCD-K/ML cadres remained in key posts, such as heading customs offices at border posts.

A second example concerns an emblematic case of militarised mining that occurred in Bisie under the control of the FARDC's non-integrated 85th Brigade between 2004 and 2008. Considered one of the world's largest cassiterite deposits, Bisie became a mining hub from 2002 onwards and was controlled by Rwanda-associated networks until 2004. After the wars and the creation of a new, national army, the 85th Brigade, composed of former Mai-Mai units, was assigned to the area. Bisie emerged as a flagship example of how militarised control of mines can foment a particular style of experimental security governance, with economic and political stakeholders tied in through fine-grained, implicit patterns of cooperation.[60] In North Kivu, the 85th Brigade was the only unit not integrated with others during the *brassage* and *mixage* exercises to unify belligerents into the FARDC, the post-war Congolese army (besides ex-CNDP units that eventually replaced them in Bisie, triggering the creation of Sheka's NDC in 2008).[61] The 85th Brigade was led by Colonel Samy Matumo, whose role in mining is legendary.[62] Matumo ran a differentiated strategy of direct exploitation and indirect measures, including taxation and control of trade routes. The 85th Brigade had amicable relations with political and customary leaders, local state officials and nearby FDLR units in Walikale territory. In addition, it exploited the artisanal miners' fears of foreign mining companies interested in industrialising Bisie's tin mines. Like the RCD-Goma, or large cohesive armed groups such as the FDLR that controlled vast mining areas until the 2009 Umoja Wetu operations, the example of the 85th Brigade showcases that the militarisation of 3T mining is not a one-way street of plunder, but features negotiation amidst tenuous, fragmented authority and overlapping networks.

The third example highlights that control over mines and trading routes and the actual influence of armed actors vis-à-vis other stakeholders are more contested than we may think. The more belligerents compete over control or lack the capacity to set up more than aleatory rackets, the less stable their control. In some cases, such as in the remote, sparsely populated Kivu lowlands bordering Maniema Province, the influence of belligerents on mining is marked by a relative weakness when it comes to spatial authority beyond neuralgic points such as settlements or roads. Paradoxically, this can help armed groups to survive largely undisturbed for longer. However, it prevents them from establishing greater political and economic clout owing to geographic isolation and low population density compared to the highlands around Lake Kivu. The Raia Mutomboki, for instance, are a highly decentralised militia that have been operating in Shabunda territory since 2012. Regularly involved in local mining sites, no faction has developed governance practices comparable to the lasting control of the 85th Brigade over densely populated Bisie. The faction under Donat Omari Kengwa and Ngandu Lundimu, for instance, operates small coltan mines in secluded, remote patches of the Kahuzi-Biega National Park. While they successfully co-opted local authorities and populations in mutual arrangements, their mines are economically irrelevant to both the government and iTSCi.

These three cases are just a selection of situations that illustrate the ambivalent, multifaceted interplay between mining, violence and taxation since the end of the Second Congo War in 2003.[63] As opposed to orthodox assumptions about state failure, neopatrimonialism and greed in civil wars, the opportunity to benefit from natural resources does not always trigger insurgency in the first place. Moreover, these vignettes question dominant thought about the relation of taxation and armed mobilisation, in which it is argued that international demand of resources triggers violent taxation.[64] Rather, the contrary seems to be the case: on many occasions, opportunity depends on the capacity of armed actors to establish a modicum of authority, including a degree of compliance on the side of the population, in order to engage in taxation beyond sporadic looting. Hence, what the 'greed school' calls looting may upon closer inspection turn out to be a 'governance experiment', in which accumulation is part of a broader arrangement and thus not a unique driver of armed mobilisation. Such a reading resonates with a broader historical and empirical basis: armed mobilisation in eastern Congo predates any link between conflict and resources. Even the Rwandan- and Ugandan-backed rebellions from the late 1990s only engaged in mining over time. One of the most significant recent rebellions in eastern Congo—the M23—did not operate any mines but earned significantly from customs. The FDLR, composed of remnants of the Rwandan genocidal forces, lost most of their access to mines from 2010—yet they show remarkable resilience, specialising in a range of other legal and illegal businesses. Others, including Mai-Mai and Raia Mutomboki, flexibly adapt their sources of income.

Questioning the cliché of miners held 'at gunpoint',[65] the three cases above stress the ambiguity of protection rackets and the extent to which they rely on an ounce of compliance that goes beyond mere imposition. This somewhat echoes the idea of Congo posing 'an important analytical problem: although it appears to lack every requirement for qualifying as a functioning state, its political system has persisted in most surprising fashion' and has been thriving in post-war eastern Congo.[66] This creates a paradox: while illegal taxes and protection rackets subvert the very state within whose boundaries they occur, they implicitly 'contribute to its capacity to exercise power over wealth and people'.[67] The example of mineral governance is a case in point, given how a multitude of stakeholders keep 'seeing and doing the state'.[68]

Academic misunderstandings

The three examples discussed above also help to clarify a few more academic misunderstandings. Arguably, the rule of the RCD-Goma over large parts of the Kivus, including the short-lived SOMIGL episode, framed the key assumptions of much that underpins the 'conflict minerals' paradigm. However, reading the RCD-Goma story against other empirical cases, we can critically assess the validity of these assumptions. Focusing on coltan peak and subsequent instances of militarised mining, neo-classic theory was a main inspiration for international policy debates on resources and conflict from the 1990s. Based on large-N datasets and econometric regression, this strand of scholarship developed the 'greed theory'. This idea suggests that the availability of lootable natural resources increases the likelihood of conflict.[69] The founder of this school, Paul Collier, consulted international organisations including the World Bank to develop his theory. However, there is growing recognition that this approach limits our analysis of individual and collective agency, market connections and power configurations in mineral markets in conflict and post-conflict contexts.[70]

In recent decades, prolific literatures have deconstructed the hypotheses of 'greed theory', exposing various methodological shortcomings, including ambiguous proxies and the conflation of causation and correlation.[71] Data linking resource abundance to the outbreak of violent conflict is often 'appearing on the surface very scientific because of the numbers and the algebra' while being an 'oversimplification that gives us the illusion of having understood a complex world'.[72] Classified as 'arbitrary', 'spurious', 'inadequate', 'reductionist', 'speculative' or 'misleading', the theoretical foundations of the greed theory rely on random proxies that would generate diametrically opposed results if their place in the equation were to be changed.[73] Still, the dominant view—inspired by Orientalist and colonial perspectives—remains that natural resource economies in conflict areas are fragile and open to criminal intrusion given their unregulated and informal character. While this downplays the potential of alternative, indigenous forms of market regulation, the misguided focus on economic agendas and the role of natural resources in civil wars has spurred nothing less than a revolution in conflict studies, leading to radical policy innovations.

The 'greed theory' was particularly salient in areas of protracted armed conflict, where institutions are presumed to be either weak, antagonistic or generally 'malfunctioning', bearing in mind the value-laden judgements in these terms. Artisanal mining is often depicted as generally unruly, illegal and dominated by militaries,[74] downplaying the complexities of civil-military interaction.[75] Since 2001, the link between conflict and mining in eastern Congo has been stressed in a range of reports. A flagship reference is the 2001 UN Panel of Experts on the Illegal Exploitation of Natural Resources in the Congo.[76] One of its recommendations to the UN Security Council was an immediate embargo on minerals originating from eastern Congo given the pervasive involvement of armed groups and foreign armies during the coltan peak. NGO research corroborated the panel's findings and thus strengthened the problematic epistemics of transnational advocacy on 'conflict minerals'. In subsequent Western advocacy, the complexity of primary reports was watered down to fit dominant narratives.[77] This oversimplification was discursively embedded in a white saviourism pitch that enlarged the campaigns' public appeal and bandwidth thanks to increasing digital mobilisation potential for humanitarian and human rights advocacy.[78] Consequent campaigns forged a simple yet compelling argument that suggested conflict parties would provoke war to benefit from chaos and violently pillage natural resources, and in order to do so, enrol children and rape women. Hence, a highly political and historically rooted set of contingent local, national and regional conflict dynamics was—to accommodate a global public—condensed into one single, flat argument.[79]

Once formulated, it had to be transported out of the remote Kivutian forests into the minds of Western consumers. The mobile revolution that kicked in around that time offered a solution: although only minuscule amounts of tantalum are needed for a cellular phone and most of the world's tantalum does not originate from Congo, mobile gadgets were construed as the epitome of human rights violations in a far-flung African war zone. Depicted alternately with child soldiers or victims of sexual violence, campaigns targeted the conscience of Western consumers like earlier advocacy on 'blood diamonds'.[80] Western advocacy relied on mindsets reminiscent of Said's definition of 'Orientalism' as an attitude that 'enables the political, economic, cultural and social domination of the West, not just during colonial times, but also in the present'.[81] Rather than acknowledging the ambivalent character of war and violence,[82] media and public debates painted Congolese either as greedy, bloodthirsty warlords and young, brainwashed male recruits or defenceless female victims lacking agency. 'Conflict minerals' campaigns thus translated hand-picked pieces of a larger puzzle, interspersed with a decidedly Orientalist undertone, to a global audience: one element of a larger story—warlord greed—was foregrounded to justify a white saviour-style intervention.

Western campaigns on 'conflict minerals' found their perfect narrative complementarity in the campaigns on sexual and gender-based violence (whose by-product is a generalised stigmatisation of Congolese women as victims) and the emerging trend of militarised fortress conservation around Virunga National Park and the protection of mountain gorillas in eastern Congo and its neighbour states.[83] The narratives supporting these advocacy themes rely on a colonial image of Black and African savagery that requires white saviours—more often than not Hollywood celebrities—to bring peace, order and development.[84]

These images not only dismiss historical and political continuities of imperialist and capitalist relations—unsurprisingly, perhaps, they also do not match with empirical observation. In my many years of researching and living in eastern Congo, I observed an impressive level of individual and collective agency amongst Congolese women. To offer but one example: in 2010, I met a group of women representing local associations. *En passant*, they told me how they had organised marches—on foot!—to Kigali and Kampala to protest against the involvement of neighbouring governments ravaging their livelihoods.

Having told me their story, one of the women noted how little interest their initiative generated with campaigners and policy-makers back then. A similar picture exists in the realm of conservation, where Congolese grassroots organisations working on community-driven nature protection are not only erased in public discourse, but occasionally seen as adversaries in the eyes of the white saviour-led multinational Virunga machine. Over the years, I regularly heard such stories when in eastern Congo. Sadly, the agency and dedication of women's rights and biodiversity activists are blatantly underestimated and underfunded by global publics as well as—with some exceptions—among humanitarian and peace-building actors.[85]

3

A CIVILISING MISSION 2.0?

Based on the intellectual and political foundations of the 'conflict minerals' paradigm, this chapter traces its evolution from advocacy into policy and intervention, and introduces the panoply of attempts to regulate the exploitation and trade of 3T minerals. It pays particular attention to the US law known as the Dodd–Frank Act, the OECD guidance on responsible sourcing and the regional certification mechanism of the ICGLR. These policies are informed by a decidedly neoliberal approach and a *mission civilisatrice* ideology, and rooted in an Orientalist discourse of the Congolese conflict as violent, backward, driven by greed and therefore requiring white saviours. Such readings have a long tradition, and painting

> ... the Congo as a primitive, chaotic 'heart of darkness' has made certain things happen in the political world. For example, Henry Morton Stanley, an American writer turned explorer, violently conquered and colonized the region in the name of Belgian King Leopold II, in part because he believed he was bringing 'order' to a chaotic space. Seeing the inhabitants as primitive savages allowed Stanley and other colonizing agents to exact brutality against them.[1]

CONFLICT MINERALS INC.

The struggle against 'conflict minerals' emphasises formalisation and due diligence to reassert control over mineral production, curb 'illegal exploitation' and deliver assurance to consumers. 'Conflict-free' laws and guidelines evolved into practical policy in the shape of 'private indirect government'.[2] Through the prism of iTSCi, a corporate traceability scheme run by a lobby of the world's major tin industries, this chapter analyses 'conflict-free' sourcing and takes a critical look at the epistemological cleavages between humanitarian discourses and consumer-oriented advocacy. The simplistic foundations of the 'conflict minerals' paradigm notwithstanding, its policy relevance cannot be underestimated as it provided a basis for numerous laws, regulations and practical initiatives in eastern Congo's mineral markets.

Table 3.1: Timeline of key events in the evolution of conflict minerals policy

Date	Event	Role
April 2001	UN Panel Report on 'conflict minerals'	Agenda-setting
July 2009	iTSCi test in Nyabibwe (aborted due to ban)	Creation of 'clean supply chains'
April 2010	First OECD draft guidance	Standard-setting for due diligence
July 2010	Adoption of section 1502 of the Dodd–Frank Act	Changing legal framework
September 2010	Mining ban in eastern Congo	Pre-empting international embargos
November 2010	UN Group of Experts due diligence	Standard-setting for due diligence
December 2010	ICGLR Lusaka Declaration	Established six ICGLR tools

December 2010	Adoption of OECD guidance	Standard-setting for due diligence
April 2011	iTSCi begins operating in Tanganyika Province	First regular operation
August 2012	Publication of SEC rule for section 1502 of the Dodd–Frank Act	Implementation of section 1502 of the Dodd–Frank Act
October 2012	iTSCi pilot project in Nyabibwe (re-)starts	Creation of 'clean supply chains'
February 2014	First ICGLR certificate issued in eastern Congo	Implementation of due diligence
March 2014	iTSCi Rubaya project begins	Expansion of 'clean supply chains'
June 2014	iTSCi Lemera and Nzibira projects begin	Expansion of 'clean supply chains'
June 2015	iTSCi Numbi project begins	Expansion of 'clean supply chains'
May 2017	Adoption of EU 'conflict minerals' regulation	Changing legal framework

The OECD due diligence guidance and section 1502 of the Dodd–Frank Act are two of the major policy developments with regards to the struggle against 'conflict minerals'. While the OECD guidance is a classic 'soft law', the latter is part of a US law package and legally obliges companies registered with the US Securities and Exchange Commission (SEC) to disclose their activities in case of implication in 3T and gold supply chains allegedly fuelling armed conflict in eastern Congo. Temporally, the OECD process and the US legislative process significantly overlap, as the above timeline illustrates. However, for the sake of clarity, I will discuss them one by one and flag key points before turning to practical implications.

CONFLICT MINERALS INC.

From advocacy to laws

Since the mid-2000s, advocates of 'conflict minerals' have begun to more virulently address politicians. At the forefront of this group was the Washington-based NGO Enough Project, who were instrumental in lobbying legislators to draft a law on 'conflict minerals'. Powered by simple pitches and led by John Prendergast, a fervent liberal-interventionist advocate and Clinton-era spin doctor known for his ambiguous engagement on the Sudans, the Enough Project made significant inroads into US law-making circles.[3] An original draft bill featured a mix of punitive and supportive measures to stem the illegal trade in 3T and gold sourced from eastern Congo. However, it was never brought to the floor. Instead, it got recycled by its authors Sam Brownback, a Republican senator, and Democratic congressman Jim MacDermott. The revamped draft law retained only its penalising parts as it got re-introduced as section 1502 of the magnanimous Wall Street Reform and Consumer Protection Act sponsored by Senator Chris Dodd and Congressman Barney Frank (nicknamed the Dodd–Frank Act). On 21 July 2010, President Obama signed it into law, leading Congolese miners to refer to it as *loi Obama* ('Obama's law'). Around 850 pages long, Dodd–Frank is one of the largest pieces of US legislation in recent history. Its 'conflict minerals' section comes at 1502 out of 1601 and is part of a rather plethoric 'miscellaneous' provisions chapter. Among other things, it states: 'the exploitation and trade of conflict minerals originating in the ... Congo is helping to finance conflict characterized by extreme levels of violence in [the] Congo, particularly sexual- and gender-based violence'.[4]

Besides summoning the US Agency for International Development (USAID) to develop a regional plan for peace and security and the US State Department to produce a map of 'conflict minerals', section 1502 mainly targets private companies, whom it requires to regularly report whether or not their activities involve 3T and gold sourced from eastern Congo or any neighbouring country.[5] In strict terms, this does not outlaw 'conflict minerals', but does oblige US stock market-listed companies to publicise their use of these minerals and outline the due diligence measures they employ to avoid financing conflict. Some provisions of the law led to criticism, most notably the narrow geographical and geological approach in the definition of 'conflict minerals' as only 3T and gold from eastern Congo and the region. Moreover, the definition of 'armed groups'—although ambiguous in wording—excludes state security forces. The reality on the ground, however, suggests that, both in the heydays of the coltan boom and after, national armies do figure among the key protagonists of militarised mining in Central Africa.

Box 2: What is due diligence?

Both hard and soft law on 'conflict minerals' require 'due diligence' as a mitigation mechanism. A fashionable notion in corporate social responsibility, due diligence is an umbrella term rather than a fixed set of rules, and can be translated as factoring a reasonable degree of carefulness and research into economic action prior to a decision. In the context of 'conflict minerals', due diligence means companies exercising ongoing checks of potential risks (e.g. human rights violations) within the supply chains of which they form a part. Due diligence precisely describes the practice of knowing about risks and finding ways to alleviate them. While due diligence is more an attitude than a particular practice, several initiatives have developed specific ways in which companies can exercise due diligence as legally required by the US since 2012 and the EU from 2021 onwards.

, In 2009, the OECD set up a project to develop a due diligence guidance for the responsible sourcing of minerals, following requests by the ICGLR (see Box 3 below) and the G8. The process happened largely in collaboration with the UN Group of Experts, which had been tasked by the UN Security Council to develop similar guidelines.[6] The Group of Experts succeeded the 2001 UN Panel to monitor the sanctions regime defined in Security Council resolution 1533 of 2004. Resolution 1896 of 2009—one of the annual extensions of the UN's sanctions regime on Congo—asked the Group to elaborate guidelines for 'conflict minerals', resulting in the UN due diligence guidelines annexed to the Group's 2010 final report.[7] In May 2011, the first in a series of OECD–Group of Experts–ICGLR forums took place, where the OECD officially published the first edition of its 'Due Diligence Guidance for Responsible Supply Chains of Minerals from Conflict-Affected and High-Risk Areas'. The guidance was approved upon request by the ICGLR in December 2010 after a series of consultations and subsequently endorsed by Congolese authorities in February 2012.[8] (The current version is the third edition, issued in 2016.) The UN and OECD guidelines are mutually inspiring and overlap in definitions and recommendations. In August 2012, the US Securities and Exchange Commission (SEC) published its rule to implement section 1502 of Dodd–Frank, noting that the OECD guidance would serve as a baseline for required due diligence procedures.[9]

Box 3: The International Conference on the
Great Lakes Region

A regional body, the ICGLR convenes Congo and its neighbouring states on security, economic and humanitarian issues. At the Lusaka summit in 2010, ICGLR heads of state and government endorsed the OECD guidance and set up the 'Regional Initiative against the Illegal Exploitation of Natural Resources'. It combines six tools: (1) a regional certification mechanism (RCM); (2) harmonisation of member state legislation; (3) a regional database on mineral production; (4) ASM formalisation; (5) adherence to the Extractive Industries Transparency Initiative; and (6) a whistle-blowing mechanism. While most tools were only partly implemented, the most relevant is the RCM, introduced in 2014 as part of the due diligence schemes for eastern Congo.

The EU developed its own regulation to counter conflict minerals, stipulating a mix of compulsory and voluntary compliance. As with section 1502 of Dodd–Frank, it is inspired by the OECD guidance. The European Parliament adopted it in March 2017 based on the EU Commission's proposal negotiated since 2014. It has legislative character and was ratified by the Council of the EU in May 2017 as EU regulation 2017/821.[10] Similar to Dodd–Frank, it focuses on 3T and gold; however, it does not have a specific geographical focus and applies across the globe (although primarily to EU-based companies). Entering into force in 2021, it is unclear whether the EU regulation will have much impact given that many European companies cross paths with SEC-listed companies somewhere in the supply chain and have thus been bound to section 1502 of Dodd–Frank since 2012. However, since compliance with Dodd–Frank and SEC rules has been patchy in the past decade, advocates voice hope that the EU rule may see more thorough enforcement. Similarly, potentially constraining legislation has been debated in other countries, such as in Switzerland. In a 2020 referendum, the Swiss population approved a proposal which was later rejected by Switzerland's upper chamber.[11]

From laws to policies

As a result of this international legal and regulatory architecture, eastern Congo's artisanal mining sector would begin to face a far-reaching reorganisation. Inspired by the belief in a neat equation of resources and conflict, policymakers went to save eastern Congo from 'conflict minerals' with 'new frameworks of intervention, aimed at cutting the supposed links between armed groups and resources and at promoting transparent models of resource governance'.[12] Most of the resulting initiatives implicitly rehash colonialism and draw legitimation from the 'greed' paradigm, whose parsimonious design informed the underlying logics imbued in the policies to address 'conflict minerals'.[13] Among these techniques, for instance, is the formation of rigid regulatory frames to trace, formalise and certify mineral sourcing. These frameworks largely ignore existing institutional and legal pluralism in their belief of entering a space free from regulation. Other techniques, as listed in Table 3.2 below, also came with important shortcomings.

Table 3.2. Overview of resource governance techniques in eastern Congo

Technique	Short definition
Formalisation	Inventory of market participants and their activities into bureaucratic, legible, legal frameworks
Standardisation	Merger of multiple access regimes into a standardised one, often coupled with formalisation
Validation	Categorisation of access regimes between 'conflicted' and 'conflict-free' (through a traffic light system)
Qualification	Official acknowledgement of the validation process by the Congolese government
Traceability	Establishment of oversight systems in supply chains to trace minerals from pit to exportation

| Certification | Legalisation of exports through a regional scheme, pending validation and traceability |
| Due diligence | Determining the origin of minerals and circumstances of sourcing, including through audits |

Standardisation is inspired by a belief that transnational reform can establish a unique, easily accepted, overarching set of rules over an ASM sector hosting multiple orders and legal pluralism with roots not only before, during and after colonialism, but also before, during and after war. Formalisation, in turn, assembles different policies to have artisanal miners receive legal permits, organise in cooperatives or be employed by registered mining firms. It relies on a kind of double-teleology that conceives of individuals as unable to decide for themselves what shape or type of economic engagement is beneficial to their specific situation, and the belief in a superiority and imagined legitimacy of Western economic order. Moreover, formalisation eliminates a range of advantages of informal trade such as its flexibility (e.g. the ease for artisanal miners of hopping from one mine to another), yet without guaranteeing any socio-economic benefit. Both standardisation and formalisation come with a white saviour mentality that dismisses situated knowledge and requires outside solutions. Validation and qualification insinuate a static, flat geography of stable conditions for a mine over time and rely on the unlikely scenario of a security situation that remains identical over the course of several years. Traceability, insofar as it is defined by iTSCi, assumes that physical tracking with barcoded plastic tags can provide reliable assurance that no human rights violation or fraud affects a supply chain. In these circumstances, certification and due diligence end up being just as credible—or not—as the lowest common denominator of the preceding techniques upon which they are based. Most of the initiatives pay lip service to the OECD guidance. On the ground, however, they clash with long-standing trajectories of unrecorded trade and institutional pluralism.[14] Like the bodies of hard and soft law discussed above, the techniques to help businesses perform due diligence were thus founded largely on 'unsupported assumptions regarding how natural resources are linked to the motivations of combatants and the dynamics of conflict, and rarely consider the populations in conflict-affected regions'.[15]

These assumptions omit the extent to which ex-combatants turned to mining as an alternative livelihood and, inversely, how miners may take up arms when facing embargo due to 'conflict minerals' advocacy.[16] Moreover, and paradoxically, interviewed miners stated that while they appreciate working without armed interference, their revenues in regions under rebel control during the RCD-Goma era were more amenable to meeting subsistence needs, including the schooling of children. Moreover, years into the roll-out of traceability, the national army remains factionalised and responsible for much of the violence and illegal trade, and the number of armed groups has multiplied from a few dozen to a kaleidoscope of over 120.[17] Resource governance is therefore intrinsically intertwined with security sector reform (SSR) and disarmament, demobilisation and reintegration (DDR) policies, both of which are 'essential to improve security in the mining regions of the hinterland'.[18] In recent years, however, none has been credibly addressed: while SSR has been non-existent, most DDR programmes brought limited success but numerous lacunae.[19]

Before describing the key practical due diligence approaches, one key event needs to be added to the equation: in September 2010, a few months after the adoption of Dodd–Frank yet before its provisions entered into force, the Congolese government declared a ban on ASM in North Kivu, South Kivu and Maniema. This ban put a temporary halt to emerging traceability efforts and amplified the Dodd–Frank-inspired embargo tendencies, causing devastating effects on Congolese mining communities.[20] While Dodd–Frank does not directly prohibit trade—it merely demands disclosure—production plummeted. During the ban, mining continued mostly under the control of clandestine, militarised patronage networks operating through contraband, causing losses in public revenue and reducing supply and mobility in remote areas, most notably Walikale and Shabunda but also elsewhere. Moreover, the ban's

> ... impact was clearly reflected in the number of school dropouts, because the parents and children (who sometimes went into the mines themselves to pay for their fees) could not afford the school fees anymore. In some mining sites ... people were not able to afford the costs of going to the hospital.[21]

Hence, if the relation of ASM and conflict in eastern Congo is more complex, most of the initiatives implementing Dodd–Frank and the OECD guidance did not account for this. As such, being the broader public–private governance architecture for clean sourcing, the ICGLR's regional certification mechanism became the sole legal channel to export minerals listed in the law. According to the OECD guidance and section 1502 of Dodd–Frank, these certificates' value hinges on whether due diligence has been exercised before exportation. However, which technique of due diligence has to be performed is not specified.[22]

From policies to practice

In sync with regional initiatives, bilateral cooperation also took up the issue of conflict minerals. A flagship example is Germany's Institute for Geosciences (Bundesanstalt für Geowissenschaften und Rohstoffe [BGR]), a federal agency for resource governance. In Congo and its eastern neighbours, BGR developed two complementary approaches: an analytical fingerprint (AFP) system and the certified trading chains (CTC) project. The CTC project focuses on traceability prior to export certification, similar to iTSCi, but has not seen significant implementation as iTSCi imposed itself as monopolistic traceability operator.

The AFP is a geo-chemical technique to identify the origin of minerals. It offers a possibility to perform random sampling tests (e.g. auditing ICGLR certification), and requires reference samples for any potential 'clean' mining area that can be used to test shipments before export, as they are often mixed afterwards. As of late 2015, the AFP was sufficiently developed to identify up to five substances of different geological origin within a single shipment based on three factors: geochemical composition, geological age and ore variability. As a result, it would have made the life of smugglers more difficult, as they would need to mix over five shipments to blur the traces of one specific origin. While not infallible, the AFP is one technique to help clarify the identity of a mineral shipment beyond reasonable doubt.

On the industry side, different platforms (including a 'joint extractives workgroup') became a gravitation point for 'conflict minerals' initiatives. While US producers gather in the Responsible Business Alliance (formerly the Electronic Industry Citizenship Coalition), European producers have created the Global e-Sustainability Initiative, which converges in the Responsible Minerals Initiative (RMI, formerly the Conflict-Free Sourcing Initiative), an open coalition of companies interested in improving transparency and traceability, which focuses on the mine-to-smelter supply chain via iTSCi and the Conflict-Free Smelter Programme (later renamed Responsible Minerals Assurance Process [RMAP]). Taken together, this forms a combination of upstream and downstream due diligence. The RMAP runs an audit-based scheme to improve due diligence at the level of smelters, which are a key bottleneck of global 3T supply chains.

What most initiatives have in common is a focus on ostensibly objective, technical solutions to problems deeply entrenched in

---

Box 4: The smokescreen of auditing

Initiatives against 'conflict minerals' rely on auditing as part of due diligence. The ICGLR commissions third-party audits and has its own 'independent mineral chain auditor'. iTSCi also performs internal and third-party audits. Smelter audits happen in the frame of RMAP and RMI. Such audits, however, can be a broken promise: they risk transposing the qualitative, case-by-case logic of due diligence into mere compliance standards driven by a tick-box mentality. In many cases, audits are commissioned by private sector stakeholders themselves, such as iTSCi, which means their independence is not guaranteed. Moreover, the character of artisanal mining in eastern Congo—marred by 'unrecorded', 'clandestine' practices—would require seasoned specialists, while audit teams often include business consultants with little intricate knowledge of local economies. This has led to spurious assessments as auditors at times fail to unpack the 'invisible' dynamics characterising artisanal mines. In other cases, auditors are under pressure to not disclose breaches of due diligence, such as the presence of armed groups in iTSCi-operated mines. In further cases, audits are undermined by prior announcement leaked to local stakeholders.

---

contested politics. To paraphrase James Ferguson, transnational regulation efforts depoliticise the issue of 'conflict minerals' by making the struggle against them appear like 'an administrative apparatus organising development projects', and hence an 'anti-politics machine' that operates within the entangled Congolese conflicts which are anything but apolitical.[23] More concretely, the push against 'conflict minerals' is thus driven by the assumption of a *terra nullius*, a free space or open frontier in which regulation must occur—much like colonialism's justification as a 'civilising mission'. In contrast to such a technical reading, I argue, with Raeymaekers, that the advent of certification and traceability enacted yet another 'constant mediation between global capitalism and local forms of governance'.[24]

Worse still, 'conflict minerals' initiatives neglect the participants in mineral markets and upstream supply chains, such as miners, intermediary traders and cooperatives: this 'low level of consultation with some of the most important actors in the supply chain' led to ignoring 'the bridge between producers (artisanal miners) and industry buyers (both national and international)' as well as to misunderstandings as to how ASM generally works.[25] While powerful actors are co-opted into 'conflict-free' sourcing, the subaltern are left out of the equation and have little to gain from the implementation of reform. However, while eastern Congo's civil society is vibrant, it suffers from scarce resources and political divisiveness. The lack of collective action and consultation has contributed to neglecting the multiplicity of views, legal systems and respective contradictions, such as between mining, customary and land laws.[26] The combination of this neglect with white saviourism, colonial mindsets and profit-oriented extractive imperatives has complicated what was sold to the global public as a consumer-driven path from war to peace.

From war to peace?

Corporate start-ups like iTSCi have become a fashionable tool in conflict resolution strategies and neoliberal peacebuilding ideology. Inspired by neoclassic economics and Orientalist campaigning, and led by profit-driven white saviours, such and similar projects have gained traction not only in eastern Congo but in a range of conflict-affected countries over the past 15 years, including Liberia, Sierra Leone, Angola and South Sudan. While the foundations of these interventions are fraught, they produce important consequences for artisanal mining communities in Africa. Overtaken by a capitalist logic of enclosing so-called resource frontiers—the Kivus being seen as such—the advent of supposedly 'conflict-free' sourcing in eastern Congo triggered a major transformation, imposing external modes of extraction that seek to deplete alternative forms of accumulation by describing them as 'informal' or 'illegal'.[27]

This discursive criminalisation justifies new regulation that reifies marginalisation and exclusion in economic and epistemic terms. Yet, in practice, artisanal mining in eastern Congo features just another situated mix of legal pluralism. It is not as deviant as 'conflict minerals' advocates posit but fits the empirical patterns of most economic and political markets in the world.[28] Like similar initiatives before it,[29] the transfusion of a number of entrenched assumptions about the causes of and possible solutions to war economies into actual policy frameworks not only profoundly transforms the configuration of local production networks, but also affects governance patterns more widely.[30] Against publicly stated expectations of advocates and campaigners, the dynamics of transnational market regulation have not enhanced the prospects for 'structural peace' as in an absence of injustice and violent accumulation in eastern Congo. Instead, they have fed into and exacerbated existing dynamics of exclusion, marginalisation and violence.[31] Transnational intervention such as iTSCi—as Chapter 4 will show in detail—radically alters the conditions of economic accumulation and can thus seriously jeopardise the livelihoods of the very people transnational intervention figuratively sought to rescue from warlord abuse. As Walter Rodney poignantly noted, certain periods and areas in history have known situations where this has occurred:

> [T]he capitalist system increased the well-being of significant numbers of people as a by-product of seeking out profits for a few, but

today the quests for profits comes into sharp conflict with people's demands that their material and social needs should be fulfilled.[32]

Rekindled as a 2.0 version of a *mission civilisatrice*, the reform of artisanal 3T mining in eastern Congo casts a myopic lens on the intricate relationship between formalisation and accumulation. Sold as a prerequisite for 'peace', reforms fanned the monopolisation of trade in a closed-pipeline supply chain, with a few recalcitrant transnational military-commercial networks offering the only alternative. 'Conflict-free' sourcing not only reinforced dynamics of monopsony (a buyer-end monopoly) at the expense of the Congolese workforce, but also allowed for violence in eastern Congo to continue under the veil of a 'conflict-free' illusion. This resembles other examples of violent expansion in the margins of capitalist markets,[33] where '"joining the world economy" [is] a matter of highly selective and spatially encapsulated forms of global connection combined with widespread disconnection and exclusion'.[34] It is a tale of extractable reservoirs versus expendable bodies: while the former are finite, the latter are renewable and can be replaced anytime. As long as they are powerless enough to be reduced to what Polanyi called 'fictitious commodities', their labour can thus be re-inscribed in a centralised mode of accumulation—just to find itself as an accessory ingredient in the public recipe for the ethical sourcing of so-called digital minerals.[35]

Despite what advocates suggest, the result of this process is a mixture of war, profit and white saviourism.

INTERLUDE

GODFATHER'S TALES

Once upon a time under the sunlight, thither wast a fellow, honest and bright.

Neither king nor knight, his name wast Musemakweli and he worketh day and night.

Beneath the lands, the ancestors did betoken those folk, wast the riches of a poor present,

but these riches, would beest graveyards of the unborn children, they did doth sayeth with resent.

The years did doth cometh and did wend, so did doth big and bawbling armies, ripping kith and kin,

runneth, runneth faster, Musemakweli, wend and encave, once they catcheth thee the chance is thin!

Distaff, men and children did doth carryeth their sorrow 'longside their shovel, too busy, oft fainting.

Some wast silent, others did want to speaketh but their colours did maketh them those folk dainty.

Not after long, inconspicuous and gentle, arrived the Muzungudanganya brotherhood.

They did doth endue a letter from King Barack, with a gage still misunderstood.

Wrapped in clean jewellery like royal heralds they did doth sayeth 'rejoice, peace is coming, war is ov'r'.

Musemakweli did doth clepe Bahatimbaya, 'cometh did let's go wend hark and moveth closer.'

We maketh thee and giveth thee cannot refuse, they did whisper, but Musemakweli denied.

They looketh at each other, enraged, blood shooting like a tantalising gaze in their eye.

Beware, the end wilt justify the means, and thee wilt feeleth't, they did tout.

One day anon, all bloody phones did buzz, 'it's-he,' they did shout.

But the brotherhood wast did maketh of many cunning fellows, and Bahatimbaya did giveth in,

they maketh him writeth a 'free' wonderland yond hath nev'r been, but thither wast just a new prison.

Time wast fluid, January becometh June, in the brotherhood's quest for the permission,

to narrate the story of Black villains and White Saviours with Musemakweli in chagrin.[1]

4

ETHICAL MONOPOLIES

This chapter draws from ethnography and survey data to gauge the socio-economic impact of traceability and formalisation. As of 2019, according to the Antwerp-based thinktank the International Peace Information Service (IPIS), the 'increasing regulation of the artisanal mining sector and responsible sourcing efforts, have rather had a negative overall effect on the socio-economic position of artisanal miners'.[1] Through the prism of iTSCi, the main private sector-led mineral traceability scheme, the chapter traces the evolution of livelihoods, market access and subsistence, demonstrating how iTSCi reconfigures supply chains mostly to the detriment of local producers and communities.[2] Justified by ethical sourcing, iTSCi traces mineral bags to follow their route, incorporating selected mines into clean supply chains (or not, as the case may be). This has major implications: in iTSCi mines, given the lack of competition among trading houses and smelters, producers face what is known as a monopsony (a buyer-end monopoly), whereas in mines not (yet) partaking, miners are de facto excluded from legal market access. Both scenarios can lead to decreasing revenue for producers, illustrating the disjuncture between demands of Western consumers and the livelihoods of mining communities in eastern Congo. The results of this mixed-methods approach are an empirical illustration that the definition of universal values and morality is a contested and diverse playing field.

> A gradual but decisive shift took place toward more interventionist ... development assistance: from simply funding development policies and programmes; to influencing aid recipient countries' policy frameworks under stabilisation and structural adjustment programmes; to directly transforming political and administrative institutions under the rubric of good governance for market-based development.[3]

While iTSCi did not yet exist in 2004, Luckham's words—and the reference to the World Bank's structural adjustment—are intriguingly pertinent. A primary initiative to trade and market 'conflict-free' 3T minerals in the Great Lakes region, iTSCi is run by ITA Ltd. (previously ITRI Ltd.), the world's largest lobby organisation of global tin industries, which is mostly comprised of companies in the 'downstream' part of the supply chain ('upstream' is the part from mine to smelter). In a bid to allow these companies to apply due diligence and meet the requirements of Dodd–Frank, iTSCi transformed the threat of regulation into a business opportunity, forming a closed-pipeline supply chain under the slogan of 'conflict-free' sourcing. iTSCi is a member-based programme, with downstream industries joining as 'associate members' while upstream stakeholders (e.g. cooperatives or *comptoirs*) are considered 'full' members. While it is not a due diligence programme writ small, it claims to support companies sourcing minerals from conflict areas to perform due diligence.

The making of a monopoly

iTSCi traces mineral supply from mines to smelters. This works through the sealing of mineral bags with a barcoded tag that accompanies each shipment along its journey. There are two physically identical but functionally different tags. The first—*tag mines*—are applied after initial purification as bags leave their mine of origin en route to nearby peri-urban trading centres. When a bag gets picked up by intermediary traders, the second tag—*tag négociants*—replaces the *tag mines* to accompany the bag until it is resold to a *comptoir*, often in a city, where shipments are further refined to be exported. The tagging is reflected in logbooks that register time, place, seller, buyer and content. To perform assurance, iTSCi runs third-party audits and logs are kept in a proprietary database where incidents are recorded and followed. In so doing, iTSCi establishes a 'closed pipeline' of mineral sourcing to seal off the supply chain against outside interference. A first pilot project happened in 2009 in Nyabibwe, South Kivu, but a planned formal launch in 2010 was aborted due to the mining ban, making Tanganyika Province in former Katanga (Mayi Baridi and Kisengo) the official launch area in 2011.[4]

The main requirement for iTSCi to run is mine site validation. This process involves the provincial mining ministry, its Service for the Assistance and Supervision of Artisanal and Small-Scale Mining (Service d'assistance et d'encadrement des mines artisanales et à petite échelle [SAEMAPE]), iTSCi and other partners, such as the International Organisation for Migration, BGR and civil society organisations.[5] For its 'conflict-free' validation, this process uses a traffic light categorisation: green for clean mines, red for mines with armed presence or human rights violations, and yellow for minor infringements. Once done, the mining ministry confirms the validation through decrees (called qualification), on the basis of which iTSCi operates. This 'legalising' logic rests on an inverted *in dubio pro reo* approach, considering mines guilty until proven innocent; in other words, each mine is red by default until validated otherwise. Clumsy in essence, the process has many shortcomings: at best, it provides an approximate judgement of the situation at the moment of validation, with little validity over time and space, since the situation can change within days. Validation narrowly focuses on mines, casting a blind eye on events on roads and at customs, where the bulk of illicit taxation occurs. Hence, validation and qualification provide no absolute certainty as to whether a mine is conflict-affected.

The system favours mines that are profitable and accessible from major trading hubs. This reflects 'the two different Africas that French colonialism once distinguished as "*Afrique utile*" and "*Afrique inutile*"',[6] and excludes thousands of remote mines, many of which are not militarised, from legal markets. While less than 10% of eastern Congo's known 3T mines were included as of late 2017, a full assessment is difficult given the lack of a comprehensive mapping of all actual and potential 3T mines.[7] Inversely, economically attractive mines remain part of iTSCi even in the event of armed influence—suggesting a profit-oriented rather than a development- or human rights-focused approach. Traceability is financed almost exclusively by Congolese upstream actors and outsourced to SAEMAPE and an American NGO called Pact. iTSCi staff only occasionally work on the ground.[8] This leads to a situation whereby

> ... outsiders bring money ... on which officials from impoverished states are highly dependent, as well as new skills and technologies that are essential to increasingly sophisticated forms of territorialisation, [creating] an emerging class of 'hybrid' actors who maintain their positions in developing states while simultaneously working for transnational institutions that can pay them much more remunerative salaries and higher consultancy fees .... Often these individuals are torn between the agendas of transnational institutions and the interests of their constituents.[9]

By operating based on a memorandum of understanding with the government, iTSCi taps into Congolese sovereignty in subcontracting government agencies like SAEMAPE,[10] with its operating cost borne by upstream companies. Officially, *comptoirs* pay a fee per exported ton. Juxtaposing iTSCi's Congo tonnage with collected fees, the latter broadly range around 0.3–0.4 USD/kg.[11] However, many *comptoirs* indicate that they pay flat-rate subscriptions, hinting at a practice of bespoke arrangements. As with additional costs (e.g. audits), these fees trickle down the supply chain, with *comptoirs* and smelters offsetting them proportionally to shipments they acquire from *négociants*, who in turn do the same with local suppliers.

Mineral pricing depends on many factors, including global pricing, domestic exchange rates, distance to trading centres, ore quality, local governance and taxation.[12] However, iTSCi's levies also shape pricing, with the system forming a bottleneck through which all legal 3T supplies must flow. Its financial report for 2016 shows that most of its costs are borne by Congolese producers—'conflict-free' minerals thus come at literally no cost for international industries and Western consumers. More precisely, iTSCi's budget was composed of only 0.7% (or 68,000 USD) downstream industry contributions, whereas the Congolese side of the supply chain shouldered a total of 80.1% of costs, representing more than 7.3 million USD (the remaining 19.4% were contributed by donors and donations).[13] In consequence, prices for cassiterite can be around 0.25 USD/kg less than in an assumed competitive market, *ceteris paribus*.[14] In the first three areas operated by iTSCi by mid-2014 (Nyabibwe, Rubaya and Lemera), this resulted in a decrease or stagnation of prices compared with pre-iTSCi and pre-Dodd–Frank levels. Local prices in Nyabibwe halved from 8–12 USD/kg in 2010 to 4–6 USD/kg in 2014 (global tin prices only fell by roughly 20% during this period). While part of this bust relates to geology, such as the levels of arsenic in Nyabibwe's mines, the Nzibira area experienced periods with prices as low as 1–2 USD/kg without these geological problems. Hence, the 'iTSCi tax' can amount to up to 15–20%, rendering livelihoods more precarious. The slow implementation of alternative systems applying the OECD guidance and section 1502 of Dodd–Frank gave iTSCi a pole position to hammer out an initially exclusive deal over the legal sourcing of 3T in eastern Congo. Bolstered by the ethical demands of international consumers, iTSCi forged a monopsony justified by a need to streamline opaque and 'criminal' supply chains while the actual aim was total market control. This had a twofold outcome: in iTSCi mines, prices were imposed on producers, while others were excluded from legal trade—regardless of whether or not they were conflict-affected (see above for the validation process).

Technical shortcomings also undermine the effectiveness of mineral traceability in a situation of low state capacity. Despite tackling fraud in 'digital minerals', iTSCi itself is not very digital as it relies on barcoded tags to manually control the itinerary of shipments, whilst outsourcing on-site oversight to sparsely equipped and understaffed teams at an NGO and un(der)paid Congolese civil servants. This strategy of 'at arm's length' monitoring in a sector with enormous local political stakes backfired. Fraud and contamination with minerals from outside 'green mines' became common patterns, entangling the dream of conflict-free minerals with the very conflict economies it set out to take apart.

While iTSCi remains the dominant purveyor of traceability, other schemes have timidly begun. Founded in 2013, the Better Sourcing Program (BSP) is part of a US-funded joint venture with GeoTraceability, a digital geotagging start-up. As BSP was testing an alternative to iTSCi in mid-2015 in the mines around Numbi in South Kivu, bureaucratic and political tensions would delay its entry into Congolese mineral markets. However, it was successful at implementing its first supply chain traceability projects for coltan and wolframite in Rwanda between 2016 and 2017. Two main differences exist between BSP and iTSCi. Technically, BSP aims at lessening traceability's dependence on human factors through a digitisation of tracking. Politically, however, BSP suffered from iTSCi's close relations with the Congolese mining ministry and a lack of customers—not surprisingly, given that most relevant tin producers and end users are regrouped in ITA Ltd. and share an interest in curtailing competitors. Given the lack of efficient labour unions and competitive local markets, producers are compelled to sell at synthetically reduced prices or bypass traceability altogether, turning to 'illegal' trade.[15] Many *négociants* told me they traded both inside and outside iTSCi in order to weigh business risks. Moreover, tensions over iTSCi fees have in some places triggered conflict between cooperatives and exporters. In meetings, iTSCi operatives have defended the system's high cost in eastern Congo with reference to logistical challenges and the downstream industry's refusal to contribute. When I was invited to the OECD's 2014 annual minerals meeting in Paris to provide an empirical snapshot of the socio-economic conditions in iTSCi mines, a senior iTSCi staffer accused me of lying in front of hundreds of 'conflict minerals' professionals from the fields of politics, industry and civil society. It would take until 2018 for the same person to admit to me in private that my figures were accurate, not without adding that iTSCi still struggled to lobby its own international members to increase their financial commitment to the system. In 2019, at the first annual OECD gathering in years that I did not attend in person, my phone buzzed with messages from other meeting participants: OECD specialists and Congolese officials for the first time had publicly confirmed that iTSCi had contributed to decreasing revenue for Congolese artisanal miners.

All of this undermines the credibility and legitimacy of traceability: UN reports found evidence of black markets for Rwandan iTSCi tags to obfuscate the origin of minerals and circumvent iTSCi's high Congo levies. In consequence, trans-border fraud

Figure 4.1: Geographical distribution of mines and violence[21]

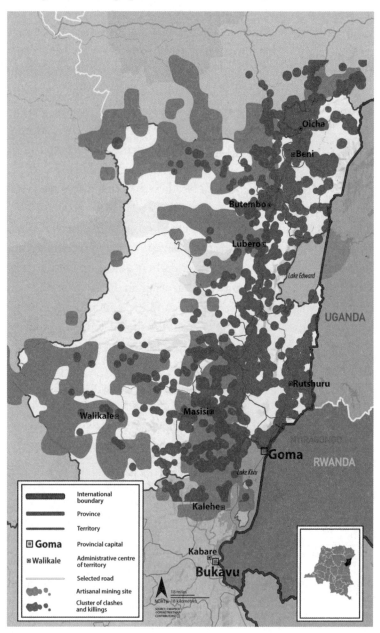

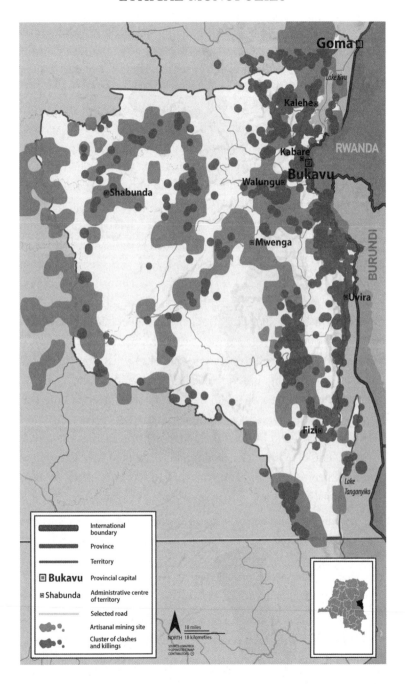

increased. While this is difficult to enumerate, a growing trend of arrests offers some impressions.[16] Sometimes, Congolese tags are not sealed properly in order to recycle them for one shipment after another. This allows traders to bring minerals from non-validated sites into the 'closed pipeline', as was the case from Numbi to Nyabibwe between 2012 and 2014. Meanwhile, mining officials used the opportunity of regulatory change to develop new taxes.[17] This questions the claims that the establishment of iTSCi would lead to a reduction in violence and corruption.[18] Most research indeed suggests the opposite is the case, particularly regarding violence.[19] An unpublished UN report noted in 2013 that even before the reforms, only 8% of the conflicts in eastern Congo were linked to resources. This is echoed in research by IPIS from 2019, suggesting that most of the armed conflict appears to be geographically and causally unrelated to mining. The Kivu Security Tracker, a project monitoring violence in eastern Congo, regularly backs up these findings.[20] Figure 4.1 above combines these datasets to illustrate the spatial disparities of mining and violence in North and South Kivu.

Finally, given the lack of complementary socio-economic and labour safety measures, the shiny corporate social responsibility blurbs on iTSCi and other stakeholder websites read as shallow.[22] In sum, iTSCi's main socio-economic impact is to have Congolese producers pay for the right to pass through its bottleneck so as to internationally sell their minerals. Meanwhile, the local

> ... economy remains beyond the pale, forced into either illegality or collapse as certain international buyers have responded to the legislation by going 'Congo-free'. Large numbers of Congolese miners ... lost jobs or businesses or had their incomes significantly reduced, with some (re-)joining armed groups.[23]

Having looked at how iTSCi fosters their monopoly, I now illustrate what this means for artisanal miners and their communities. Combined qualitative and quantitative evidence shows how corporate responsibility, if only geared towards Western consumers, can reify colonial logics of extraction and accumulation.[24] This illustrates how conflict minerals policies forgot, or merely paid lip service to, complementarities fostering livelihoods, missing an opportunity to generate inclusive reform and legitimate bottom-up solutions.

The local impact of conflict-free minerals

Little systematic attention has been paid to the impact of 'conflict-free' sourcing on livelihoods of mining communities, although the sector sustains an estimated 200,000–550,000 workers and around 1–4 million dependants in eastern Congo.[25] Instead, the focus of mineral reform has come with a push to formalise and thus eliminate the perceived 'illegal', 'inefficient' and 'fraudulent' practices of non-Western economies.[26]

> Official state policies, transnational governmental organizations, and international legal frameworks typically portray illegal activities as being bereft of moral value, economically inefficient, and ultimately threatening to the modern nation and the expectations of modernity wrapped up with its social, political, and legal construction.[27]

Questioning industry and advocacy claims, the incompatibility of artisanal mining and corporate extraction seems to prevent a more positive impact of conflict-free sourcing in local mining economies.[28] Worse still, human rights violations and extreme poverty continue under the label of 'ethical sourcing'.[29] In addition, the normative push to clean up the region's supposedly illicit mineral trade obfuscates how resource economies in eastern Congo are embedded in a delicate web of complementary relations and regulations that often make sense in and of themselves.[30] This is echoed in the observation that '[s]ocial scientific application of categories such as ethics and legality can obscure the generally fluid movement of subjects and objects across networks of value and contexts of exchange'.[31]

This section explains how formalised 'ethical sourcing' smashed existing complementarities in so-called informal markets and how closed-pipeline schemes triggered stagnation or decrease of local revenue. Linking ethnography with a quantitative survey exercise conducted in 2016 and 2018, it demonstrates how corporate claims to ethical mining were transformed by iTSCi into a bid for total market control.[32]

A result of international requirements for companies to apply 'due diligence' when sourcing minerals from conflict-affected areas (as per the OECD guidance), iTSCi is designed to provide proof of the origin and trading route of minerals (complying with section 1502 of the Dodd–Frank Act) through closed-pipeline supply chains. In orthodox thought, such a chain is believed to offer transparency, enclosing decentralised, hardly traceable production networks; in other words, making things readable to oversight.[33] However, conflict-free sourcing's more significant impact lies in altering socio-economic dynamics, affecting patterns of choice by which producers (miners, cooperatives, traders) navigate livelihoods.[34] Looking at how communities were suffocated by new regulation, one cannot help but think of the infamous analogy of the 'miner's canary', the bird that used to be taken down the shafts to serve as an early indicator of a lack of oxygen:

> Miners often carried a canary into the mine alongside them. The canary's more fragile respiratory system would cause it to collapse from noxious gases long before humans were affected, thus alerting the miners to danger. The canary's distress signalled that it was time to get out of the mine because the air was becoming too poisonous to breathe.[35]

While canaries are not used anymore (and possibly never were in Congo), the socio-economic well-being of Congolese artisanal miners is itself a figurative canary when it comes to the impact of 'clean sourcing'. They are an indicator to understand how live-lihoods in artisanal 3T mines evolve under formalisation, trace-ability and certification in volatile socio-economic environments facing persistent, protracted violence and displacement that has reduced rural households' subsistence capacities. Taking this angle sheds light on miners' agency and their views on legiti-macy, authority and formalisation.[36] Here, formalisation is defined as the ensemble of policies, techniques and practices to make people and things legible to oversight by regulatory insti-tutions.[37] Eastern Congo's ASM workforce (miners, auxiliary workers and intermediary traders) fluctuates and 'a large share of these individuals [are] educated and/or skilled victims of purges in other sectors'.[38] There are many reasons for this, including insecurity, migration, the six-month presidential mining ban, and boom and bust cycles on the global commodity market, among others.[39] Here, however, the focus is on formalisation via traceability and certification. (Formalisation can be a job machine or a socio-economic trap depending on its complementarities, so it is important to have a close look at the empirics.)

In our survey, 52% of respondents believed that formalisation and traceability have an impact on their socio-economic situation, and 35.5% believed this strongly. Artisanal mining is a mostly low-skilled sector in which most tasks do not require higher edu-cation or specific training, yet 47.5% of survey respondents enjoyed some secondary or university-level education. While this indicates that, previously at least, mining has been one of the better opportunities to make ends meet in a crumbled economy, 58% of survey respondents said their children would not or only intermittently go to school. In other words, the children of min-ers are on average a little less likely to attend school than their own parents. This an indirect but significant reversal of inter-generational development gains in terms of education.

Only 16% of survey respondents indicated they had regular access to healthcare. In the absence of an efficient redistributive social system and reliable insurance, access to basic services depends on private capital and community solidarity. Moreover, 55.5% of respondents noted their revenue had strongly (23.5%) or moderately (32%) decreased, while only 16% noted an increase since the onset of iTSCi. 40% had witnessed their access to health and education declining, while 22% reported stagnation. Only 14% had experienced positive developments in these fields. Finally, 72.5% estimated their current livelihoods as 'very bad' or 'bad', compared with 17.5% who perceived them as 'good' or 'very good'.

At the same time, 69% thought that traceability lessened fraud in the mines and 57% thought it reinforced state presence and authority in mining areas. Yet, this must be taken with a grain of salt: while dynamics *in* the mines changed, fraud *around* the mines did not substantially reduce, and so-called 'parafiscal' practices are on the rise, as is smuggling. This ambivalence is embodied in the pairing of service delivery with extortive and rent-seeking practices. While less than 20% reported illicit taxation by administrative and military actors, 38% are taxed by a cooperative, 42% by customary authorities, 56% by SAEMAPE, and 61% by mining ministry officials.[40] Illegal taxation by 'others' was reported by 32% of respondents, including government anti-fraud services.[41] 6% claimed iTSCi staff levied illegal taxes. Furthermore, SAEMAPE, iTSCi's implementation partner, was accused of coupling formal taxation (collecting access fees and duties) with various parafiscal practices that involve negotiable contributions for placing iTSCi tags on the mineral bags prior to transport (usually between 0.5–1.5 USD per bag).[42]

Corporate violence replaces military violence

While eastern Congo's mines were infamous for their apparent militarisation in the first decade of the twenty-first century, this image—generated as a consequence of the struggle against 'conflict minerals'—is gradually being replaced by the frame of 'responsible sourcing'. However, the notion rests on a thin base: responsibility merely refers to a presumed absence of armed actors and human rights violations, as outlined by the OECD guidance and the broader international legal and regulatory architecture. Despite claims of coupling the validation of mines with comprehensive livelihood improvements, this has not been a primary concern of reform. Nyabibwe's Kalimbi mine was validated in June 2011 and began exporting 'conflict-free' tin through iTSCi in October 2012. However, since it was validated 'conflict-free', human rights violations have continued—including forced labour, arbitrary arrests, beatings by soldiers, illicit taxation and safety incidents. The nearby Numbi area validated after this, meanwhile, remains under the occasional influence of Nyatura armed groups. Nonetheless, conflict minerals advocates declared that Kalimbi 'represented an important milestone towards conflict-free mineral trading in Congo, proving that due diligence and traceability is possible, even in the most challenging circumstance'.[43] Independent research, however, suggests that current 'trends are ... a strong reminder that the current situation is not sustainable'.[44]

This fixation on consumer-oriented PR is a result of policies designed in response to Western-led advocacy efforts. It gravitates around the question of how Congolese ASM production can be fed into a verifiable supply chain in order to offer Western consumers a 'conflict-free' seal of approval for digital gadgets. While in theory this could improve oversight at the transmission points along the upstream supply chain, it comes with the burden of monopsony, excluding local producers even if they are not associated with conflict.[45] As a result, monopsony is accepted—if not desired—by key global tin producers in their attempt to exclude parallel supply chains to maximise market control.[46] It is the adverse effect of a for-profit system sold as assurance for 'clean' minerals, while its immediate effect on communities is price dumping. Congo's artisanal miners 'are most likely to receive less money for the minerals they extract once traceability schemes are rolled out in the Kivus, as trading houses will have to start paying a fixed amount per ton of minerals'.[47]

While as many as 60% of respondents to the 2016 survey confirmed the prediction made a couple of years before, there is not just one explanation for the price collapse in Congo's mines. As mentioned, a decline in global demand at the London Metal Exchange (LME), the lead indicator for tin prices, was felt all the way down the supply chain. Nevertheless, discussions about international pricing are—despite miners' extensive knowledge of the supply chains they work in—not always easy for them to grasp,[48] partly due to their temporality (local prices would often not rise or fall concurrently with international ones), which can lead to conspiracy theories or feelings of powerlessness.[49] Industry websites illustrate the recent price carousel: while tin peaked at over 30,000 USD/ton in early 2011, prices plummeted to less than half of that in 2015.[50] In addition, as mentioned above, other factors influence local pricing, including iTSCi fees.

These fees depend on the amount, quality and type of minerals, and the contract under which *comptoirs* join iTSCi, with some paying monthly fees and others paying per exported ton. Testimonies vary between 180 and 480 USD/ton, meaning that 'levies can exceed the amount of taxes [paid] to the government'.[51] While it is difficult to calculate the depreciation of cassiterite at local levels, estimations range between 0.2 and 0.4 USD/kg, or 10–20% of the local price.[52] The levy fees are part of the reason mineral prices are higher at some non-validated sites than at iTSCi sites (up to 1–1.5 USD/kg higher for cassiterite and up to 10–12 USD/kg higher for coltan), encouraging smuggling, including to Rwanda, where iTSCi levies are lower.[53]

Another explanation is monopsony: while two international smelters buy the lion's share of iTSCi cassiterite, upstream supply chains are an oligopoly of Congolese iTSCi members that are encouraged to forge monopoly situations on the ground in each mining area included in the system.

The Lemera mines are but one example. There, a combination of global prices, supply chain monopolies, iTSCi levies and local politics have affected the socio-economic environment; for example, the local food market that used to be the area's economic pivot has shrunk by around two-thirds in size since iTSCi's inception. Traceability consequently coincided with endogenous and exogenous developments that have had a negative impact on the local economy. While certain mines saw a short-term price stabilisation or slight increases with the advent of iTSCi, these instances were limited and could not reverse the trend of miners migrating from 3T mining towards gold and gemstones since 2014.[54] This speaks to the miner's canary: before total collapse, warning signs point to the impending 'failure of vital organs', in this case local pricing and market access. As in other African ASM contexts, formalisation focused 'on monitoring, regulating and tracking mining activities, in the hope of channelling more revenue to a central government authority'.[55] However, this does not always happen by default—reality is often messier. While governments have an interest in maximising tax and customs revenues, this may not necessarily lead to a coordinated approach as revenue maximisation can be decentralised to satisfy patronage networks and defuse bottom-up pressures in a proverbial 'fend-for-yourself' fashion.[56] In eastern Congo, SAEMAPE's role is particularly illuminating:

> The example of SAESSCAM [SAEMAPE] is reflective of a broader structural challenge experienced by all the agencies and technical services operating within the Ministry of Mines .... Under-resourced, they find themselves unable to effectively fulfil their mandates, which

require significant logistical capacity to traverse the vast distances between and to mine sites and significant technical capacity to effectively carry out their work once there. Underpaid or unpaid, the agents who are in the field find themselves needing to resort to alternative strategies to survive, often including extortion or theft.[57]

Formalisation in the guise of traceability has changed little in relation to SAEMAPE's situation. A senior official of the agency lamented that 'iTSCi uses [us] as delivery boys'. His colleague complained that 'iTSCi is creating a lot of extra work for our staff'. This is in part due to lack of burden sharing, whereby unpaid SAEMAPE agents are pressured to 'sell tags to miners for money'. Meanwhile, iTSCi outsources the handling of logbooks to SAEMAPE, only to recover the files later without having been present during the registration of mineral bags, leading to loopholes.[58] This raises important questions as to how formalisation—considered a technique by which governments or state actors assert control over an economy—actually supports efficient governance. As observed in other artisanal mining areas, few of the 'regulatory frameworks now in place for ASM ... are in tune with the realities on the ground. Misguided and misinformed policy, therefore, has, in large part, "created" the burgeoning informal ASM economy'.[59]

If, in its joint venture with iTSCi, the Congolese mining administration increased oversight and taxation capacity, the new rules do not emanate from an analysis of local production patterns, and thus little of the newly gained control translates into systemic change. Instead, Congolese miners face novel forms of *parafiscalité*, in line with what Oliver de Sardan called 'practical norms', thus resonating with the idea of 're-inventing institutions'.[60] The role of mining cooperatives is telling. As per Congolese mining laws, they must register in order to operate, thereby becoming key players in the realm of access and taxation. In our survey, over a third of respondents reported they had to pay contributions to cooperatives. If a few are genuine, most resemble either traders regrouped into business associations, kinship organisations camouflaged around customary leaders, or seemingly syndicalist appendices of larger companies seeking to co-opt miners. In Nyabibwe, two competing cooperatives engage in sharp rivalry; in Nzibira, two cooperatives contest one another's legitimacy over attempts of extortion; in Lemera, a cooperative founded by businessmen provoked anger by taking miners hostage, as the next chapter on the role of *incontournables* further discusses.

Reform versus development

Although the maxim that modernisation does not equal development may be hackneyed, it remains illustrative. The transnational push to reform Congo's 3T sector is rooted in a vast justification ('solving conflict') for a narrow policy goal ('ethical sourcing'). Meanwhile, it has opened an immense Pandora's box of economic subsistence, market regulation and political power, leading to five main development problems.

First, top-down formalisation is seen by some as a holy grail of ASM governance.[61] While this dismisses important social theory on resistance, attempts to escape central governance, legal pluralism and the uneven implementation of regulation, it also prevents more durable solutions, and fosters window-dressing such as Potemkin village cooperatives that stress the contradictory logics of transnational reform.[62]

Second, formalisation remained incomplete and did not feature strategies to reorganise access for miners in a context of overlapping contested rights to land and concessions.[63] In her work on gold, Geenen observes that 'legal titles are a key and necessary first step to take, but it would not be sufficient. Other aspects such as access to finance, technical expertise, education and training also need to be addressed.'[64] Moreover, the issuing of titles for land and concessions is not addressed by current reforms, although the regulation of access rights is a particularly tenuous aspect of resource governance more broadly.[65]

Third, traceability is blindly imposed upon locally existing systems of authority and regulation.[66] While many mines were (and still are) 'informal', not all of them are 'conflicted'. Nonetheless, they are excluded from legal markets due to iTSCi's slow but profit-oriented expansion: before a mine is declared 'green' and eligible for certification, a cumbersome but unreliable validation process is necessary.

Fourth, while key elements of the reform process were hastily privatised, 'corporate social responsibility' (CSR) remained an issue on paper only.[67] While company-specific CSR policies exist in many industrial mines in Congo, for better or for worse, such policies are rare in the ASM sector. There are a few exceptions, such as a government-led process known as a 'basket fund'. In collecting taxes from miners, traders and *comptoirs*, the fund aims to generate the means for health and infrastructure projects. While there are success stories, local leaders deplored that 'politicians want to channel these funds to provide for their private needs'.[68]

Finally, local development was imagined as an automatic effect of a technical approach in a highly political environment. In overtly neoliberal fashion, reformers presumed that local producers could seamlessly and vertically be integrated into transnational markets. Despite this, eastern Congo's economy—while having its own complementarities—sits at the disenfranchised end of transnational capital flows and does not have a Westphalian state-like social contract that can safeguard it against adverse incorporation.[69] Mineral reform should thus have an interest in embedding these complementarities instead of suffocating them. This includes capacity-building in Congolese institutions. As a mining official once told me, 'at SAESSCAM [SAEMAPE], we realise that we, and the state we represent, lack the capacity to fulfil our mission'.[70]

At the end of the miners' survey we conducted, there was one open response field. Independently of each other, many respondents wrote *hakuna maendeleo* ('there is no development'). While some may have described the impact of mineral reform and others their wider socio-economic situation, the picture is equally worrying. In my research for this book, as well as in my broader work on conflict dynamics, I conducted dozens of interviews with current and former miners who are or have been combatants, and with current and former combatants who are or have been miners.[71] Given the broader contours of eastern Congo's political economy, these two occupations are intimately connected in the social dynamics of 'circular return'.[72]

All of this is not a blanket anti-formalisation argument. The reasons why formalisation can harm mining communities are diverse and context-specific. While some are linked to 'conflict minerals' policy, others are rooted in the way the Congolese state works. However, in both cases they can activate registers of resistance, since 'people involved in criminalised forms of work and networks of exchange sometimes come to see the act of defying state authority as an ethical practice in and of itself'.[73] Reflecting on iTSCi, miners regularly invoke detention metaphors. One trader complained, 'the tags lock up our business like they lock the mineral bags'.[74] Another claimed that 'the tags are just like a prison'.[75] If iTSCi has been hailed as a silver bullet, armed mobilisation continues unabated, and robust data to support the idea that iTSCi reduces armed interference does not exist.[76] Geographic isolation is a more feasible cause for both armed presence and iTSCi absence, given a lack of economic interest. While armed interference continues undisturbed in remote mines, mining and armed group presence rarely overlap.[77] Conflict is thus due to causes other than mineral exploitation, and addressing illicit trade may not equate to addressing conflict.[78] The reforms' greatest impact is therefore the burden they place upon Congo's mining communities, a collective canary that national and international policymakers and advocates may want to watch closely.

The problem of unilateral ethics

The foundation of the 'conflict minerals' paradigm is rooted in misperceptions of Congolese conflicts, whose multiple root causes were folded and packaged into one easily digestible narrative. Both the 'greed' paradigm and Western advocacy helped create an Orientalist imagery that has pitted victims and perpetrators against each other to promote—similar to other examples of Western advocacy on African conflict zones such as 'Kony2012'—the idea of greedy warlords terrorising voiceless populations, requiring the help of white saviours.[79] This highlights the ethical problems of unilateral ethics. This reading of eastern Congo was picked up by international policy, justifying top-down regulation informed by another Orientalist assumption, namely that depoliticised, technical interventions can establish transparent governance in a territory perceived both as savage and as a *terra nullius* void of rules.[80] Yet, in the shape of 'conflict-free' supply chains, this new and supposedly humane face of '"the global economy," has left little or no place for Africa outside of its old colonial role as provider of raw materials', since the defence of extractive monopolies remained the main objective.[81] The result, in brief, has been translocal frictions over authority and crumbling livelihoods for Congolese mining communities despite the interveners' 'will to improve'.[82]

5

BROKERS AND PATRONS

So far I have discussed the impact of the 'conflict minerals' paradigm on livelihoods and conflict. This chapter now takes an
ethnographic look at the real governance of mining in eastern
Congo. Zooming in on two types of stakeholders—brokers and
patrons—the chapter analyses how the networked logics of mineral trade evolve during and despite transnational efforts of
'conflict-free' sourcing.[1] Brokers are the intermediary traders
connecting mines to urban centres. Known as *négociants*, they
pre-finance the trade and transport of minerals and consumer
goods. Considered 'weak spots' navigating corruption and armed
interference in supply chains, transnational regulation aims at
eliminating them. Patrons, in turn, are the kingpins of the networks, assembling economic, political and military clout in the
mining sector.[2] As *incontournables*, they have mastered the art of
recycling themselves to remain key nodes in eastern Congo's
political economy. If many of them played a vital role during the
wars, transnational reform has failed to isolate them. Instead,
they reinvented themselves to become absorbed by 'conflict-free'
trade. Investigating the role brokers and patrons play can help

one to understand how privatised governance persists and how elites, armed groups and transnational business constantly form new networks of extraction, invoking repertoires of the 'state as an idea' while they erode the 'state as a system' by having one foot in the system and one foot out.[3]

Brokering mineral wealth

Boissevain has defined brokers as entrepreneurs who place 'people in touch with each other, either directly or indirectly, for profit'.[4] This, so the argument goes, creates both connection and friction: brokers reify boundaries and, 'to avoid redundancy, they have to simultaneously maintain the tension' that justifies their presence.[5] Like 'big men', brokers thus need a 'large network with a high score for multiplexity and exchange content'.[6] Their in-betweenness creates room for manoeuvre for which, Boissevain continues, three factors are central: (1) centrality; (2) time; and (3) power. Centrality refers to position, such as the *négociant*'s shuttle-like role in space and embeddedness in social networks. Time means to move unrestrained from social or economic obligation that requires constant presence at one place. Indeed, *négociants* have the time to travel across supply chains and to connect them. Power is the capability to acquire 'first-order' resources—in the *négociants*' case, this means cash to buy minerals or pre-finance mining to keep extraction running. Hence, rather than immediate gain, the idea of future revenue characterises brokers, which makes them somewhat similar to patrons.[7] Such gain is rooted in credit and debt schemes. For *négociants*, this is a two-sided coin: while they pre-finance *creuseurs*, their role as middlemen trading between mines and urban trading hubs—selling on behalf of *creuseurs*—also brings a surplus of revenue, kept as a sort of debt payment, or rent, in cash or kind.[8] The concept of 'development brokers' also stresses their relevance as intermediaries. In contexts of polycephaly and legal pluralism, politics are often framed by competition and coalition, whereas social interaction is characterised by negotiation. In spaces of contested or fragmented authority, brokers are thus the go-betweens 'between social units who benefit from this mediation'.[9]

Négociants fulfil vital functions inside and along supply chains.[10] As brokers, they operate between and within the networks in which material (minerals, consumer goods, money) and immaterial (access, power, networks) resources are negotiated. Given the rise of the 'informal' economy and the asphyxiation of bureaucracy during Mobutu's reign and its aftermath, the political and economic importance of networks has notably increased since the 1980s, as has concomitant uncertainty.[11] As connectors, brokers articulate exchange with both business partners and others, but the power relations in such arrangements are not always even; for instance, *négociants* hold more power than *creuseurs* due to familiarity with trade and pricing, and their mobility. Yet, while *négociants* outdo *comptoirs* with regards to local knowledge, they lack transnational connections. The locus of a broker's clout is never the person itself; it is activated in spatial terms. Exposed to uncertainty, brokers 'surf on the edges' of human interaction, reifying and re-bordering. They can be patrons towards some, like *creuseurs*, and clients towards others, like military commanders.[12]

> For it does seem that mobility, and control over mobility, both reflects and reinforces power. It is not simply a question of unequal distribution, that some people move more than others, and that some have more control than others. ... Differential mobility can weaken the leverage of the already weak.[13]

While many analyses perceive *négociants* as motors of 'criminal' and 'illicit' trade, less attention is paid to how they perform vital functions of subsistence too. As recent attempts to regulate artisanal mining curtail their reach, it is important to remember that *négociants* do both harm and good to the economies of which they form part. Understanding this ambiguous role is crucial for a nuanced analysis of how mineral trade evolves in a context of crisis, framed by competition, survival and uncertainty. Looking at how brokers straddle different networks and render imagined dichotomies (state versus non-state, armed versus unarmed, economic versus social, etc.) can thus offer a more adequate picture of mineral trade. *Négociants* purchase minerals at the mines and re-sell them in urban centres, connecting production with trade. They link miners (*creuseurs*) and cooperatives with trading houses (*comptoirs*). Those focusing on local trade around the mines are also called *managers, chachouleurs, commissionaires* or *fournisseurs,* and are known locally as 'category B' *négociants* ('category A' refers to *négociants* operating from urban hubs like Goma or Bukavu). Due to their place, mobility and ability to access resources, their position comes with a higher status than that of *creuseurs* or category B traders. However, these *négociants* usually still depend on *comptoir* owners, who are wealthy enough to send *négociants* to buy shipments instead of going themselves. Figure 5.1 situates the different actors just introduced and highlights the role of *négociants* in connecting other stakeholders.[14]

The upper part shows the mine level, with different actors often but not always convening in cooperatives. The light arrows in the upper part indicate the flow of raw minerals, while the lower part features state agencies (light arrows) and security forces (dark arrows) intervening in the *négociants'* everyday business.[15] With the *négociants* in the centre, the double-line arrows are key transmission points leading to the point of exportation. To buy minerals, *négociants* need to gain access, which is understood as an 'ability to benefit from things'. Two types of access are relevant to *négociants*: market access means 'to gain or maintain entry into exchange relations' by way of acquaintance with *comptoirs*, credit institutions or (kinship) networks;[16] legal access, meanwhile, was regulated in the 2002 mining code with the

Figure 5.1: Locating the *négociants* in the supply chain

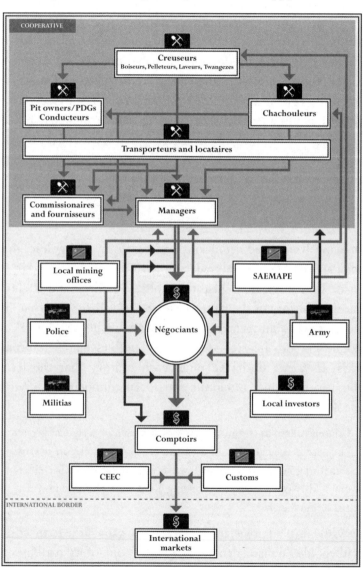

introduction of a permit to trade minerals for 250 USD per year and substance (i.e. coltan), known as a *carte de négociant*. Financial and legal access is further shaped by the liquid, oligopolistic character of authority, requiring *négociants* to negotiate within an environment of rapidly evolving power relations.[17] If the 'analysis of ... production, distribution, and exchange in Africa requires more than describing and tracking individual or group strategies in the present economic crisis', research on *négociants* thus fills a gap between existing studies on *comptoirs* and *creuseurs*.[18] In a context of real and perceived economic crisis, 'the power structures that condition the position of middlemen and miners' are crucial to understanding how trade works.[19]

The meaning of crisis

Drawing from emic definitions and usages by Congolese, this book approaches mineral traders in Kivu through the concept of crisis. In a meticulous historiography, Koselleck and Richter trace the history of the Greek *krísis* and its verbal root *kríno*. Its oldest retrievable meanings are 'separate', 'choose', 'judge' or 'decide' but also 'quarrel' or 'fight'—often in eschatological contexts. It wasn't until the nineteenth century that the term obtained a distinct economic and social connotation, often a teleological one:

> Conceptualized as chronic, 'crisis' can also indicate a state of greater or lesser permanence, as in a longer or shorter transition towards something better or worse or towards something altogether different. 'Crisis' can announce a recurring event ... or become an existential term of analysis.[20]

While its ubiquitous, tautological usage gained the term 'crisis' epithets like 'transcendental placeholder', one of its attributes is the allusion to uncertainty and transition, relating to a sociospatial idea of crossing boundaries, such as between risk and opportunity.[21] This is linked to the idea of something begun yet uncompleted—a 'permanent or conditional category' or 'immanent transitional phase'.[22] Just as 'wars of the nineteenth century were only a part of [a] larger crisis', cyclical violence and recurrent socio-economic challenges in eastern Congo represent more chronic and sustained uncertainty.[23] The ways in which seemingly punctual crises are a rather stable state of affairs is also picked up in other theoretical work:

> [It] is in everyday life that the crisis as a limitless experience and a field of the dramatization of particular forms of subjectivity is authored, receives its translations, is institutionalized, loses its exceptional character and in the end, as a 'normal,' ordinary and banal phenomenon, becomes an imperative to consciousness.[24]

The notion of crisis also informs Vigh's work on the navigation of urban youth. Seeing crisis as cyclical rather than exceptional, he develops the image of countless ruptures that form a continuum as crisis becomes steady.[25] Vigh writes that navigation is therefore the simultaneous movement of actors and their environment; it is 'motion within motion', like a moving boat in moving waters. This alludes to infinite aleatory iterations between structure and agency. Emirbayer and Mische define agency as 'temporally constructed engagement by actors of different structural environments ... which, through the interplay of habit, imagination, and judgment, both reproduces and transforms those structures'.[26]

Vigh's metaphor remains somewhat voluntarist as to whether countless ruptures 'produce' normality—or might just simply *be* normality. One needs to also account for structural factors allowing *négociants* to act as brokers. They are exposed to environments of uncertainty, both physically (checkpoints, war zones, hazards, etc.) and socio-economically (markets, villages, mines, etc.). In response, they need to make immediate but informed choices. Through the notion of *la crise*, Congolese refer to the struggle for survival (*la survie*) as mixing conflict-related insecurity with economic uncertainty. This emic conceptualisation is on a par with Roitman, who suggested that 'the very idea of crisis as a condition suggests an ongoing state of affairs'.[27] Noting that 'war is not a matter of "all terror all the time" *all over the place*',[28] eastern Congo can thus be considered as a 'crisis economy' rather than a flat 'war economy'. The concept of the crisis economy helps overcome neoclassic assumptions about resources and violence, and paints a more realistic picture of the contested, fragmented spaces of authority—similar to what Michael Watts termed 'governable orders'—where 'normative pluralism is the rule and not the exception'.[29] A governable order can be defined as a 'non-territorial, social figuration of power, norms and rules that transcends spatial scales'.[30] Other scholars teach us how such authority is (un-)made, agreeing that in most of the world '"state order" is only one of a number of orders claiming to provide security, frameworks for conflict regulation and social services'.[31] Roitman's work on the Chad Basin highlights how contested authority works at the 'intersections of "informal" activities with the "formal" economy by way of mediators'.[32] Like the Chad Basin, the crisis economy of Congo's mineral markets and its larger political economy complicates the debate on formal and informal. Rubbers' polemic quip on 'formalised informality' and 'informalised formality' shows that this dichotomy faces severe theoretical and empirical limitations to understanding state–market relations in a (postcolonial) political order.[33] As arbitrary as it is artificial, the binary is further unmade by the very emic Congolese notions of *système D* or *article 15*.[34] In short, these terms describe how interactions 'between members of state administrations like police, customs and army, and the range of cross-border entrepreneurs and smugglers active in the "informal" economy have given rise to new patterns of authority and regulation'.[35]

This is not to say that there is nothing but uncertainty in eastern Congo's mining economy. Despite rampant legal pluralism, the networked struggles over authority can lead to fairly foreseeable, even if spatially and temporarily limited, certainty. However, more often than not, the *négociants'* uncertainty finds its echo in fluctuating networks of sellers and buyers, and interlocking spheres of authority in which they circulate with minerals and money. In an environment of poverty and insecurity, this is exemplified by the *négociants'* struggle to make ends meet against opportunities to amass wealth, and the exposure to physical insecurity against collusion with armed forces. Within the 'ragged, unstable dynamics of multiple systems of authority', *négociants* thus 'navigate a perilous terrain and contribute at the same time to its re-shaping'.[36] As brokers of risk and opportunity, they are thus agents of crisis. It is in this context that they have emerged as a professional class and have come to form an obstacle to closed-pipeline supply chains.

Living mysteriously: Everyday uncertainty in the mines

To understand the *négociants*, we need to return again to Congo's ASM liberalisation in 1983.[37] Pressured by the International Monetary Fund to apply structural adjustment policies, Mobutu allowed the creation of private mineral trading houses. In sequence with the 1973 Zairianisation policies, this led to state-sponsored privatisation of a state that had already 'abandoned any pretence of formality'.[38] While the decay of the Zairian state would prove irreversible, privatisation was paralleled by infrastructural bust. Empowered by the breakdown of parastatals and agrarian transformation, populations went on to conquer the crumbling concessions of SAKIMA, SOMINKI and MIBA. The emergence of private *comptoirs* provided a springboard to the *négociants* (even if their status was only later officialised in the

2002 mining code). Since *comptoirs* were structurally and legally unable to access remote mines, *négociants* came up as intermediaries. Despite this, there were no reports of immediate violence; this only occurred 15 years later, when mineral trade became enmeshed with war. By that point, Mobutu had long since been ousted by the Rwandan-supported AFDL and the Second Congo War was in full swing. While the militarisation of mining was ascribed to greedy militias, things were more complex: even if violent exploitation skyrocketed around 2000—following a long history of Zairian army involvement in the sector[39]—this was not a 'war economy' per se, but a crisis economy in which artisanal mining became a precarious form of subsistence for many and a cornucopia only for some:

> [I]nsecurity reinforced the isolation of far-flung rural areas and made markets inaccessible, leading many communities to retreat into subsistence farming. Others were pushed towards the exploitation and trade of natural resources[;] violent modes of appropriation and economic collaboration with armed actors became institutionalised practices.[40]

Recurrent displacement made farming less viable, and people were unable to securely work their fields anymore nor wait until the harvest was ready. While the relicts of a parastatal economy continued to evaporate throughout the Second Congo War from 1998 to 2003, 'coltan remain[ed] the only survival strategy in response to a local economy profoundly destroyed' by subsequent waves of conflict.[41] Nevertheless, international discourse on the wars focused on what became known as 'conflict minerals', leading to the simple but compelling narrative that 'greed' for resources motivated violence.[42] The ensuing pressure and its strong appeal in public opinion—epitomised by the 'no blood in my mobile' campaign pinpointing the use of coltan capacitors in cellular phones—unleashed a chain of political consequences.

Driven by the idea that minerals were the cause of the wars (and sexual violence a main consequence), international policy reacted with three tools: (1) benchmarks such as the OECD guidance; (2) laws such as section 1502 of the Dodd–Frank Act; and (3) practical interventions such as iTSCi. Meanwhile, heightened scrutiny informed a presidential mining ban by Joseph Kabila on 3T and gold in eastern Congo in 2010.[43] While the ban and the incoming transnational regulation put *négociants* and other stakeholders out of jobs *de jure*, it quickly became clear that these interventions might 'fail to achieve their intended purposes [being] thrust upon social arrangements'.[44] In the following years, iTSCi became a de facto requirement for legal mineral trade. In its ambition to trace shipments 'from mines to markets', iTSCi established a monopsony that led to a decrease of local prices and fostered new 'parafiscal' practices.[45] Within this, the *négociants'* uncertainty was accentuated in their uncomfortable position between formalised 'clean sourcing' and 'illegal' informal trade. Echoing the critique of the formal versus informal binary, Hart observed:

> Rule-breaking takes place both within bureaucracy and outside it; and so, the informal is often illegal. This compromise attempts to promote the informal sector as a legitimate sphere of the economy, since it is hard to draw a line between colourful women selling oranges on the street and the gangsters who exact tribute from them.[46]

Transnational reform did not spend much time locating miners and traders on the spectrum of 'women selling oranges' and gangsters. Instead, it embraced a technical, market-centred logic through which it sought to delink violence and mining. Singling out minerals, the reform eclipsed root causes such as the politics of land and identity.[47] While this approach did little to reduce violence, it fundamentally changed the position of *négociants* as brokers of mineral wealth, leading to the exclusion of 'informal' participants from mineral markets and new incentives for fraud, violence and illegal taxation.

There is no predefined CV necessary to become a *négociant*, but a few factors do matter: while education is no ultimate condition, many *négociants* have completed some years of secondary schooling. However, beyond formal registration, a good address book (including ties to customary power or local militias) is a *sine qua non*. Many *négociants* are former pit owners, but occasional soldiers of fortune can also be found. To be successful, *négociants* need to link urban business with local mining economies and bail out *creuseurs* under strain. Fundamentally, the certainty of uncertainty that frames a crisis economy is paramount, as *négociants* operate a terrain that is constantly in motion. Despite—or perhaps thanks to—illicit activities, *négociants* can be motors of local development: the social dynamics of a 'primordial public' oblige them to operate in a way that doesn't solely benefit them.[48] Most of Kivu's remote mines depend on them for the supply of cash and consumer goods, which serve as lifelines for local markets: 'When I bring money, everyone benefits. When there is no [mining] work, businessmen and farmers are idle too; if the money does flow, shopkeepers weep for not selling anything'.[49]

The nexus of *madeni* ('debts') and *madini* ('minerals') underpins this crisis economy: miners depend on credit to cover expenses, but 'only middlemen are really aware of what is in demand at any given time and they try to fool diggers'.[50] These debts range from tiny sums to thousands of US dollars.[51] *Négociants*, in turn, voice unease in dealing with Rwanda-based traders: once, having made an illegal export via Rwanda due to Congo's global reputation, one of them recalled how he lost 60,000 USD as he could not pursue legal action. At the same time, he stressed how cross-border connections once played to his advantage:

In RCD times, I worked for high-level Rwandan authorities. Once in 1999, I was held in Minova by a colonel unaware of that. I called and after a few hours, soldiers came and arrested him. I even cuffed him on the cheeks! I could do that because I traded for these authorities. Once, an RCD colonel gave me a gun and a Motorola handset for my security.[52]

In sum, despite unequal power, miners appreciate the *négociants'* role: 'when a *négociant* comes with francs, business soars. Without money, even eating is a challenge.'[53]

This credit-debt system is an example of 'formalised informality'.[54] While debt is a source of uncertainty, it builds trust: sophisticated arrangements and clear rules govern pre-financing, 'exist within a clear framework of cooperation and obligations and serve both an economic and a social purpose' rooted in the structural marginalisation of miners.[55]

> Miners cannot leave ... to sell their material. The risks of losing their site and the opportunity cost of not digging during that period are too high. Traders provide a source of finance, cost efficiencies on transport, provision of merchandise to be traded in the mines. Miners don't have the network or expertise to command a significantly improved price than the négociant would have paid them.[56]

Miners lack leverage in this pre-financing, which sometimes covers over 50% of the operations. However, *négociants* depend on miners too: 'if a *creuseur* is arrested for debt, I will not be able to buy minerals. If I have money, I can bail him out and he will pay me back as he goes to work again.'[57] This relationship became increasingly difficult in the context of traceability. In South Kivu, local economies crumbled as iTSCi-associated *comptoirs* imposed local prices and co-opted *négociants* as sub-contractors—eliminating a key element of the supply chain.[58] In Nyabibwe, iTSCi's pilot site, the lack of capital led *négociants* to buy minerals through a 'lottery' buying system that excluded a prior verification of the purity of ore.[59]

Box 5: Testimony of a female *négociant* in Nyabibwe in early 2015

I have been a *négociant* since 1992, but it has become harder and harder in the past months. I sub-contract several people but they do not always pay back debt. My income does not cover my children's schooling anymore. The price for cassiterite here is between 6 and 7 USD. I used to secure 0.2–0.4 USD/kg, but nowadays less as local prices are almost equal to Bukavu. Taxes are 0.38 USD/kg, not counting those in Bukavu, so in the end I lose. Since few *comptoirs* joined iTSCi, I lost bargaining power. Previously, the Chinese paid decently, but they closed. Colleagues from Numbi or Ziralo go via Rubaya to sell in Goma. These tags lock down our business in the same way they lock the bags.[60]

Rubaya is a mining town in Masisi territory, an area that has known conflict and insecurity since the 1990s.[61] The violence in the region influenced Rubaya's development as a shantytown mining hub. Alongside Kitchanga, it is Masisi's largest urbanised area, and is dependent on mining and connected to Goma through a thriving network of *négociants*.[62] Conflicts persist, although security has improved since many Nyatura militia recently demobilised to become miners. While the 'concessionaire-cum-*comptoir*' Société minière de Bisunzu used to be linked to CNDP, the 'cooperative-cum-*négociants*' Cooperative of Artisanal Miners of Masisi (Coopérative des exploitants miniers artisanaux de Masisi [COOPERAMMA]) had ties to PARECO. While Rubaya's history is particular, its *négociants* face similar consequences as elsewhere, claiming their 'problems are because of [iTSCi] tags'.[63] As one of them said, 'before the tags, we were all fine';[64] however, following their introduction, his average monthly revenue dropped from 250 to 50 USD, and the number of *négociants* serving the area from 400 to 100. As monopsony triggered payment delays (in June 2014, for instance, 50 tons of coltan were unpaid), many *négociants* turned to passenger transport, running bars or NGO jobs. Others went into the unrecorded tourmaline trade, where prices are calculated in debt, or in the words of a *négociant*, 'like Russian roulette'.[65]

Despite iTSCi's arrival in March 2014, it is difficult to discern 'clean' from 'unclean' minerals. Since the '*tag mines*' are given at the *guichet unique* (central taxation counters; that is, not at the mine) and the *tag négociant* only in Goma (not at the *guichet unique*), fraud thrives through the mixing of coltan from nearby non-validated mines. While traceability reduced options to navigate, revenue from coltan in Rwanda is 10–20% higher, in part because iTSCi levies are lower. Many *négociants* thus consciously combine 'legal' (iTSCi) and 'illegal' trade, called *kuchoresha* ('make something go out') or *hélicoptère*, a term used to describe 'lifting the minerals up and away'. Often, smuggling operations involve collusion with security forces earning a percentage for facilitating nocturnal transports to Goma, avoiding or offering bribes at roadblocks. One *négociant* explained how, in Bihambwe, he first passes a checkpoint of intelligence agents and SAEMAPE. He then has to stop at an army roadblock in Mushaki before reaching Lutobogo. The last control is in Mubambiro, but there are alternative pathways. Often, tags are not properly sealed so that they can be re-used afterwards. Other tactics include army escorts, pretending the shipment 'had already been seized' or lacustrine smuggling.[66]

In Rubaya and elsewhere, plethoric taxes are a key feature of the crisis economy. Comparing contextual variation of official and other taxes is thus a helpful prism to analyse the *négociants*' relation to state and similar actors. Most taxes are negotiated. In some cases, state agencies acknowledge parastatal actors (and vice

Figure 5.2: The coexistence of legal and illegal trade

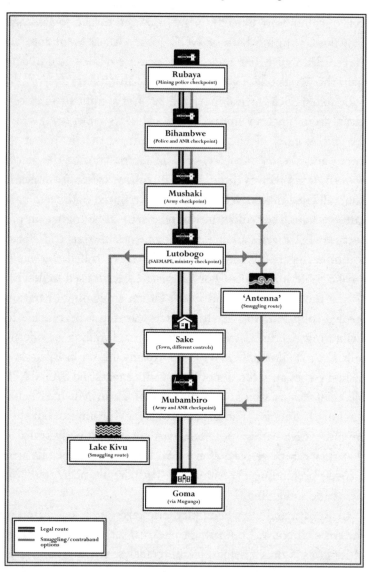

versa): at the *guichets uniques*, some taxes are forwarded to customary authorities. Some taxes are collected through rackets while others are fees for weighing or transporting minerals. Many *négociants* complain over SAEMAPE: 'we are told they are an assistance service but in fact they are a taxation racket and intelligence outfit'.[67] Some of its agents demand 500–1,000 CDF per tag. In South Kivu, an anti-fraud unit demanded clearance fees in addition to transport waivers of up to 30 USD per vehicle. In one case, fees were determined by the number of drinks the clerk had had beforehand. The same clerk also invented a new registration form as the old one became obsolete with the onset of iTSCi. Table 5.1 offers a non-exhaustive overview of taxation.

Furthermore, iTSCi levies and new taxes curtail the margins for *négociants*; hence nocturnal operations are legion. While charging vehicles for transport at night is officially forbidden, SAEMAPE agents facilitate it against a newly invented tax. Wherever armed groups control mines, such as the Raia Mutomboki in South Kivu, 1–2 USD has to be paid per bag and checkpoint.[68] Insisting on equal shares, certain armed groups allow state agencies like SAEMAPE to tax alongside them. Taxation is uncertain due to volatile conflict dynamics and the lack of clarity regarding to whom, where or when taxes are paid. While some taxes are more standardised, others are fairly haphazard. Collaboration with armed groups thus helps to attenuate uncertainty to a degree. Moreover— with state symbolism transcending areas of government control— armed group taxation paradoxically tends to be lower if paperwork is in order. Confronted with this taxation, *négociants* often seek *a priori* agreements, although not without negotiating prices. There are solidarity funds to pool risks, known as *horoscopes*, a term by which *négociants* literally mock the uncertainty of the situation.[69]

In certain cases, former *négociants* have taken up administrative jobs (e.g. at SAEMAPE), which strengthens ties between *négociants* and their bureaucrat counterparts and offers avenues for

Table 5.1: The panoply of taxation along the mineral supply chain

Tax type	Paid by/to	Rubaya (Ta)	Nyabibwe (Sn)	Lemera (Sn)	Nzibira (Sn)
1) Carte négociant	Négociant/division	250 USD/year	250 USD/year	250 USD/year	250 USD/year
2) Identification	Négociant/(variable)	60 USD	60 USD	60 USD	60 USD
3) Identification	Négociant/SAEMAPE	15 USD/year	15 USD/year	15 USD/year	15 USD/year
4) SAEMAPE fee	Négociant/SAEMAPE	3 USD/kg	0.5 USD/kg	0.5 USD/kg	0.5 USD/kg
5) Transport waiver	Négociant/division	0.5 USD/kg	10 USD/load	15 USD/load	10 USD/load
6) Customary tax	Négociant/chefferie	N/A	0.08 USD/kg	0.1 USD/kg	0.05 USD/kg
7) Police or intelligence	Négociant/police or intelligence	(variable)	(variable)	20 USD/day	(variable)
8) Army	Négociant/army	(variable)	Phone credits	30 USD/load	(variable)
9) Militia taxation	Négociant/militia	N/A	N/A	5,000 CDF/load	-20%
10) Road construction	Négociant/cooperative	10 USD/year	N/A	N/A	N/A
11) Transport fee	Négociant/driver	0.5 USD/kg	0.1 USD/kg	0.1 USD/kg	0.1 USD/kg
12) Cooperative tax	Négociant/cooperative	0.5 USD/kg	10%/load	N/A	0.05 USD/kg

13) Basket fund*	Négociant/ministry	50 USD/ton	50 USD/ton	50 USD/ton	50 USD/ton
14) 'Fiche Controle'	Négociant/division	N/A	1.5 USD/tag	5 USD/load	N/A
15) 'Late charging tax'	Négociant/SAEMAPE	0.5 USD/kg	10 USD/load	N/A	N/A
16) SAEMAPE fee	Comptoir/SAEMAPE	1%	1%	1%	1%
17) Export taxes etc.	Comptoir/CEEC	3%	3%	3%	3%
18) Prov. government	Comptoir/division	1% (repartition)	1% (repartition)	1% (repartition)	1% (repartition)
19) Carte creuseur	Creuseur/division	10 USD/year	10 USD/year	10 USD/year	10 USD/year
20) Registration	Cooperatives/division	100 USD/year	100 USD/year	100 USD/year	100 USD/year
21) Pit tax	PDG/division	(unknown)	100 USD/year	100 USD/year	100 USD/year
22) Processing tax	Comptoir/division	(unknown)	60 USD/ton	60 USD/ton	60 USD/ton
23) Anti-fraud	Négociant/anti-fraud	N/A	30 USD/car	(unknown)	(variable)
24) 'Tag fee'	Creuseurs/SAEMAPE	N/A	500 FC/tag	N/A	N/A
25) iTSCi levy	Comptoir/iTSCi	360–480 USD/ton	180–250 USD/ton	180–250 USD/ton	180–250 USD/ton

*Plus 30 USD from creuseurs, 35 USD from transporters, and 75 USD from comptoirs, per ton.

bespoke deals. Stressing that extortive state agents and armed groups undermine their capacity to supply consumer goods to mining areas, *négociants* refer to their social role to justify 'defying state authority as an ethical practice in and of itself'.[70] Nonetheless, many *négociants* define their relations to state agencies (and armed groups) as cordial, for the latter 'also need to light their stoves'.[71]

Négociants confront myriad challenges beyond business writ small. After decades of conflict, practices of Othering are common. As brokers in contested spaces, where belonging is a political repertoire and source of animosity, they face many problems.[72] This is not limited to autochthonous-versus-Rwandophone cleavages; it also occurs within so-called 'autochthonous' communities or groups.[73] Protection arrangements sometimes form responses, with *négociants* straddling such risks:

> In many cases, military protection takes place in the framework of more comprehensive economic collaboration between the military and civilians. [T]he FARDC possesses specific qualities as an economic actor. As well as being a combat organisation, the FARDC is an economic network with wide geographical coverage.[74]

Most *négociants* are aware of their relational power in such situations, and differentiate between military ranks and functions when dealing with armed actors. They attempt to identify key individuals with whom they can strengthen ties, thus increasing predictability. Usually, these relations are constantly revitalised due to military reshuffles and parallel hierarchies. Collaborations depend on familiarity with involved actors and the seniority of commanders. Some *négociants* carry—like humanitarians—*enveloppes de sécurité* containing cash in case of ambushes, but whenever possible, arrangements are made in advance. *Négociants* may pay one institution to avoid (higher) taxation by another, or to garner protection—a 'commodity that lubricates economic exchange in situations where legal sanctions are either absent or difficult to enforce'.[75] Such collusion with security actors can have important effects: in August 2014, a FARDC colonel confiscated a vehicle with illegal mineral cargo despite a rank-and-file soldier from another unit intimidating him not to do so, resulting in a clash between said parties' two units. The next day, the colonel was summoned and sanctioned by his hierarchy.[76] In 2010, the presidential mining ban provoked increased smuggling, heightening the posture of FARDC and other security forces. At the same time, the ban was an era of 'anything goes', often in partnership with military commanders. *Négociants* with names as emblematic as *Carré Magique* ('magic bluff') or *Madollar* (the Swahilised plural of dollar) made their livings in this period. Certain state agents turned into part-time *négociants*, brokering their way across state services and re-investing landslide gains in real estate or, in some cases, losing them all again. In the presence of competing armed actors, *négociants* navigate the crisis economy, paying one side to be protected from another, such as in areas where police and army units compete. Such navigation is relational: from one moment to another the adequate course of action can be different. The example in Box 6 is illustrative.

As much as the proverbial use of the word *crise*, which underpins the idea of a crisis economy, the *bon mot* 'we live mysteriously' is a famous Congolese saying that often features in discussions with *négociants* when it comes to defying uncertainty.[77] While they perform a gatekeeper position and connect markets, traceability efforts aim to cut them out of supply chains. This ever shrinking room for manoeuvre has strongly encouraged fraud in the sense of *kuchoresha*. In one *négociant*'s words, 'as iTSCi and state agencies reinforce their grip, they actually provoke fraud'.[78] Adding to the socio-economic impact of this—as illustrated in the rise in school dropouts and unemployment, both of which can lead to militia recruitment—analysis of how

Box 6: Testimony of a Lemera-based *négociant*

As the [new] concession owner arrived, they confiscated our goods. I asked whether they had authorisation to do so. I pay eight people. I pay my rent. I am here in Lemera. I have to send money to my family in Bukavu. I paid my fees to SAEMAPE, the mining police, FARDC, the mining division to receive all necessary paperwork. I paid everyone! As I prepared my cargo, the concession owner called a senior FARDC commander and I was arrested with my minerals. I called the local commander, a FARDC major, and asked if my payment of 30 USD had arrived. I called my elder brother who is an army commander in the same military sector. He called me back and said I should 'let things go, his units would take the matter on within FARDC'. Afterwards, we drove to the military base where I left my minerals. I found that the officer who had me arrested was the one keeping the concession owner's farms, against a monthly 'salary' of 1,000 USD. I returned with my brother who told his colleague it was illegal to confiscate my minerals. Two days later, I got my goods back.[79]

négociants have responded to the threat posed by iTSCi further demonstrates how formalisation and transnational reform can have unintended consequences. This ethnographic account of the *négociants* shows that 'conflict-free' sourcing, at the very least, coincides with continuing fraud, the fragmentation of armed groups and a new peak of violence. Even if *négociants* are an integral part of the game over 'power, profit and protection', such a lens alone obscures their vulnerability.[80] Moreover, it also trivialises the constant interplay of risk and opportunity that frames eastern Congo's crisis economy where only few succeed in conserving gains.[81] The danger of exclusion from legal markets has weakened *négociants* to the extent that one of them told me he would join a militia if offered a mere 100 USD for doing so.[82] In dozens of my interviews and independently of each other, *négociants* used prison and handcuff metaphors to describe how they keep 'living mysteriously' despite the radical shifts affecting eastern Congo's crisis economy.

The evolution of patronage in Congolese politics

The *négociants* are not alone in operating 'mysteriously' in eastern Congo's changing minerals markets. The remainder of this chapter is dedicated to those known as the *incontournables*, a term Congolese use for the purveyors of de facto power in mining and beyond. However, the same term is used in French to positively describe outstanding people and things, such as exceptional wines, cultural performances or artists. This emic prism thus helps us revisit political patronage in situations of privatised governance without necessarily succumbing to Orientalist imagery and pejorative metaphors. While there is a rich literature on patronage in African politics, a majority of texts largely reinforce dominant epistemologies.[83] Moreover, the role of social and spatial dynamics of patronage is only marginally addressed in scholarly debate, and virtually absent in the realm of conflict studies.[84] The 'conflict minerals' case is an opportunity to critically assess the logics and language of patronage, as well as how it shapes political order and public authority. Having become part and parcel of transnational mineral reform, many of eastern Congo's wartime power brokers and entrepreneurs persist and reinvent themselves, mastering the art of becoming *incontournable*; in other words, they become indispensable, unavoidable and impossible to sideline in their given environment.[85]

The following pages look at the *incontournables* and their networks of mineral trade through the evolution from 'war' to 'peace' and from 'chaotic' to 'regulated' trade. They examine how traceability affects and reshapes these networks as well as the role of customary authorities, politicians and security providers therein.[86] Three case studies illustrate how *incontournables* deploy their clout, relying on spatial dynamism and the ability to transcend and connect networks of political, economic and military power. This helps explain how networks of mineral trade resist efforts at external regulation and continue to operate at the heart of violent politics. Patronage, in its contemporary emanations, finds roots in the violent character of colonialism wherein a pretence of public authority was performed by private (government-linked) entities, as Mbembe illustrates in the notion of 'private indirect government'.[87] Examples like the British East India Company and the Congo Free State speak intimately to that, as much as iTSCi does today.

I neither presume linear evolution from colonial to postcolonial rule, nor claim that patronage has no precolonial antecedents. Indeed, as Ekeh conceptualised through the 'tale of two publics' in postcolonial Africa, patronage is a long-standing social phenomenon that predates colonisation.[88] He contends that colonial rule established a 'civic public' that follows Western-type patron–client relations, which coexists with a 'primordial public' rooted in precolonial, indigenous social dynamics; these consequently perform a socio-moral guarantee function which members of society can rely upon.[89] This contribution remains highly pertinent—it not only describes precolonial patronage but converges with the Western, colonial duality foregrounded by Mbembe. Therefore, and given the broader colonial character of the struggle against 'conflict minerals', this book focuses on the continuities of externally led extraction: in other words, if colonialism was violent plunder disguised as civilisation, postcolonial patronage logics operate a similar masquerade whereby 'informal' networks transcend both of Ekeh's two publics while foregrounding official attributes. Similar dynamics radiate into the realm of development, where the 're-ordering of the various modes of government'[90] is rooted in 'modern' transnational and 'traditional' situated politics:

> [C]lientelism, as a concept, has a heuristic value generally missing from the conceptual arsenal of either 'modern' or 'traditional' polities; it directs attention to processes of adjustment between traditional and modern patterns of behavior, expectations, and normative orientations to politics which otherwise go unnoticed.[91]

Patronage and clientelism are often 'employed as shorthand for corrupt, dysfunctional regimes, but ... this usage threatens to dilute the concept beyond analytical utility, perpetuating normative judgments based on ideal-type government structures that do not exist', including, one may add, in the West.[92] While the terms are a moving target, the idea of personalised relations between actors with 'unequal wealth, status or influence, based on conditional loyalties and involving mutually beneficial transactions' is central.[93] Patronage requires patrons and clients to bring resources to the table: patrons command skills, information and capital, while clients offer economic, political or military support. Analysing the FARDC, Verweijen sees patronage as 'social networks cemented by patron–client ties, which are asymmetric but reciprocal relations'.[94] Other than transactions writ small, patronage involves 'exchange ... usually effected by a "package-deal."'[95] While this is manifest in family or kinship ties (as Ekeh's proposition implies), it can also be enacted through other categories of belonging, such as membership of a political party or a social movement, economic ties such as networks of mineral trade in eastern Congo or, to dispel definitions thriving on Orientalism, Western governments brokering arms deals on behalf of their military-industrial complexes. What these cases have in common is a redistribution of profit (to patrons) and protection (to clients). Members of patronage networks often define these 'in flowery terms as an enactment of community relations and civic solidarity'.[96] The 'reciprocal legitimacy' such systems achieve depends on whether they rely on a 'stable or growing pool of rents'.[97]

While it is true that 'the discourse on Africa's marginality is nonsense', orthodox theories of patronage do not tell us much more about how patronage works in transnational contexts.[98] With the exception of the predominant French school, there was scant further theorisation until neo-institutionalist writing rehearsed patronage as 'relations of exchange between individuals of unequal status' that are 'fragmented, crisscrossing all sorts of organisations in which elites exerted power and competed for supremacy'.[99] Nonetheless, these literatures essentialise Africa, casting a blind eye on sovereignty and the 'assortment of power struggles between the elements that permit statehood to occur'.[100] If space is 'a constellation of different, co-existing ongoing social, economic, and political dynamics', spatialising patronage can enrich our understanding of authority.[101] Investigating the *incontournables* and their registers of power in the context of mineral reform is key to understanding how formalisation challenges so-called 'informal' networks or ends up blending into them, as well as how militarised political economies intersect with such processes.[102] The idea of a marketplace where 'provincial elites secure the support, including votes and guns, of their constituents in return for money, jobs and licences to trade or pillage' is a rare pointer to questions of space.[103] Yet, it remains theoretically insufficient to understand how elites create boundaries, how they manage networks in the shape of 'rhizomes', but also how patronage spatially operates, transcending scale (as highlighted by transnational 'extraversion').[104] Here, we go a step further by conceptualising the *incontournables* as impossible to sideline, as spatially unavoidable and socially indispensable. As gatekeepers, *incontournables* are invested with an authority to represent at different scales—from a 'local arena' to an 'international one', often taking the role of 'a voice from the field'. Inversely, inasmuch as they can 'meet the demands of clients', this bestows *incontournables* with the prestige of being 'accepted abroad'.[105] The clout of *incontournables* materialises in the capability to either facilitate or spoil interests across networks.[106] The more exclusive these aspects are, the more *incontournable* a person is. However, a person cannot be *incontournable* at any time and in any place: the role requires strong back-up from allies, as it often creates envy and engenders sabotage.

Figure 5.3: Matrix of scaled and networked patronage dynamics[107]

Field of operation ⟍ Structuring principle	Scale ('extraversion')	Network ('rhizome')
Scale ('extraversion')	Clout or influence of eastern Congo's *incontournables* within (trans-)national politics in the sense of 'jumping scales.'	The relevance of transnational acceptation on the *incontournables'* local authority in the sense of 'scaled feedback loops' and resulting recognition or legitimacy.
Network ('rhizome')	Capacity of nuisance and facilitation of patronage networks deployed as spoilers impacting across different scales.	The topological power of brokering between and flowing through different networks as *incontournable* nodes of rhizomes.

In that sense, *incontournables* are a social version of Callon's 'obligatory passage points', embodying both unique power and vulnerability.[108] This blurs the lines of authority, since power is rooted not in formal hierarchy but in the nodes of networks and multiplied by scale.[109] Hence, authority is an outcome of competing attempts to govern and patronise a self-perpetuating type of 'formalised informality' across networks and other bounded social spaces.[110] Congo's mining sector and the transnational reforms tackling 'conflict minerals' have given rise to scenarios in which *incontournables* are able to become the 'obligatory passage points' from where a 'network radiates outward, mapping a delineated topological space'.[111]

> Mobutu preferred to circulate his principal elite rivals in and out of favour, making them compete against one another. Since the late 1990s this system has been replaced by a regionalized political market-place in which organized violence has become a major instrument.[112]

The transnational but glocal character of eastern Congo's wars offered a genuine arena for patronage networks to employ violence as a currency of political bargaining, forming part of broader complexes of power, profit and protection. These complexes result from an inscription of local conflict landscapes framed by 'traditional' patterns into international 'modern' political arenas—allowing *incontournables* to jump scales and connect 'local' strongholds to international arenas. The concomitant fragmentation of authority has engendered a networked logic of elite politics. Considered the 'ability to define and enforce collectively binding decisions', public authority in Congo is exercised by a multitude of actors, of which the state is no more than empirically the strongest.[113] This fostered a 're-routing of competition practised in a legal market'.[114] In the interstitial and fragmented spaces that characterise Congo's crisis economy, *incontournables* walk a thin line between reliability and ambiguity, maintaining ties with other power brokers as much as their clients.[115] The temporal coincidence of continued violence and 'post-conflict' policies, such as international peace-building, is fertile ground for them. While international conflict resolution and stabilisation aim at harmonising public affairs and 'returning' to an imagined ideal of uniform, state-projected public authority, recent Congolese history featured the de facto 'outsourcing of central state functions ... to influential individuals in post-civil war settings'.[116]

Underpinned by a lack of settlement resources and with extractive rents outweighing productive ones, this favours militarisation and the survival of wartime networks built around the *incontournable* kingpins. In eastern Congo, peacekeeping and peacebuilding feature a variety of approaches, including transition and peace deals, demobilisation, the integration of conflict parties into unified security forces, peacekeeping forces, and transnational efforts for ASM reform. Although the latter produced 'conflict-free' mineral markets under a smokescreen of transparency, this reform contributed to the further fragmentation of contested authority. While political power-sharing and army integration deals absorbed a number of elites, some business-people, disgruntled politicians, customary chiefs and mid-range commanders had little to gain.[117] The subsequent 'post-conflict' conjuncture framed by both watchdog scrutiny and 'peace dividends' thus co-opted spoilers, encouraging 'illegal' wartime *incontournables* to morph into 'legal' ones.[118] While this has not lessened violence, it has strengthened the position of wartime elites by increasing their options.

Patronage and conflict minerals

The following three snapshots demonstrate how patronage lubricates the friction between violent politics and the new rules of the mineral game. Each offers an example of the networked dynamics of patronage that underpin conflict-free sourcing. The first ('boat busting') is rooted in historical ethnopolitical conflict that plays out between a mining company and local traders. It shows a collusion of rebels turned army commanders who became *incontournable* during a smuggling operation. The second ('Fuliiro fault lines') describes a customary succession conflict involving local militia and businesspeople that has formed into an *incontournable* complex. The third ('conflict cooperatives') narrates the rivalry between cooperatives, with one customary chief trying to position himself as *incontournable* even if he is ultimately unsuccessful. Together, all the cases portray the resilience of patronage, questioning the tenets of clean supply chains.

Boat busting: Contraband and militarised patronage

It is time to return to North Kivu's highlands west of Goma, where forced colonial labour and migration has formed a fertile basis for tensions over citizenship and land. Throughout recent history, Kinyarwanda-speakers' citizenship has been 'switched on and off', cultivating resentment against the perceived invaders in the struggle over local political power.[119] A hotbed of mobilisation since 1993, the Masisi area has experienced spates of violence giving birth to Rwandophone and 'autochthonous' militia (the *combattants* and Mongol, and Batiri and Katuko, respectively). Since 1996, Laurent-Désiré Kabila's AFDL rebellion and the anti-Kabila RCD have integrated Masisi into eastern Congo's wider conflict topography, deepening old rifts and creating new ones. Decades of violence have eked out networks linking politicians, businesspeople and commanders. While armed mobilisation has fragmented in recent years, these networks keep thriving around mineral trade. Rubaya, the key hub for coltan in Masisi, is surrounded by 17 mines, seven of which are in a concession owned by the Société minière de Bisunzu (SMB). Miners, including many ex-combatants, and traders organise in the COOPERAMMA.

Since Rubaya joined iTSCi in 2014, the COOPERAMMA have denounced both the monopoly created by iTSCi and SMB's refusal to tolerate other buyers.[120] In mid-2015, this added up to 6 million USD in unpaid deliveries. While the cooperative is

Figure 5.4: Boat busting

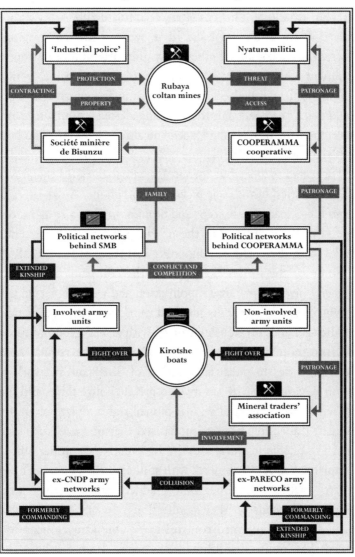

believed to have had ties with one armed group, SMB used to be close to another. Within this broader set-up, the following happened: in the early morning of 16 October 2015, seven lorries carrying around 50 tons of coltan, accompanied by army escorts, arrived at the shores of Lake Kivu, where boats were waiting. There, they encountered other army units attempting to stop the shipment and were met with gunfire. Soon afterwards, a high-ranking officer called off the intervening troops so the lorries could reach the boats, but the shooting alerted a nearby navy unit who found the boats being loaded and also opened fire. Two boats capsized with cargo. While one boat managed to leave, three lorries retreated to a nearby hideout. Eyewitnesses called the provincial authorities, but no one picked up the phone. A day later, the cargo was reloaded onto jeeps and brought to Goma at night, only to end up being parked at the provincial branch of the central bank. From there, the mining police lost track of the cargo.[121]

Some of the lorries belonged to the company of a general formerly involved in Hutu mobilisation and well-connected with provincial elites. The units involved were under the command of another general, previously involved with armed groups opposed to Hutu mobilisation before integrating into the regular army. Both have ties to politicians critical of SMB and networks of coltan *négociants*. SMB has its own private police force, and they too have been accused of regular human rights violations. In this context, traders repeatedly emphasised that one needs to 'know the right people to work with'.[122] In interviews, mining officials complained about 'transports with military escorts we can't even control', while one police officer added, 'we can't just arrest people, it depends on their connections'. In one case, a convoy opened fire on unarmed controllers.[123] One army officer confessed that 'politicians sabotage my work. I am a soldier they are not my superiors, but they are *incontournable* [sic].'[124] In this case, ostensible ethnic antagonism subsided around shared interests. However, operations of such magnitude are unlikely to be conducted without the buy-in of senior military officers and their army patronage networks. It was this entanglement of commanders, business circles and political elites that offered a chance to become *incontournable* in a supply chain clean only on paper.

Fuliiro fault lines: Custom and business

Stretched along the Congo–Burundi borderland in South Kivu, Uvira territory regroups three customary entities, including the Bafuliiro chieftaincy headquartered in Lemera on the hills that dip down towards the Ruzizi Plain. The area is home to conflicts over 'ethnic territory', cattle and other scarce resources between and within communities.[125] This case study shows how customary conflict has become enmeshed with armed mobilisation and mineral governance. Shortly after the death of *mwami* (chief) Ndare Simba in 2012, the validation of the Kigunga and Mugerero mines introduced Lemera to iTSCi's 'conflict-free' supply chain. Meanwhile, a stand-off over Ndare's succession evolved between his son and his half-brother. The *mwami's* prerogative to tax in an impoverished chieftaincy was a fertile basis to antagonise the two camps. This split scaled up to provincial and national politics, with the son initially garnering government support through a decree declaring him *mwami* by the then governor.[126] The half-brother, meanwhile, relied upon support from opposition stalwarts. The confusion was compounded by the half-brother's possession of customary insignia (the *lushembe*), which many took as explanation for a temporary, 'magical' disappearance of cassiterite. A local militia partly composed of family members of the *mwami's* son (called *biloko*, Lingala for 'things') joined the contestation, leading to a militarisation of customary and economic competition: 'Molière, the previous commander-in-chief, was firmly in

Figure 5.5: Fuliiro fault lines

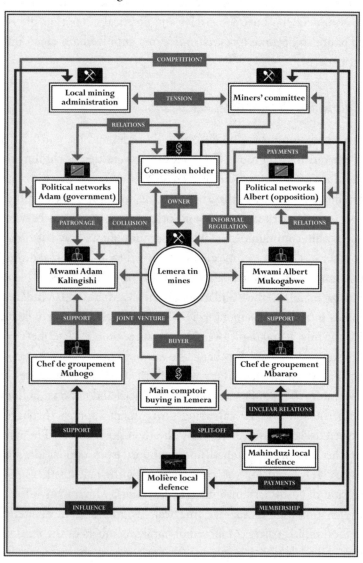

the mwami Adam camp, obeying his orders became a political act. Consequently, local defence commanders preferring to stay neutral or harbouring sympathies for Albert tried to distance themselves from Molière's command'.[127]

The arrival of iTSCi transformed Lemera's economy. Magical or not, the reconfiguration of local mineral markets resulted—based on an erstwhile deal with the late chief—in monopoly access for a joint venture by the concession owner and a Bukavu-based trading magnate. Yet, as local traders remarked, 'the joint venture was firmly in the hands of the *chefferie*'.[128] Members of the *biloko* militia close to the late chief's son were able to occupy positions in the local mining committee and were paid monthly allowances by the joint venture, which had signed a memorandum with the customary leadership as a shareholder.[129] The local mining administrator protested and called for a suspension of the committee. Subsequently, *biloko* looted his office, chased him away and replaced him with a militia member on the joint venture's payroll. Not much later, armed *biloko* introduced themselves as a customary security outfit to an iTSCi audit team. The customary militia business network, iTSCi's operating costs and falling global tin prices aggravated the monopoly situation and led to economic crisis, with local cassiterite prices shrinking by two-thirds, and Lemera's market by the same factor. In light of dwindling opportunities, the patronage networks linking customary power, local militia and business elites emerged as a powerful yet explosive tool: pits were allocated—by the miners' committee—to *biloko* who supported the *mwami*, thereby making the network *incontournable*. Garnering support from Congo's presidential majority and provincial business elites, and co-opting a local militia heavily intertwined with the local mining community, their network was reinforced by the authority to tax as well as the financial clout of the involved entrepreneurial interests.

Conflict cooperatives: Networked political power

Ngweshe in Walungu territory, South Kivu, is one of the main chieftaincies of the Shi. Because their 'ethnic territory' encloses the provincial capital Bukavu, other communities voice grievance about Shi dominance in provincial politics. One distinct trait of the Shi is a centralised political organisation with powerful chiefs (as opposed to segmentary communities such as the Rega or Tembo). In Shi custom, *kalinzi* regulates land use, whereby usufruct rights are leased to a user against a tribute.[130] Based on a contract, these rights are inheritable via kinship and alienable pending *mwami* consent.[131] However, under *kalinzi*, the king can also take back and offer another plot in exchange—unless a state title triggers ambiguity, as several key land laws (including the 1966 Bakajika Law and the 1973 Land Law), mining legislation and customary law can contradict each other. Unlike land and customary laws, the 2002 mining code differentiates between soil and subsoil, an ambiguity that nurtures patronage, as the case of Chaminyago shows.

Located in Nzibira, the Chaminyago tin mine was validated 'conflict-free' and joined iTSCi in 2014. Two cooperatives competed over access to the mine: the Mining Cooperative of Artisanal Exploiters (Cooperative minière des exploitants artisanaux [COMIDEA]), founded in 2010 by local *négociants* and registered in 2012; and the Mining and Agricultural Cooperative of Ngweshe (Cooperative minière et agricole de Ngweshe [COMIANGWE]), founded and registered in 2014 by the then provincial mining minister (formerly the royal secretary of Ngweshe chieftaincy, before being appointed by the then governor, also a Shi). According to a local pundit, staff 'nominations [were] a family affair. Even at the lowest levels, people [sought] for umbrellas by *incontournables*.'[132]

Both cooperatives are recognised by ministerial decrees but, as of 2015, only COMIDEA had provided documentation to the

Figure 5.6: Conflict cooperatives

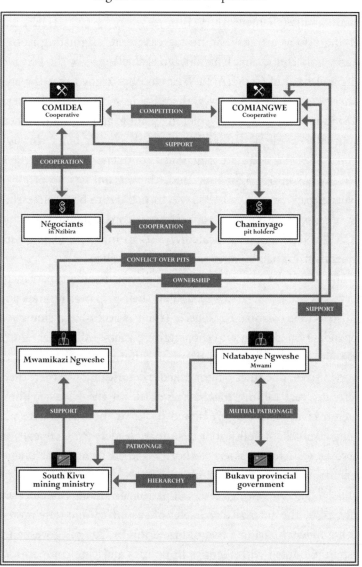

cadastre. Legal on paper, COMIANGWE exhibits what Olivier de Sardan called a 'double game practiced by the political elite, in mastering both the law (official norms) and their obligation-based relationships (clientelism)'.[133] Run for years by COMIDEA and serving also as a transit site to tag cassiterite originating from a nearby gold concession, Chaminyago is challenged by the *mwami's* wife and head of COMIANGWE, who has argued that the area is her personal land. However, there is a lease agreement between the *mwami* and a local sub-chief in Chaminyago.[134] Many miners eventually acquired land from the sub-chief's heirs through *kalinzi* or *bugule* and state-sanctioned contracts. Besides his theoretically absolutist right over land, the *mwami* has no proof of ownership. While COMIANGWE turned out to be unsuccessful, the *mwami* continues to collect taxes from Chaminyago, and COMIANGWE have repeatedly tried to infiltrate iTSCi with minerals from neighbouring, non-validated sites.[135]

The Ngweshe case shows how politico-customary patronage networks use cooperatives to tighten their grip over revenue and redistributive patronage resources (such as access) as a club good dependent on allegiance to cooperative owners. Influential figures in politics and custom contribute to a burgeoning landscape of cooperatives: one interlocutor asked, rhetorically, whether 'there were any real mining *cooperatives* at all' in the Kivus, while a veteran civil society figure stated he knew 'no cooperative not being a vehicle of political or customary leaders'.[136] Cooperatives serve as vehicles to assert authority and to tighten patronage, benefitting from close relations with high-level provincial politicians.[137] The intertwined levers of patronage among Shi elites are boosted by the entangled character of customary and state power, with a *mwami* having a twofold function in Congo's governance system. Coupled with identity in politics and elite competition, this forms a powerful basis for patronage networks with multiple gravitation centres.[138]

Another lease on life: The incontournables

With an economy always embedded in its social and political context, and bearing in mind Ekeh's 'tale of two publics', the persistence of networks and *incontournables* comes as no surprise in eastern Congo or other places characterised by contestation.[139] However, within a broader (post-)conflict—as misleading as the label may be—deadlock, the fragmentation of authority also serves as a self-fulfilling prophecy in maintaining the networks of mineral trade that shape eastern Congo's crisis economy. In the absence of predictable law enforcement, patronage provides a 'space of complex interpersonal relations creating confidence through a process of learning by doing'.[140] Ethical sourcing allowed for these networks (as 'permanent fixtures' rather than short-term foreign interveners) to reinvent themselves while paying lip service to the struggle against 'conflict minerals'.[141] In this conjuncture, they have adapted to changing realities of governance at large, and 'conflict-free' mining in particular. While this is often analysed from Manichean perspectives (reporting on eastern Congo more often than not focuses on either hope or despair), a deeper look reveals contradictions. For instance, none of the savvy *incontournable* actors openly rejects reform when partaking in international meetings. However, parallel operations are legion and subvert reform.

The three cases above illustrate how *incontournables* use their networks to assert authority. In all cases, 'conflict-free' sourcing provides new legitimation, even if this is only achieved by outside recognition. While all cases emphasise the socio-spatial dynamics rendering individual or collective actors *incontournable* in a given context, they show—like Callon's 'obligatory passage points'— that this is always tenuous and context-dependent. Nonetheless, given the capacity to operate across multiple scales and networks, *incontournables* can hardly be sidelined altogether. The ambiguity of the cases and their protagonists also speaks to analysing eastern Congo (including its mineral markets) as a crisis economy framed by uncertainty—as conceptualised above in this chapter—rather than a stereotypical war economy in which top-down violence and extortion are the sole patterns.

As political order and economic power are neatly intertwined in eastern Congo's mineral markets, such dynamics at best result in the harmonisation of 'external' reform and 'local' practice. In less favourable scenarios, they result in a Potemkin village of transparency where those who participated in past violent accumulation now operate refurbished, whitewashed 'complexes of power, profit and protection'.[142] While the struggle against 'conflict minerals' and the corporate approach to 'ethical sourcing' portrays Congo's mineral sector as notoriously criminal and in need of Western governance, these studies demonstrate how fraudulent and violent trade is paradoxically encouraged by 'conflict-free' initiatives such as iTSCi. The works of civil society activists and researchers like Josaphat Musamba, Claude Iguma, Safanto Bulongo, Marline Babwine, Philippe Ruvunangiza and other Congolese authors mirror this worrying trend. Their analyses paradoxically demonstrate how the violent and unruly practices ascribed to Congolese have become a defining feature of Western efforts to regulate the trade in 3T minerals.[143]

In sum, the *incontournable* patrons—and, to a lesser degree, the mineral brokers—are 'capable of generating and enforcing their own norms, in semiautonomous relation to other social fields'.[144] This not only stresses the limited ability—both in terms of political will and actual capacity—of policies and institutional frameworks to evenly impose regulation (in the words of one minerals trader, 'there is "the system," and another system, and some people are *incontournable* in both');[145] it also opens further debate as to the fluid character of state-sponsored disciplinary and sovereign power, not least because 'social relations, rather than institutional arrangements or generalised morality, are mainly responsible for the production of trust in economic life'.[146] This is particularly true in the contexts of a crisis economy, where mechanisms of trust and predictability are eroded. In that sense, the *incontournables'* clout within and between networks makes them, to paraphrase Mario Puzo's *Godfather*, those whose offers others cannot refuse.[147]

6

CONFLICTED CERTIFICATION

The previous chapters addressed the social and economic impact of 'conflict-free' sourcing. Another yardstick is how it intersects with the evolution of violence in eastern Congo.[1] Looking at how mineral traceability coexists with armed conflict and insecurity, as well as with continuing smuggling and fraud, this chapter illustrates how conflict parties and 'conflict-free' sourcing providers mimic and permeate each other in their parallel quest for authority. Wrangling over access and taxation, the result of this uneasy cohabitation is a deepening fragmentation of political order.[2] This reflects John Allen's work, suggesting that

> In place of the conventional assumption that the central state is the only actor of any real import, the institutional playing field is now shared with non-governmental organizations, multinational enterprises and others .... At any one point in time, the relative significance of each scale may change, in that the power can be scaled up or down through the different units of spatial authority, both transnational and sub-national.[3]

As opposed to orthodox thought around the resource conflicts nexus, the following pages not only show that mining does not necessarily correlate much with conflict, but also that 'conflict-free' sourcing has not notably reduced human rights violations or armed group activity.[4] After a brief recap of key points, this chapter dives into two case studies that analyse how mineral reform has affected dynamics of conflict and authority in the Kivus. While the first concerns iTSCi's role in the competition for authority, the second looks at the Raia Mutomboki ('citizens in anger'), a decentralised militia that governs a number of mines in South Kivu. If underlying conditions differ—an industry–NGO joint venture compared to an armed group—this comparison unearths a set of structural similarities between transnational regulation and rebel governance: 'The privatization of authority, the shift from government to governance and the proliferation of regulatory bodies are among those changes that made it ... difficult to pin down the institutional geography of power'.[5]

For decades, artisanal mining has served as an arena for the contestation of authority between state agencies, customary power, businesspeople, armed groups and other non-state actors in eastern Congo. Formal state institutions in the (post)colonial Congolese state never developed textbook Weberian governance capacity in terms of a legitimate monopoly of violence.[6] However, the conflict minerals paradigm and the subsequent advent of traceability to satisfy due diligence and ethical sourcing demands add another layer in a nested game of authority. The interplay of domestic struggles and transnational encroachment has contributed to a growing democratisation of claims to authority. State institutions and their transnational (iTSCi) and domestic (Raia Mutomboki) challengers command similar repertoires of taxation, often considered a prerogative of 'modern states' as well as their emerging or intermittent variants.[7] Moreover, these diverse actors show striking parallels in their broader everyday governance.[8] It is in this context that 'conflict-free' sourcing found itself 'conflicted' by colluding with fraud and ignoring human rights violations; moreover, it also came to resemble the very actors it set out to eliminate, and contributed to weakening the state institutions to which it claims to be allied. If the postcolonial Congolese state architecture was already easy prey for military-commercial networks and predation from within, it is now confronted with yet another threat to its sovereignty in the shape of iTSCi. In that sense, ethical sourcing risks being no more than a chimera of legitimacy to producing countries and consumers interested in ethics.

Conflict without certification

The political economy of the Great Lakes region links violence and wars with abundant reservoirs of 3T, gold and other minerals, most of which favour artisanal exploitation.[9] Since the early 1990s, cycles of conflict have dominated politics and social reality. From 1993 onwards, tension over land and identity erupted into political violence in North Kivu, only to merge into a regional war a year later when the influx of Rwandan refugees and *génocidaires* set the countdown for Zaire. In 1996, Kabila's AFDL and its Rwandan and Ugandan backers went on to conquer the country bit by bit, forcing Mobutu into exile a year later. In 1998, Kabila kicked out his foreign partners, leading to the Second Congo War, which pitted dozens of rebel groups and neighbouring armies against each other until a 2003 peace deal.[10] This period featured the coltan peak, triggering unprecedented scrutiny of minerals, when several factors helped make minerals a key source of revenue for military entrepreneurs. While wartime insecurity favoured violent accumulation and prevented investment, displacement pushed significant labour from farming to mining.[11] In addition, international speculation triggered windows of opportunity. Finally, an ailing state allowed commercial-military ventures to operate parallel customs. However, not all

Figure 6.1: Geographical distribution of mines and armed groups[12]

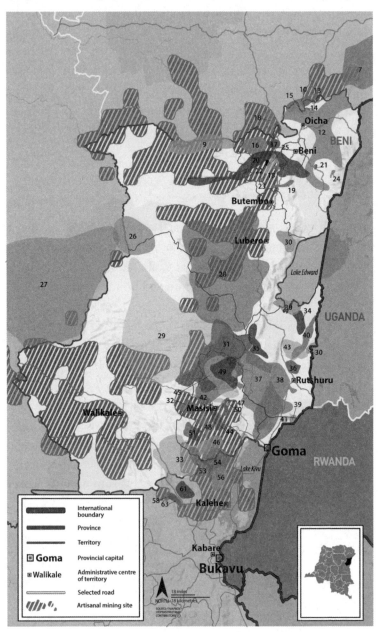

CONFLICTED CERTIFICATION

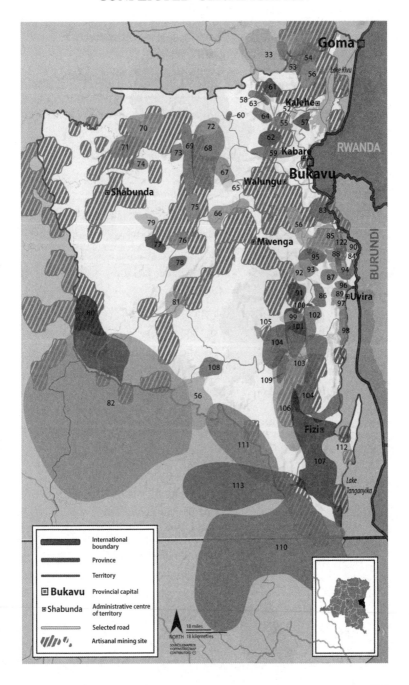

7	FRPI	(Front de résistance patriotique de l'Ituri)
9	Mai-Mai Simba Mangalibi	(Mai-Mai group under Mangalibi, ex-Manu/ex-Morgan)
10	MNLDK-Kyandenga	(Mouvement national pour la libération durable du Kongo)
11	Mai-Mai Barcelone	(Mai-Mai group under Baraka Lolwako)
12	ADF	(Allied Democratic Forces)
13	FLEC/NG	(Front de libération à l'Est du Congo/ Nouvelle génération)
14	Mai-Mai Ngolenge	(Mai-Mai group allied to UPLC, formerly under Jackson Muhukambuto)
15	Mai-Mai Uhuru OAPB	(Organisation d'autodéfense pour la paix à Beni)
16	Mai-Mai Shingo Pamba	(Mai-Mai group under Matabishi, MNLDK split-off)
17	Mai-Mai Mandefu	(Mai-Mai group with roots in the earlier Front de résistance populaire de Lubwe-Ruwenzori, led by Mandefu)
18	Mazembe-APASIKO	(Alliance des patriotes pour le salut intégral du Kongo)
19	Mai-Mai Léopards	(Mai-Mai group emerging from Léopards-Muthundo and Nzirunga groups)
20	UPLC	(Union des patriotes pour la libération du Congo)
21	APRC	(Armée du peuple pour la reconstruction du Congo)
22	Mai-Mai Ninja	(Splinter faction of the UPLC)
23	FAP	(Force d'autodéfense populaire)

24	APR	(Armée patriotique de Ruwenzori)
25	RNL	(Résistance nationale Lumumbiste, aka 'Mille tours par seconde')
26	Mai-Mai Simba UPLD	(Union des patriotes pour la libération et le développement)
27	Mai-Mai Simba Forces Divines	(Mai-Mai group led by Mando Mazeri, with roots in the 1960s)
28	FPP/AP	(Front populaire pour la paix/Armée du peuple, ex-Mazembe)
29	NDC-Rénové/ Guidon	(Nduma Defence of Congo-Rénové/ Guidon)
30	Mai-Mai FMP	(Front des mouvements populaires, led by Jackson Muhukambuto)
31	NDC-Rénové/Bwira	(Nduma Defence of Congo-Rénové/ Bwira)
32	Guides-MAC	(Mouvement d'action pour le changement)
33	Mai-Mai Kifuafua	(Mai-Mai group under Delphin Mbaenda)
34	AFRC	(Alliance des forces de résistance congolaise, ex-Mai-Mai Charles)
35	Nyatura FPDH	(Force de défense du peuple hutu)
36	Amka Jeshi	(Urban militia in Kiwanja led by Kasereka Celestin)
37	Nyatura CMC	(Collectif des mouvements pour le changement, ex-Nyatura Domi)
38	FDLR	(Forces démocratiques de libération du Rwanda)
39	Former M23	(Former Mouvement du 23 mars)
40	RUD-*Urunana*	(Rassemblement unité et démocratie)
41	Nyatura Turarambiwe	(Umbrella term for several small Nyatura factions)

42	APCLS	(Alliance des patriotes pour un Congo libre et souverain)
43	Nyatura FPPH	(Forces pour la protection du peuple hutu)
44	Nyatura GAV	(Groupe armé les volontaires)
45	Nyatura APRDC/ Abazungu	(Alliance des patriotes pour la restauration de la démocratie au Congo)
46	Mai-Mai Kifuafua Maachano	(Kifuafua faction under Maachano)
47	Nyatura Bagaruza	(Nyatura group with unknown leadership)
48	Nyatura Delta FDDH	(Forces de défense des droits humains, led by Delta Gashamare)
49	Nyatura Jean-Marie	(Nyatura group under Jean-Marie)
50	Nyatura Musheku	(Nyatura group under Musheku)
51	UPDC-Kapasi	(Union des patriotes pour la défense du Congo)
52	Raia Mutomboki Soleil	(Raia Mutomboki group under Soleil)
53	Mai-Mai Kirikicho	(Mai-Mai group under Kirikicho)
54	Nyatura-Kalume	(Nyatura group under Kalume)
55	Raia Mutomboki Shabani	(Raia Mutomboki group under Shabani)
56	CNRD	(Conseil national pour le renouveau et la démocratie)
57	Groupe JKK/ CCCRD	(Coalition congolaise pour le changement radical et la démocratie)
58	Raia Mutomboki Mungoro	(Raia Mutomboki group under Mungoro)
59	Raia Mutomboki Blaise	(Raia Mutomboki group under Blaise)

60	Raia Mutomboki Bralima	(Raia Mutomboki group under 'Bralima')
61	Raia Mutomboki Butachibera	(Raia Mutomboki group under Butachibera)
62	Raia Mutomboki Bipompa	(Raia Mutomboki group under Bipompa)
63	Raia Mutomboki Hamakombo	(Raia Mutomboki group under Bwaale Hamakombo)
64	Raia Mutomboki Lance	(Raia Mutomboki group under Lance Muteya)
65	Raia Mutomboki Lukoba	(Raia Mutomboki group under Lukoba)
66	Raia Mutomboki Ndarumanga	(Raia Mutomboki group under Ndarumanga)
67	Raia Mutomboki Mabala	(Raia Mutomboki group under Mabala Mese)
68	Raia Mutomboki FPP	(Forces populaires pour la paix, under Donat Kengwa/Ngandu Lundimu)
69	Raia Mutomboki Walike	(Raia Mutomboki group under Walike)
70	Raia Mutomboki Kazimoto	(Raia Mutomboki group under Kazimoto, ex-Kikuni)
71	Raia Mutomboki Kabazimia	(Raia Mutomboki group under Kabazimia)
72	Raia Mutomboki Musolwa	(Raia Mutomboki group under Musolwa)
73	Raia Mutomboki Charles Quint	(Raia Mutomboki group under Charles Quint)
74	Raia Mutomboki Kabé	(Raia Mutomboki group under Kabé)
75	Raia Mutomboki 100kg	(Raia Mutomboki group under '100kg')

76	Raia Mutomboki Kimba	(Raia Mutomboki group under Kimba)
77	Raia Mutomboki Kampanga	(Raia Mutomboki group under Kampanga)
78	Raia Mutomboki Bozi	(Raia Mutomboki group under Bozi)
79	Raia Mutomboki LeFort	(Raia Mutomboki group under LeFort)
80	Raia Mutomboki Musumbu	(Raia Mutomboki group under Jean Musumbu)
81	Mai-Mai Makindu	(Mai-Mai group under Makindu)
82	Mai-Mai Malaika	(Mai-Mai group under She Assani)
83	Mai-Mai Rasta	(Mai-Mai group under Rasta)
84	FNL-Nzabampema	(Nzabampema wing of the Front national de libération)
85	Mai-Mai Buhirwa	(Mai-Mai group under Buhirwa, split-off from Mwenyemali)
86	Mai-Mai Ilunga	(Mai-Mai group under Ilunga, split-off from Mushombe)
87	Mai-Mai Kashumba	(Former Local Defence, led by Kashumba)
88	Mai-Mai Kijangala	(Mai-Mai group under Kijangala)
89	Mai-Mai Makanaki	(Mai-Mai group under Makanaki)
90	Mai-Mai Mbulu	(Mai-Mai group under Mbulu)
91	Mai-Mai Issa Mutoka	(Mai-Mai group under Issa Mutoka)
92	Mai-Mai Ruma	(Mai-Mai group under Ruma, formerly N'yikiribha)
93	Mai-Mai Mushombe	(Mai-Mai group under Mushombe)
94	Mai-Mai Nyerere	(Mai-Mai group under Nyerere)

95	RED-*Tabara*	(Résistance pour un état de droit–*Tabara*)
96	Mai-Mai Rushaba	(Mai-Mai group under Rushaba)
97	Mai-Mai Réné	(Mai-Mai group under Réné)
98	Mai-Mai Réunion FPLC	(Forces pour la libération du Congo)
99	Mai-Mai Ngalyabatu	(Mai-Mai group under Ngalyabatu)
100	Mai-Mai Mupekenya	(Mai-Mai group under Mupekenya)
101	Twirwaneho	(Banyamulenge self-defence groups)
102	AFP–Gutabara	(Alliances de fédéralistes patriotes, aka Android and Abakenya)
103	Gumino	(Banyamulenge group)
104	Mai-Mai Mutetezi FPDC	(Forces populaires pour la défense du Congo, led by Ebu Ela, ex-CNPSC)
105	Mai-Mai Bishake	(Mai-Mai group under Bishake)
106	Biloze Bishambuke	(Umbrella term for militia in Fizi)
107	Mai-Mai Yakotumba	(Mai-Mai group under Yakotumba)
108	Mai-Mai Aochi	(Mai-Mai group under Aochi, ex-CNPSC)
109	Mai-Mai Shoshi	(Mai-Mai group under Shoshi, ex-CNPSC)
110	Mai-Mai Apa na Pale	(Mai-Mai group under Mundusi)
111	Mai-Mai Mulumba	(Mai-Mai group under Mulumba, ex-CNPSC)
112	Mai-Mai Alida	(Mai-Mai group under Alida, ex-CNPSC)
113	Mai-Mai Brown	(Mai-Mai group under Brown)

Note: For operational reasons, our 2020 mapping included other provinces beyond the Kivus; as a result, some numbers are missing here.

mining was absorbed into violent markets: during and after the Second Congo War, hundreds of artisanal mines in the Kivus remained outside the grasp of armed groups. Twenty years later, studies still find no robust correlation, with reports lacking coherent and complete baselines:[13] 'In 2009/10 the percentage of 3T workers engaged at mines affected by interference from non-state armed groups and public security forces was 57%, compared with 26% of workers at sites visited in 2013/14'.[14]

These figures, however, probably exclude the bulk of remote, inaccessible mines.[15] As discussed previously, Western 'conflict minerals' advocacy began dominating international conflict analyses of eastern Congo. What these analyses ignored is that it is not just minerals that contribute to war, but any resource. In Congo as elsewhere, the prevalence of minerals and their impli-cation in violent networks are the symptoms rather than the causes of more profound political and social rupture.[16] This did not prevent campaigners insisting that networks of mineral trade were the key drivers of violence. But while it is true that conflict parties commercialised minerals, only some, like the RCD-Goma, had success.[17]

As Figure 6.1 above indicates, a majority of known mining sites are (and have been over time) outside of armed group influ-ence. Most of these sites had marginal profits: conflict parties did not initially wage war over minerals, and mining them was for subsistence rather than profit.[18] If the 2003 transition brought a formal end to the war, the Kivus remain a 'Matryoshka doll' of conflicts.[19] Meanwhile, a set of transnational policy interventions kicked in, aimed at cleaning up what they defined as a 'war economy'. Laws, guidelines and initiatives—most notably iTSCi—set foot in a fragmented landscape of authority, where conflict over land, identity and political power is legion, inter-secting with weak state capacity and a colonial hangover.[20] Against this backdrop, it is vital to look closely at how mineral reform interacts with these dynamics and compare how trans-national traceability and formalisation differ or align with the broader logics of contested public authority.[21]

Contested statehood in eastern Congo

Studying the 'state', its character, reach and limits, is an unending challenge in social theory, regardless of whether we are focusing on a particular region or theme.[22] This book neither replicates existing scholarship nor suggests a new theory of the state. It merely acknowledges two main observations: those of the state as an idea and as a system. As an idea, the state links violence to legitimacy through imagery and performative techniques.[23] As a system, a state is made of different socio-spatial and functional networks that are bound by territorial confines.[24] Theorists of 'stateness' by and large agree that the symbolic emanation of a state contributes as much to its claim to authority as its material structure.[25] However, as the example of eastern Congo's mineral markets illustrates, states face 'pressures from both "above" and "below," which have resulted in the displacement of their authority'.[26] This happens not only when non-state actors employ state imagery and performances, but also when they become part of the networks a state claims exclusivity for, such as taxation or the imposition of rules. Following this, both state and non-state actors claim authority, which as Lund wrote, is 'always in the making',[27] and, one may want to add, in the unmaking too. Hence, 'state authority is not so much "up there" or indeed "over there", as part of a spatial arrangement within which different elements of government, as well as private agencies exercise *powers of reach*'.[28]

Authority is a fuzzy matter in the Kivu provinces and largely affects the ways in which market participants negotiate taxation and access to resources. Home to the better part of conflicts in the region, they are the landing site of transnational mineral reform. Amidst protracted insecurity, different factors underpin the growing fragmentation of authority. Civil servants often juggle multiple allegiances, partly towards non-state (armed) actors but also towards parallel hierarchies. Foreign intervention dilutes the authority of state institutions. Putting state authority into question is a broader legacy of legal pluralism and so-called 'informality', shrinking livelihoods and the erosion of trust.[29] It is under these circumstances that the struggle against 'conflict minerals' has forged a situation whereby domestic and transnational non-state actors alike intervene with new policies in an arena already saturated with competing claims to authority.[30]

As Lund notes, 'there is no shortage of institutions attempting to exercise public authority' in African political economies; as a result, such authority often becomes 'the amalgamated result of the exercise of power by a variety of local institutions and the imposition of *external institutions*, conjugated with the idea of a state'.[31] In formalising a supposedly unregulated ASM sector, external interveners indeed pushed a re-conjugation of mineral governance and provoked friction between new and old rules. Throughout the past decade, eastern Congo saw both the onset of iTSCi, the first mineral traceability programme, and a notable increase of armed group activity and numbers. Starting with a short discussion of the concept of access in relation to authority, the remainder of this chapter juxtaposes these developments and analyses how different contenders for authority compete over governing access to minerals.

Regulating access to mineral markets

In contrast to property, which represents a codified, legal right to something, access is the '*ability* to derive benefits from things'.[32] From an empirical perspective, access is more relevant than property writ small when it comes to eastern Congo's artisanal mines because transnational reform has not enacted notable change with regards to property, even though that certainly is an arena for 'struggles for the recognition of a wide variety of rights'.[33] This is due to a difference between land ownership and mining concessions, which in Congolese law oscillate somewhere between a temporal property right and an exclusive access right.[34] As this chapter demonstrates, neither armed groups nor iTSCi compete over legal, recognised property, but focus instead on access. Others, in particular *creuseurs* and *négociants*, also strive for access to minerals, rather than lending themselves to the illusion of property. Hence, in asking '*why* some people or institutions benefit from resources, *whether or not* they have rights to them', access is a useful prism to understand authority in settings of contested politics, economic competition and legal pluralism.[35] To study how conflict dynamics and the implementation of transnational regulation have reshaped access to mineral wealth, it can be helpful to ask how simultaneous, intertwined, 'translocal' claims to authority have come to threaten the overall regulation capacity of state institutions in the context of mineral reform.[36]

Driven by iTSCi, transnational regulation has altered the Kivus' economic landscape by dividing their mines into 'clean' and 'conflicted' ones. However, the establishment of authority over 'conflict minerals' is not limited to the former; it also radiates beyond 'clean areas' where 'everyone intervenes [in mining], armed actors, customary power'.[37] In both cases, this is based on conceptions of legitimacy. As in other 'emerging political complexes' that have enabled 'political projects ... [that] now go beyond conventional forms of territorial, bureaucratic or juridical authority',[38] such legitimacy is fluid and depends on how claims to authority translate into actual political order. Here, the onset of iTSCi has triggered dramatic change: to comply with due diligence, a mine needs validation through joint stakeholder visits that verify the absence of armed actors and human rights abuses before it can be decreed 'conflict-free' (see above). Hence, unless validated, any mine is 'red-flagged' and denied legal access to markets, regardless of whether there are armed actors or not.[39] This is a twofold denial of access for thousands: while miners are geographically excluded from markets inside iTSCi's supply chain, they also lack legal access outside iTSCi areas of access since validation is the only game in town.[40] Despite being just one way to perform OECD due diligence, iTSCi became a requirement as it was the only operational traceability system in the early years. This is all the more surprising given its many flaws:

> Even in those mines where certification is being carried out, the [iTSCi] scheme will not record influence of soldiers either at the mine or along the trade route. Congolese organisations have also expressed concern that fraudulent traders could bribe or coerce their way into having their minerals certified as 'conflict-free.'[41]

A central institutional innovation of transnational mineral reform was the creation of a triad assembling the private-sector iTSCi, the international NGO Pact and the governmental ASM regulator SAEMAPE. As an entangled 'twilight institution' that combines 'external' policy with 'local' practice, this conglomerate came to be a de facto governing body for legal 3T trade. Although distinct on paper, it is not always easy to discern the three parties on the ground: iTSCi and Pact, for example, share staff and both their logos appear on employees' uniforms. Moreover, their presence is intermittent: in some areas, only one person covers half a dozen mines, and SAEMAPE staff ultimately do the job of tagging mineral bags, controlling weight, fil(l)ing iTSCi logbooks or giving transport clearance. These employees, however, are often unpaid, which compels some SAEMAPE staff to abet fraud.[42] State officials must navigate the friction of enforcing traceability while simultaneously undermining the system's credibility and facing pressure from trade networks to circumvent the circuit. In that sense, the Congolese mining administration is an illustration of how a state can drive formalisation as a governance technique while avoiding its own formalisation, where both individual wrongdoing and the non-payment of staff help erode its authority in the long run. Left with little material capacity to ensure a smooth functioning, SAEMAPE's catch-22 is to be both a state-sanctioned and externally legitimised custodian of traceability. Parafiscal practice (illicit but widely normalised taxation) is but one outcome of this institutional bricolage. SAEMAPE's position—namely being partner to both traceability systems and (less visibly) others navigating around them—is a neat 'blend of formal and informal, traditional and modern'.[43] It is illustrative of Sally Falk Moore's observation that 'innovative legislation or other attempts to direct change often fail to achieve their intended purposes ... because new laws are thrust upon going social arrangements [and] complexes of binding obligations already in existence'.[44]

With legal innovation lacking independent scrutiny, state agents and their associates interpret and perform claims to authority over 'conflict-free' minerals, thereby '"re-embedding" a new form of private authority'.[45] This leads to an uneven, contextualised pattern of traceability deployment, which depends on myriad factors beyond iTSCi writ small. As a result, SAEMAPE's interaction with commercial stakeholders can ultimately contradict the very idea of traceability, as the following field notes demonstrate:

> We sit in an ironmonger's backyard, talking local economy. All of a sudden, people arrive with untagged bags. One of them drops and bursts, exposing the contained coltan. As the ironmonger interrupts our discussion, a SAEMAPE agent enters the scene and calls him. The porters, the ironmonger and the agent discuss. The latter asks them to refill the minerals into new bags, which he tags. Later, it turns out that the SAEMAPE agent that facilitated the operation was previously

a trader. While his embedment into the institutional threesome provided necessary connections to cover up the deal, his socio-economic
embedment provoked closer allegiance than his formal job.[46]

The question here is not whether these specific coltan bags are
'conflicted' or not. Rather, this case shows that while they should
not access markets according to due diligence guidelines, the
involved persons worked through their ex-colleague turned
SAEMAPE official to broker access to the 'closed pipeline'. This
illustrates how the authority vested on paper in SAEMAPE
transforms into a club good shared by a network of friends. Here
and in similar cases, the way in which stakeholders react to
iTSCi shows the degree to which ethical sourcing is often 'based
on principles which bypass or contradict those inherent to local
decision-making and co-operation'.[47] Although iTSCi foregrounds a technical stance, the system actually engages a highly
political environment and coexists with the very networks it aims
to regulate. The hybrid institutional identity of iTSCi staff further exemplifies this ambiguity: employed by Pact, they present
themselves as non-profit while running a for-profit, private-
sector project. Sporting the image of a 'local development project', iTSCi further conceals its corporate identity.[48] This echoes
rebel governance, which—in Congo and elsewhere—is marketed
by political and military leaders of armed groups as a service
reminiscent of a public provision of goods while their everyday
action often turns into particularistic for-profit enterprise. The
following case studies carve out in more detail how many striking parallels exist between 'conflict-free' sourcing and governance
by armed groups, such as the Raia Mutomboki.

Ethical profits? The case of iTSCi

This section zooms in on iTSCi. Even if its implementation
remains limited, iTSCi traceability was already running in 57

mines of the two Kivus as of 2015, and effectively reshaped access logics wherever it was present. Certain new illicit taxes that emerged in iTSCi mines were paradoxically justified by traceability. Due to the vulnerability of unpaid SAEMAPE staff and iTSCi's lack of interest in monitoring, the former morphed from 'an agency to assist [to] an intelligence and taxation service'.[49] One such tax is called *encouragement*, a fee paid per tag handed out. Another cost arises when *négociants* show up after business hours and officials levy a 'late-charging fee'. These taxes are irregular and sometimes spontaneous and differ from mine to mine.[50] While this could be dismissed as a result of unpaid salaries, the power to tax is also a marker of authority; an attempt to set new rules in the shadow of iTSCi regulation. Given that working within iTSCi mines and supply chains is the only legal way to be employed in the 3T sector, for the miners this represents a restriction of legal access to markets. As the previous chapter demonstrated, SAEMAPE and the mining ministry's technical division created even more new taxes with the onset of iTSCi, many of them fluid and temporary.

Given its cost, iTSCi's fiscal impact goes beyond indirect effects. *Comptoirs* and exporters pay membership fees, which they pass on to miners; this allows iTSCi-registered buyers to mark down prices, amplifying the vulnerability of miners (due to price fluctuations) and placing the system's cost on local producers. It lessens state taxes, which are often calculated in percentages of transaction prices excluding levies. Poaching into a state's taxation monopoly, iTSCi thus undermines public revenue.[51] Controlling a buyer-end monopoly for legally exported 3T, it excludes other supply chains, denying access to miners at remote sites.[52] With the lion's share of iTSCi's production being processed by two big Asian smelters and a few Congolese trading houses, monopsony is maintained with a rule obliging *négociants* to identify purchasers *a priori*, outlawing market-based exchanges.[53] In other words, iTSCi prompted an industry cartel that vertically integrates and adversely incorporates Congolese producers into a global value chain.[54]

The criminalisation of other supply chains has created a situation in which iTSCi not only controls the terms of trade, but the '[l]egalization and institutionalization of this new ownership dispossesses commoners'.[55] iTSCi, a senior clerk quipped in disarray, 'monopolises anything; it even takes the state hostage'.[56] This grab for authority is contrasted by radical disengagement elsewhere: conflictual issues, such as concessions and land ownership, are treated as a black box. Moreover, when it comes to conflict dynamics, a mixture of a *laissez-faire* attitude and a focus on turnover marks iTSCi's due diligence.[57] In one case in Uvira territory, iTSCi implicitly legitimised one party in a militarised customary conflict. By ignoring the presence of an armed group in the mines, iTSCi tolerated due diligence violations under the pretence that this militia was 'so much accepted by the population, that it is difficult to change'.[58] In so doing, iTSCi backed a joint venture involving a *comptoir*, the concession holder and one side of a customary succession conflict that was in cahoots with the involved entrepreneurs. The tensions not only made all sides resort to armed protection by FARDC and militia, it also reinforced smuggling and human rights violations.[59]

Another case features regular violent clashes involving the police, FARDC and miners in an area that used to be a hotbed of armed conflict in North Kivu. The arrival of traceability there was preceded by the self-demobilisation of certain factions of the Nyatura militia that represented a key ethnopolitical bloc in the area. Moreover, most of today's miners are former combatants. However, regular clashes and social protest have persisted, occasionally leading to killings. One incident occurred when iTSCi was already up and running, and is illustrative of the scheme's odd relation to due diligence: in a row over the construction of a road close to a mine, two people were killed and six wounded. Local miners had protested that the works represented a land grab on the side of the concession holder, whose legitimacy is contested. Local authorities, some of whom were involved in mining activities, were able to attenuate the situation but the underlying contestation lives on.

In sum, while iTSCi poaches state authority within the confines of traceability, it looks away when it comes to violations so long as they do not affect its business. This is reflected both in iTSCi's opaque incident handling and its disregarding of armed presence in certain lucrative mines. Echoing others, one SAEMAPE agent complained that in the sector, 'even the guards at [certain] pits are militiamen'.[60] Hence, by adjudicating over what ought to be regulated and what is not, iTSCi positions itself as a form of government imposing uneven rules.[61] In mines formerly under armed influence, former and current commanders often maintain some authority, mediated by customary or political leaders who 'can make the population throw stones at the police, if the police does not consult them'.[62] In deciding where it intervenes, and where it does not, iTSCi performs sovereign power and partakes in the fragmentation of authority with regards to access and taxation prerogatives, creating monopoly or giving *carte blanche* to illicit activities.[63] This even impairs cooperation between state agencies: in one case, South Kivu's 'mining ministry and its technical division were at war against each other' over a race between iTSCi and Better Sourcing Program (BSP), as the latter tried opening up pilot sites for its own traceability scheme.[64]

Legitimate extortion? The case of armed groups

While the 'ethical sourcing' frontier in the Kivu provinces is progressing, some mines remain under direct or indirect control of armed groups.[65] This may or may not result in the violent

Figure 6.2: Comparison of an 'unregulated' and an iTSCi supply chain

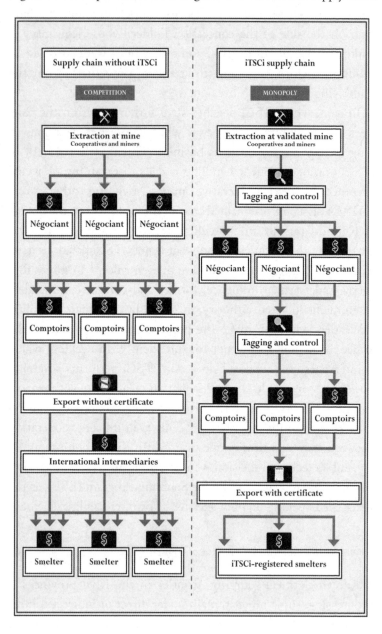

modes of exploitation that underpin the 'conflict minerals' paradigm. The reality is murkier. State institutions such as SAEMAPE, the mining ministry and police or intelligence services are sometimes present and 'even in red-flagged mines, SAEMAPE makes ends meet'.[66] Fragmented authority and governance experiments shape the interactions between combatants and civilians (as far as this distinction can be made), as well as between armed groups, customary authorities and state institutions.[67] To understand the armed groups' attempts at mining governance and their relations to state authorities, it is worth taking a look at the Raia Mutomboki, a slate of highly decentralised militia, elsewhere called an 'armed franchise'.[68] Rooted in popular insurgency against the Rwandan FDLR rebels, the Raia Mutomboki emerged around 2010 and gained control over large areas in Walikale, Shabunda and Kalehe territories.[69] Between 2012 and 2014, the numerous Raia Mutomboki factions reached the peak of their territorial influence. Contrary to the Orientalist narrative of bloodthirsty rebels holding miners at gunpoint, their combatants often worked the mines themselves.

What can their case teach us? Like other armed groups, the Raia Mutomboki impose taxes on civilians to generate revenue and instil a whiff of legitimacy. Taxation—a normalised, iterative activity compared to looting—is a key strategy in the repertoire of armed groups. In the quest for legitimacy, armed groups often reciprocate taxation with embryonic public services, such as providing security to the communities they claim to protect.[70] However, most services are not indiscriminate and have limited predictability and efficiency. In Raia Mutomboki-held mines, pits were often divided between combatants and civilians following negotiations involving customary authorities and mining officials. Taxation of minerals, meanwhile, was capped so as to not jeopardise the movement's popularity. Some factions also levy taxes for *négociants*: as one commander explained, like the

Congolese state, his group issues miners and traders with ID cards in areas under its control for the purpose of taxation.[71] Armed groups refer to their taxes with euphemisms like *effort de guerre* ('war effort') or *lala salama* ('sleep safely') to camouflage protection rackets and to perform authority and stateness. These practices are similar to those run by regular army units, who also refer to taxes with slogans.

The Raia Mutomboki market taxation as a functional, legitimate counterpart to their efforts in protecting the population against enemies such as the FDLR. Echoes of this were found at roadblocks, where males paid 500 Congolese francs (then 0.5 USD) against a stamped receipt exempting them from double taxation. The movement's commanders agreed for each faction to maintain a number of roadblocks. Attempts by some factions to increase taxes, or the number of checkpoints, were punished by other factions.[72] This ostensibly transparent, public and state-like performance—in a similar way to the issuing of receipts and miners' ID cards—embodies the Raia Mutomboki's claims to authority by employing a grammar of 'stateness' in its bid for legitimate domination. Other forms of state symbolism, such as the embryonic provision of justice, further underline this ambition. However, despite the semblance of an orderly administration, tensions are legion.[73] While SAEMAPE was allowed to collect taxes—that were subsequently divided between customary leaders and the militia's own war chest—Raia Mutomboki leaders kept a tight grip on the procedure: whenever state agents were believed to have withheld money or to have applied illicit fees, they were detained or chased away. From 2014, this changed. Subsequent army operations and internal strife fissured the Raia Mutomboki and weakened its clout. Some factions transformed into roving bandits living off looting and ambushes, while others retreated to secluded areas with insignificant small mines, where they maintain this 'state-mimicking' lifestyle beyond the reach of transnational regulation.

CONFLICTED CERTIFICATION

The case of the Raia Mutomboki shows parallels to iTSCi's approach in the push to emulate legitimacy by regulating social and economic life, in both constituencies and the outside world. However, the point here is not to equate the state-like behaviour of militias with heightened international scrutiny in the slipstream of 'conflict minerals' advocacy. Neither is the aim to legitimise armed groups.[74] Rather, the argument is to emphasise how the fragmentation of authority is driven by different non-state actors alike—transnational corporate actors as much as rebels. Like iTSCi, armed groups employ and cultivate state symbolism, pressuring state institutions from different sides and leaving them—to paraphrase a bygone and failed United Nations attempt to create so-called 'Islands of Stability'—with mere islands of authority. As with armed groups, iTSCi deploys authority in its materiality—stamps, tags and other artefacts. Both the Raia Mutomboki and iTSCi infringe their own rules by transgressing them with sovereign power whenever revenue maximisation takes precedence. Sanctions only apply for violations that run contrary to iTSCi's or the Raia Mutomboki's ambitions. These striking operational and ideological parallels between domestic and cross-border conflict parties and foreign interveners pursuing ostensibly humanitarian or development goals are not unusual in eastern Congo. Most recently, for instance, the heavy-handed Ebola operations of the World Health Organization between 2018 and 2020 earned that UN agency the unflattering nickname of 'Mai-Mai OMS' (the French acronym for the WHO) due to their sub-contracting of regular and irregular armed forces and the heavy militarisation of the overall response.[75]

7

PEACE, ETHICS AND CONGO

Good intentions and savvy marketing notwithstanding, the struggle against 'conflict minerals' has been tragically imbricated in eastern Congo's longer continuities of war, profit and white saviourism. Wrapped in ethical and humanitarian pitches, campaigners and policymakers relied on colonial and Orientalist frameworks, painting a picture of a dark war zone where Africans kill other Africans, requiring foreign goodwill to end the carnage and build peace. This allowed for international interveners not only to develop an apolitical and ahistorical approach to tackle a deeply political problem, but also to justify a neoliberal and profit-oriented fix for a problem situated in the remote outskirts of global supply chain capitalism. This echoes developments in other contexts and global policymaking more broadly, such as in the context of negotiations and initiatives to tackle the climate crisis. In a similar fashion, these too are often driven by a primacy of capital and markets, leading to paradoxical suggestions. Yet, as Teju Cole remarked, 'if we are going to interfere in the lives of others, a little due diligence is a minimum requirement'.[1] (Cole surely referred to due diligence in a broader and deeper sense than technical supply chain management procedures.) As much as it is questionable to ask Congolese miners to pay for Western thirst for 'conflict-free' minerals, market-based climate reforms that bank on offsetting the continuously enormous emissions in industrialised countries through fig-leaf projects in less wealthy countries, or Western moves to Africa in a bid to protect the biodiversity long since destroyed back home, show a remarkably resilient pattern of white saviourism and colonial, imperialist ideology.

This book has demonstrated that the story of 'conflict minerals' is not straightforward enough to rely on flat and simplistic fixes. It is a story of constant contradiction and ambiguity that can emerge in contexts where contestation is legion. As a pioneer case of regulatory intervention into the political economy of conflict zones, transnational 'clean sourcing' efforts gave priority to satisfying the conscience of Western consumers, rather than bettering Congolese livelihoods. Justifying a white saviour-style operation that enabled transnational capital to consolidate the control of supply chains, the conflict minerals campaign did not shy away from invoking mutually contradictory colonial tropes of a space that is empty of rule but full of savage politics and conflict. A cartel of major transnational industries in the shape of iTSCi then seized the opportunity of imposing a closed pipeline aimed at assuring consumer-oriented due diligence. In eastern Congo, the flipside of this lucrative PR stunt has been a monopolisation of resource access, permitting some Fortune 500 companies to secure extractable mineral reservoirs at the expense of expendable bodies. Given these global intersections, the case of 'conflict minerals' is a crucial case to rethink not only conflict and intervention, but also postcolonial orders, structural violence and power relations at large.

Ten years after the first pilot projects (and first steps for this book), the balance sheet is sobering. There are multiple reasons for that—and to give justice to professionals working hard on 'clean sourcing', it would be presumptuous to expect them alone to end violence. Nonetheless, this has been the central message of deceptive policy pitches for many years. The case of iTSCi reveals how efforts to ban human rights violations and illegal trade from mineral markets suffered from a primacy of profit, prioritising the adverse incorporation of allegedly chaotic supply chains to the boon of transnational corporate industries. As a consequence, iTSCi's record of preventing, detecting and sanctioning fraud has been imperfect at best.[2] Therefore, and despite the political impetus and scale of 'conflict minerals' interventions, iTSCi's impact on resolving conflict is below measurable. According to the UN and academic sources, the number of armed groups has multiplied over the past decade, as have incidents of violence and human rights violations—yet without systematic geographical overlaps, as Figures 4.1 and 6.1 illustrated.[3]

At the same time, 'conflict-free' sourcing helped mining kingpins and middlepersons to learn the art of recycling themselves so as to remain *incontournables* in eastern Congo's networks of mineral trade, politics and armed mobilisation. If many of these elites have long played a substantive role, transnational reform has failed to isolate them. Instead, they reinvented themselves, became absorbed into 'conflict-free' trade, and aligned their interests with transnational industries and other regional or domestic elites.

Meanwhile, the Congolese workforce faces increased hardship, securing few livelihood gains from 'conflict-free' supply chains, despite feel-good stories showcasing social projects and selling a post-conflict illusion to Western audiences on YouTube. The struggle against 'conflict minerals' is not only paternalistic, trading the erasure of subaltern epistemics against the white saviourism of knowing best what is good for others, it also has tangible impacts on the lives of Congolese: while local revenue has come under strain, armed groups have multiplied, some of which increasingly recruit former miners who lost access to mineral markets.

The case of 'conflict minerals' is an opportunity to rethink Western mindsets and policies in the face of transnational governance and postcolonial relations. Doing so requires revisiting tropes and clichés we cultivate, developing new critical analysis with political awareness and working towards decolonial, just and sound policies. This in turn requires renouncing the epistemic violence that has been inflicted—like elsewhere—on Congo and Congolese for centuries through the control of narratives, discourses and imageries but also the choice of scientific terminology that clouds our understanding.[4] This echoes Dunn's critique that it 'is not important which of these numerous labels best categorized the Zaïrian [sic] state. The main point is the realisation that the Zaïrian [sic] state was different from what Western theories expected and accepted.'[5] If Dunn's observations on the Zairo-Congolese past hold true for 'conflict minerals' as much as the broader Congolese conflict dynamics and its colonial present, this also 'requires taking the Congolese state seriously as it is, not as we would wish it to be'.[6] The closing sections of this book take turns in providing some tentative avenues on how to address this challenge intellectually and politically.

Debunking tropes

The debate on 'conflict minerals' features a series of repetitive and persistent tropes. If some of these relate to violent conflict and mining specifically, others peripherally touch on the subject but still contribute to the paradigm as such. Having discussed these clichés and stereotypes from an academic and conceptual perspective, this section offers hands-on, untheoretical summaries from ordinary people. Condensing some of the issues this book has tackled, their straightforwardness offers a different look behind the curtains of three main 'conflict minerals'-related assumptions, questioning their accuracy in reflecting how emotional and tautological truisms often cloud our collective understanding of more complicated stories.

One day in late 2012, I met with representatives of a local women's association in eastern Congo. While sexual violence and abuse of women are often wrongly cited as a direct consequence of 'conflict minerals', advocacy against gender-based violence seems to suffer from victimisation and denial of agency.[7] What the women told me was a sharp reminder of how the translation of actual ills such as sexual violence all the way from those suffering in one place to those engaging it globally can trigger epistemic erasure and unequal representation. While the women were fairly unimpressed with high-profile international campaigns featuring celebrities like Angelina Jolie or Ryan Gosling, they bitterly complained that their own voices and actions were hardly taken into account.[8] Early into the Congo wars and the concomitant history of 'conflict minerals', some had rallied for marches to Kigali and Kampala, faraway capitals of neighbouring Rwanda and Uganda respectively, whose interference was a key factor of the wars of the 1990s. The aim of the marches was to submit petitions against the abuse of Congolese women by foreign belligerents. At the end of the conversation, one woman asked me, rhetorically, why foreigners kept coming to Congo to take pictures while their own struggle, full of agency and power, received little to no recognition.

In early 2014, I first visited one of the tin mines operating under the new, supposedly clean iTSCi scheme. In our discussions, miners repeatedly told me they struggled to master the logics of price fluctuation in international trading places such as the LME. This was not because they were backward; it was simply because no one had wanted to share that knowledge—just as no one told students on American campuses about the more intricate, ambivalent character of conflict in eastern Congo. The corporate stakeholders of conflict-free sourcing (international trading and smelting companies and end users such as Apple or Boeing) bank on this information asymmetry—differentiated access to knowledge and the leverage of buyers in one single, legal supply chain—to impose artificially lower prices. One consequence is that Congolese mining communities lack both arguments and collective action capacity to represent their interests. One of the older miners, in the business for decades, gave an even more disturbing example: while his village had suffered from armed occupation and violence during the 1996–2003 Congo wars, the influx of initiatives to address 'conflict minerals' had led to local prices being lower than what rebel groups had imposed on them before. Physical, armed violence was replaced by structural violence that more strongly threatened the livelihoods of Congolese mining communities. In a 2015 survey in the different mines discussed above, colleagues and I then found that access to education and health had on average decreased between the current generation and the next.[9] A recent study confirmed this, highlighting how artisanal revenues remain largely insufficient to cover basic needs.[10]

In mid-2018, I spoke at length to a Congolese analyst who dedicated years of research to the debate around Virunga National Park. Created as a colonial institution in 1925, the park is today a flagship effort for nature conservation, with a particular emphasis on protecting Congo's mountain gorillas from extinction. While that is a noble cause in itself, socio-economic consequences are often relegated to second-tier concerns. Adjacent populations face displacement for encroaching along the park's contested boundaries in a mix of claims to ancestral lands and subsistence techniques involving cropping, charcoal production and poaching. While the park's heavy-handed militarised approach has been questioned, its ambitions are every now and then justified by invoking the 'conflict minerals' paradigm.[11] Curiously, however, there are no relevant mines inside the park, and the most prominent rebel groups threatening the park in the past decade have either never resorted to mining to finance conflict (the M23 rebellion) or not done so for years and never inside the park (the FDLR rebellion). When I asked the analyst why conservation advocates still kept the 'conflict minerals' narrative holstered in their campaign arsenals, he replied that he did not know but that we should try to 'seek answers from people outside Congo'.

Broken promises of ethical sourcing

Through the prism of 'conflict minerals', this book has investigated the nexus of transnational politics and fragmented authority, questioning binaries such as 'global' and 'local', 'legal' and 'illegal', or 'formal' and 'informal', as well as their use by Orientalist and mercantilist strategies that weaponise the struggle against 'conflict minerals'. Refuting such flat readings, this book looked to more complicated entanglements of authority, networks and white saviourism in conflict zones. This exercise highlighted the extent to which the narrative detachment of Western advocacy is at odds with a much more convoluted interplay of 'ethical sourcing', marginalisation and the concomitant routinisation of insecurity and violence in eastern Congo that defies 'ethics' in itself. In that sense, the 'conflict minerals' campaign should lead us to reflect on who is entitled to claim the 'permission to narrate' in international development and peacebuilding, and also, to paraphrase Said, the authority to implement concomitant transnational policies in eastern Congo. As political anthropologists argue elsewhere, the twenty-first-century generation of transnational corporate actors 'may play a role in destabilizing processes of hybridity by supporting compliant non-state actors over state officials without adequate attention to the effects on institutional coherence and regulatory contestation'.[12]

This contestation goes beyond borders and territories, since the 'organization of security and justice is fundamentally heterogeneous, ambiguous and contingent on the spatial dispersion and clustering of taxable economic action'.[13] As we have seen, 'conflict-free' sourcing reinvigorated a panoply of illicit taxes while also entailing hidden forms of taxation, both of which threaten local subsistence and livelihoods. Relating intimately to access and regulation, taxation is a material claim to authority—especially when coupled with protection, the provision of goods in return and mechanisms of compliance, even if only on paper. This book demonstrated how violent conflict is influenced by the politics of claiming authority in the realm of trade and commerce; that is, 'restating the political nature of the market', whose logics can 'hijack the entire statebuilding project through hybrid mechanisms of collusion'.[14] This raises questions as to what authority actually looks like, how its unmaking comes about and how 'conflict minerals' can help us to understand broader dynamics of governance in Congo and other postcolonial contexts.

When large-scale regional war rendered authority more fluid and ephemeral, the entrenched memory of colonialism and its two publics (and its sequels in postcolonial government) taught political and economic authorities how to operate through privatised and rapidly evolving networks. In accounting for the resulting claims to authority, this book's *longue durée* analysis not only defies 'conflict minerals' initiatives but also the single-issue advocacy driving them. If colonial and postcolonial mining governance were push factors conditioning intense competition over extractive rent out of a concession or plantation economy, unrecorded, unofficial economic activity, in turn, is a pull factor, a decentralised exit valve. The onset of war, while not originally revolving around economic accumulation, created friction between the push and pull factors, reshaping society more broadly, including the governance of an economy centred on artisanal mining. In order to avoid losing market control, this then required a renewed colonial 'commitment' in the guise of iTSCi whose more immediate effects have thus far indicated that 'political disorder, endemic private violence [are] not temporary irruptions, but long-term features of the political landscape'.[15]

Congo's post-war settlement and, in its context, mineral reform are two sides of the same coin of imperial governance practice. The country's recent century is a telling example: until elections in 2011, the ruling power drew extensively upon Western interference while the opposition was antagonised. Between 2011 and 2018, it was roughly the opposite, only to switch back again from 2020. Similar observations can be made with regards to 'conflict minerals', where compliance with reform is conditioned by opportunity and force. This is not limited to Congo; the making of authority relies on a motley mix of exogenous and endogenous types of legitimation. Since this is both destructive and generative of order, the outcome is often an intense presence of competing orders driving a fragmentation of authority into literal fiefdoms that overlap like iTSCi overlaps with endogenous mining regimes. Analogous to Congo's militarised politics, 'the contours of this patchwork of fiefdoms [gives] the political geography of the eastern DRC a kaleidoscopic character'.[16] In other words, the negotiation of access is connected to the recognition of regulatory institutions (through patronage or corporate relations) in 'semi-autonomous fields' at multiple, interconnected scales.[17] Between 'local' stakeholders and 'external' interveners looking to 'clean' mining, the 'control over territory and bodies that marked the nation-state model of sovereignty is now supplemented by a powerful drive to control the "legal contract"'.[18] In such a pressure cooker of contestation, it should come as no surprise that new, tenuous patterns of authority emerge, marked by collusion and contestation alike. Not unlike the World Bank's structural adjustment programmes, iTSCi is 'substituting upward for downward accountability' and co-produces authority over mineral access, with the ambition to secure and stabilise extraction in partnership with government stakeholders.[19] In a more than rational fashion, iTSCi traceability thus forged monopsony, stressing its ambitions to control 'market access [and] labour opportunities and, hence, the distribution of benefits. This is most clear under oligopsony conditions where producers are obligated—if they want to sell—to work for and sell to one buyer.'[20]

Establishing control over supply chains requires making them legible and creating an infinite, expendable supply of workforce. However, as Tsing noted, 'the diversity of supply chains cannot be fully disciplined from inside the chain. This makes supply chains unpredictable and intriguing as frames for understanding capitalism,' leading to an 'incomplete and contradictory process' of policy implementation in the not-so-empty frontier of eastern Congo.[21] The good intentions guiding traceability paradoxically ended up cementing fraud, as ethical sourcing got 'entangled with conflict economies' and created resistance.[22]

While this book offered deep insight into the theoretical and empirical logics of 'conflict minerals', certain questions remain unanswered and require future research. First, the analytical focus on Congo makes this book a contextually anchored piece of work and limits applicability to comparative cases where similar conjunctures of neoliberal and colonial extraction are at play. Extraction practices always intersect with their environment, generating different registers of resistance and collusion. Second, the fight against conflict minerals is most advanced with regards to 3T given their specific geological properties. The only comparable mineral regime is the Kimberley Process for 'blood diamonds'—even gold-related projects in Congo and elsewhere are still embryonic in comparison. As much as studies on gold, research on other minerals (e.g. rare earths), comparative work on 3T mining in places such as Colombia, or mixed-methods research to bring in more quantitative or mapping techniques would be welcome.

Lastly, the research underpinning this book focused on eastern Congo and Congolese, and Western advocacy and policy are studied through this prism. Except for a few recent works, there is a need for more research on how business, policy and advocacy intersect when it comes to the politics of 'conflict minerals' and similar, contested issues.[23]

Better policies for better lives?

These reflections lead to a call for better policies, which—as the OECD's catchy corporate slogan implies—shall lead to better lives. In eastern Congo's (post)colonial legacy, authority mostly evolves in privatised networks wherein the experience of large-scale and regionalised war led to a deep fragmentation of political order. Simplistic readings of conflict have resulted in insular strategies of conflict-resolution and peacebuilding. Politically, a flat, teleological push for power-sharing has dominated while the main military strategy has been to support hasty integration of former rebels.

Likewise, 'conflict minerals' policies were largely apolitical, rendering the political 'technical'. Guided by unrepentant advocacy, soft and hard laws have been tabled in Western capitals to spearhead programmes for 'conflict-free' sourcing. All of this has been underpinned by three problems: (1) a blind eye to local complexity; (2) single-issue advocacy for Western audiences; and (3) an Orientalist epistemic cleavage between ethical justification, consumer-oriented advocacy and profit-driven reform.

From discursive paradigm to tangible intervention, the trajectory of 'conflict minerals' problematises how global supply chains, conflict resolution and consumer ethics intersect with postcolonial friction and violence. As Potemkin-style 'façade institutions', today's existing 'conflict-free' supply chains question the tenets of transnational regulation and the white saviourism pushing it, cautioning against flat, binary readings of international development and peacebuilding.[24] Nonetheless, twenty-first-century conflicts are characterised by ambiguity, pragmatism and multiple rationalities, defying both messy and simplistic stereotypes of far-flung conflict zones. In sum, this informs three policy-relevant lessons on peace and ethics in Congo.

First, to tackle war, violence and resource extraction, it is crucial to understand the political economy of eastern Congo beyond the stubborn tropes of the 'conflict minerals' agenda. This requires a more active reckoning with previous intellectual shortcomings, additional research into the multiple causes of violence and deeper knowledge of Congo's 'crisis economy', including and beyond minerals—focusing on multiple historical continuities and analytical causalities rather than salient pitches.

Second, transnational reform policies and projects towards more transparent and equitable mineral markets need to be based on more serious analysis of artisanal mining and its fragmented but elaborate governance patterns. This requires an attempt at epistemic surrender, opening the door to more adequate and realistic assessments of social and economic dynamics.[25] Programmes like iTSCi have thus far either ignored or wilfully neglected this. Successful traceability, however, needs to be dynamic, engrained and focused on local instead of external accountability mechanisms.

Third, and last, Western consumers and policymakers need to understand that clean minerals are expensive. While they may have already done so, the intermediate conclusion is to displace the cost. However, as long as local producers pay, traceability, sustainability and compliance will remain an illusion. In other words, the problem of conflict minerals not only remains misunderstood by advocates, but actually sits at the opposite end of the supply chain to the one expected, wherein multinationals refuse solidarity. In short, and to paraphrase Sally Falk Moore, any reform is more likely to succeed with the people, rather than against them.

EPILOGUE

Like others, my identity endowed me with colonial and imperial stereotypes, and I have succumbed to these repeatedly during my work and life in Congo. Researching Congo from a Western perspective is as prone to error as interventions by a policymaker, practitioner or advocate, and writing an ethnography of artisanal mining is an artisanal exercise itself; it involves stumbling about gems and getting lost in sand. Standing on the shoulders of giants, this book has argued for discursive decolonisation. We know from Ngũgĩ wa Thiong'o, Donna Haraway and many others that decolonising oneself and situating knowledge is not easy, and this book can never be as decolonial as it aims to be.[1] This is linked to what Derrida called 'untranslatability', and what Kuhn and Feyerabend termed 'incommensurability'.[2] It also speaks to Clifford and Marcus' idea that 'ethnography is artisanal, tied to the worldly work of writing'.[3]

Humanity, despite a few universal commonalities (fewer, though, than international norms and values would have us believe), is so complex and particular that a lifetime would not suffice for total immersion into another lifeworld. It always remains piecemeal, however much we strive. Nonetheless, in the age of populism, identity politics, pandemics and planetary destruction—all of which share a tendency of promoting flat, condensed readings of immeasurable complexity—we must keep trying to understand the 'rest of the world' not only out of curiosity, but as moral obligation and practical imperative. One can be wrong in doing so, and it would be surprising if there were no mistakes or omissions in this book. However, not trying is not an option for the critical mind, and the tale of 'conflict minerals' is—as much as it concerns Congo and broader global dynamics—a good parable to understand where not trying can lead us.

This book is no tribunal to judge any individuals involved in this story. It is the attempt, with all its flaws, to make sense of mindsets, actions and consequences surrounding a story linking deep Congolese mining shafts with the skyscrapers of corporate headquarters. While any mistakes that remain are mine alone, I am thankful to everyone who spoke to me about the issue. Finally, the everyday struggles of Congolese deserve mention: even impartial voices complained, 'selling to iTSCi is flushing [minerals] down the toilet'. However vulgar, the bluntness of this statement illustrates their despair and serves as a reminder that 'understanding ideas, interests, and structures that shape or hinder Africa's development efforts requires serious work'.[4] In conflict areas, this is difficult, but 'if you stop listening to those actively involved in a war, you [have] lost your chance of intervening helpfully'.[5] The struggle against 'conflict minerals', and the ethics that inform it, has not listened to those affected by conflict, whether over minerals or not. It evolved from Orientalist assumptions and triggered a form of white saviourism that morphed into a neocolonial *déjà vu* rooted in a mix of naivety and wet dreams of accumulation.

214

NOTES

ACKNOWLEDGEMENTS

1. See Galtung 1969; Hoffman 2003; Cramer et al. 2016; Kovats–Bernat 2002; Wood 2006; Campbell 2017; Cronin-Furman & Lake 2018.
2. Hoffman & Taravalley Jr. 2014; Gupta 2014; Schiltz & Büscher 2018.
3. Vogel & Musamba forthcoming.
4. See, for example, Musamba & Vogel 2016; Vogel & Musamba 2016 and 2017; Vogel, Musamba & Radley 2018.
5. Bøås & Dunn 2014, p. 146.

PROLOGUE

1. Personal conversation, but see also JamboRDC.info 2018.
2. In this book, I interchangeably use 'DRC' and 'Congo' for the Democratic Republic of the Congo.
3. See an earlier reflection in Vogel 2013.
4. Meaning 'life is difficult here' in Kiswahili.
5. See Vogel 2012.
6. The 3T stand for tantalum, tin and tungsten, the purified forms of columbite-tantalite, cassiterite and wolframite, respectively.

INTRODUCTION

1. See Cole 2012.
2. Said 1979, p. 204.
3. Mbembe 2001, p. 241.
4. Haraway 1988; Ferguson 2006, p. 14.

5. See Said 1984.

6. See Katz-Lavigne & Hönke 2018.

7. Vlassenroot & Raeymaekers 2009; Vogel & Stearns 2018.

8. Prunier 2009; see also Dunn 2003 for a critique of such terms.

9. See Kristof 2008; Collier & Hoeffler 1998.

10. Edward Said in conversation with Sut Jhally; see Palestine Diary 2012.

11. Collier & Hoeffler 1998 and 2002.

12. Mertens & Pardy 2017; Eriksson Baaz & Stern 2013; Lewis 2021.

13. Key examples of this school are Collier & Hoeffler 1998; Keen 1998; Collier 2000; Ross 2004 and, more recently, Sanchez de la Sierra 2020.

14. Wai 2012; Mkandawire 2015; Nathan 2005; Cramer 2002; Korf 2006; or—after a U-turn—Keen 2012.

15. Ferguson 2006, p. 9.

16. This book differentiates between (foreign, Western) advocates and activists that are part of a community, as suggested in De Waal 2015, p. 32.

17. Vogel & Raeymaekers 2016.

18. Collier 2000, p. 91.

19. Henceforth colloquially known as the Dodd–Frank Act. See US Congress 2010.

20. See Organisation for Economic Cooperation and Development 2016.

21. See Chase 2019.

22. Personal communication with the author, February 2014.

23. See http://icglr.org/index.php/en/, https://www.internationaltin.org/ and https://www.itsci.org/.

24. See for instance https://www.kivusecurity.org.

25. Stearns 2010; Vlassenroot & Raeymaekers 2004a.

26. Themnér & Utas 2016, p. 256.

27. This is intended to enclose unrecorded economies for the sake of taxation. However, many cooperatives are subcontractors of concession owners. While their *petites mines* are foreseen in national legislation and hailed as a step towards more 'efficient' industrial mining, several of the respective firms and their cooperative offshoots are rooted in or connected with former *comptoirs* or local politico-military networks.

28. Said 1979, p. 357.

29. For a similar argument in the context of Sierra Leone, see Peters 2011.
30. Philipps 2011.
31. Vogel & Raeymaekers 2016.
32. Ferguson 2006, p. 198.
33. Haraway 1988.
34. See, most notably, the contributions in De Waal 2015.
35. Most advocacy eclipses the fact that conflicts had emerged before the violent exploitation and trade of minerals, e.g. in Masisi.
36. Bulongo 2016; Babwine & Ruvunangiza 2016.
37. Mkandawire 2015, p. 602; Ekeh 1975.
38. Weber 1980 [1922], Ch. 1, §16, §17; Ch. 3, §2. See also Lund 2006 and Hoffmann & Kirk 2013.
39. Lentz 1998, p. 63; see also Hoffmann, Vlassenroot & Marchais 2016.
40. Abrams 1988; Mitchell 1991; Dunn 2010.
41. Agnew 1994; Ferguson & Gupta 2002, p. 982.
42. Ferguson & Gupta 2002, p. 988.
43. Lund 2016, p. 1,200; see also Dunn 2010, p. 82.
44. Allen 2009, p. 201; Tsing 2004, p. 5.
45. Allen 2009, p. 201.
46. Allen 2009, p. 207.
47. Mbembe 2001, pp. 66 & 90; see also Tilly 1985.
48. Ribot & Peluso 2003, p. 153.
49. See for instance Scott 1998; Rubbers 2007; Hart 2008.
50. Allen 2009, p. 201.
51. Jessop, Brenner & Jones 2008; Swyngedouw 1997.
52. De Certeau 1984; Granovetter 1973. See also Olivier de Sardan 2008a; Bayart 2000; Roitman & Mbembe 1995; Vigh 2008; Boissevain 1974.
53. Borgatti & Kidwell 2011, p. 9.
54. Granovetter 1985; Polanyi 2001.
55. Laumann, Galaskiewicz & Marsden 1978, p. 470. See also Ekeh 1975; Mkandawire 2015. See below for a more detailed discussion.
56. See Cole 2012.
57. See Budabin & Richey 2021.
58. See Invisible Children 2012.
59. Schomerus 2015; Bex & Craps 2016; Yu 2020; De Waal 2015. For rebuttals, see Mengestu 2012; Mamdani 2012; Kagumire 2012.

60. See https://congostories.org, Enough Project 2009 and 2011.

61. Shringarpure 2020, p. 178. See also Blomley 2008; Dunn 2003; Moore 1973.

62. Benton 2016; Shringarpure 2020; Thiong'o 1987; Said 1979; Fanon 1970.

63. Hall 1995; Crenshaw 1991; Haraway 1988; Spivak 1988; Achebe 1977.

64. See also Dunn 2003, p. 30 on the *longue durée* of using such binaries to create the colonial Other.

65. Go 2020; Mazur 2021; Mihai 2018; De Sousa Santos 2007; Mignolo & Escobar 2010.

66. Clifford & Marcus 1986, p. 2.

67. Wendt 1999; Taussig 1980; Rabinow & Sullivan 1988.

68. Scheper-Hughes 1995; Gledhill 2000a and 2000b; Arendt 1963; Levi 1986; Nordstrom & Robben 1996.

69. Haraway 1988; see also Rose 1997.

70. Greenhouse, Mertz & Warren 2002, p. 388.

71. Geertz 1973; Haraway 1988; Bourdieu & Wacquant 1992; Burawoy 1998; Sambanis 2004; Hann & Hart 2011.

72. Gledhill 2009, p. 29; Wacquant 2012.

73. Ferguson & Gupta 2002, p. 996; see also Mosse 2015.

74. Kopytoff 1987; Harvey 2006; Pereira 2015; Korf & Raeymaekers 2013; De Soto 2000; Hall, Hirsch & Li 2011; Tsing 2004.

75. Raeymaekers 2007, p. 30.

76. Swyngedouw 1997; Cook et al. 2004; see also Olivier de Sardan 2008b and 2015.

77. Das & Poole 2004, p. 4.

78. All interviews and discussions relied on informed consent, and inter-viewees could present their own questions as to my intentions. While interviews are numbered and referenced with date and place, informal discussions are not, due to heightened anonymity assurance. Based on previous research on topics considered sensitive in eastern Congo, I decided to not record interviews. Various interviews were repeated as a technique to triangulate information, both with the same interlocutor over time and asking the same questions to a maximum number of interlocutors. The sampling of interviewees followed a threefold tech-

nique combining prior identification of key stakeholders, randomly approaching people at field sites, and snowballing from the two previous categories. This resulted in a range of respondents, stretching across all rural and urban field sites and including respondents from all segments of the upstream supply chain, Congolese and international experts, mining officials, members of the security sector, politicians, UN and NGO representatives, customary and other local leaders, indirect stakeholders in the mining sector such as non-mining businesspeople, elders and members of non-state armed groups.

79. This led to (expectedly) lengthy and repetitive observation of 'usual'—eventually almost boring—patterns as well as (unexpectedly) witnessing 'spectacular' events, including flagrant attempts at smuggling and fraud, and clashes involving armed groups and the army.

80. Cook et al. 2004, p. 642; see also Marcus 1995.

81. Vlassenroot 2006, p. 196.

82. Ellis & MacGaffey 1996, p. 25.

83. Schouten, Murairi & Kubuya 2017.

84. Roitman 2005.

85. Vigh 2009.

86. Vlassenroot 2006, p. 192.

87. Wood 2006, p. 377.

88. Wood 2006, p. 380.

89. Verweijen 2015b, p. 9, paraphrasing Jackson 2003.

90. Scheper-Hughes 1995, p. 411.

91. Cramer, Hammond & Pottier 2011, p. 12.

92. Gledhill cautioned researchers to 'be circumspect about throwing ourselves [sic] into various kinds of activism in fieldwork and ... about the difficulties of adopting a partisan stance in complex situations' (Gledhill 2000a, p. 3; see also Gledhill 2000b, pp. 227–34).

93. Kuper, in Scheper-Hughes 1995, pp. 424–26.

94. A brilliant example making a similar argument can be found in Porter 2017.

95. Richards 2005; Kalyvas 2006; Jamar & Chappuis 2016.

96. Cramer, Hammond & Pottier 2011, p. 5.

97. Wood 2006, p. 384.

98. Verweijen 2015b.
99. Raeymaekers 2014, p. x.

1. VIOLENT CONTINUITIES

1. Dunn 2003, p. 5.
2. An exuberant collection of such metaphors has been put together in Dunn 2003, pp. 84–88 & 166.
3. Doty 1996. For key historical works on Congo, see Vansina 1966; Newbury 1992; Hochschild 1998; Hunt 2015; Young 1967.
4. Bhabha 1984, p. 88, in reference to observations in Naipaul 1967; Fanon 1970; Césaire 1972.
5. Mathys 2017; Newbury 2009; Vansina 1990.
6. Henriet 2021.
7. Parts of the following sections draw from a series of papers I have co-edited. See https://www.gicnetwork.be/insecure-livelihoods-series/.
8. See, for example, Dunn 2003; Vansina 1966 and 1990; Newbury 1992 and 2009.
9. French 2021. See Kopytoff 1987 on African frontiers, or Bierschenk & Olivier de Sardan 2014 on trajectories of African statehood.
10. Hoffmann 2019; Verweijen & van Bockhaven 2020.
11. Colonial decrees in 1885 and 1890 forced customary entities under colonial administration, and instilled extra-customary taxation practices, even though no Europeans had arrived in the area yet. For more background, see Mathys 2017.
12. See for instance Hochschild 1998; Mudimbe 1994 and 1988.
13. Rwandophone is a shortcut for speakers of Kinyarwanda and its variations. Banyarwanda (Hutu and Tutsi) have lived in Rutshuru and Masisi since precolonial times. Many Hutu who are neither refugees nor *transplantés* are familiar with Hunde custom and language. A second group consisted of the MIB-era *transplantés*. A third group of Tutsi refugees fled pogroms in Rwanda in 1959, mostly settling in the former Gishari chieftaincy, where they joined *transplantés* and others. Domestic trans-chieftaincy migration also occurred as people moved in search of land, due to customary struggles, or because of work-related staff rotations in the public sector. Many have since intermarried, but stigmatisation lives on.

14. Hunde chiefs also recuperated land leased to Banyarwanda, invoking an argument that land unused for a month would go back to the chief. This move was accompanied by the mass appointments of Hunde in local administration.

15. Dunn 2003, p. 107. See also seminal works by Anderson 1983 on 'imagined communities', by Hobsbawm & Ranger 1983 on the 'invention of tradition', and by Mudimbe 1988 on the 'invention of Africa'.

16. For a broader context of politics in Zaire, see Verhaegen 1966 and 1969; Jewsiewicki 1977; Callaghy 1984; Schatzberg 1988; Gondola 2002; MacGaffey 1987 and 1991; Young & Turner 1985; Nzongola-Ntalaja 2002; Reno 2006; Kennes & Larmer 2016.

17. Jackson 2007; Dunn 2003.

18. See Callaghy 1984.

19. A 1971 constitutional revision reconfirmed the Bakajika Law and clarified all land belonged to the state. The 1973 Land Law further cut customary rights to land (Law 73-021 of 20 July 1973, later supplemented by Law 80-008 of 18 July 1980). As Banyarwanda could buy land, they stopped paying customary taxes, leading chiefs to mobilise youth brigades known as *masomo siyo nyama* ('school is not meat').

20. See Gobbers 2016.

21. This was only reversed in the 2006 constitution, reinstating citizenship rights of anyone living on Congolese soil since 1960.

22. Ordinance 25/552 of 6 November 1959, Ordinance-law 71-020 of 26 March 1971, Law 72-002 of 5 January 1972.

23. Later, Kinyarwanda speakers and other eastern populations were lumped together by slogans like *opération botika mboka* ('return to your country'). Non-Rwandophone communities expressed their resentment in slogans such as *bulongo ya baba* ('land of the fathers').

24. Bucyalimwe 1997.

25. These groups emerged in southeast Walikale, and were inspired by the Mai-Mai Bangilima, a heteroclite formation of Nande militia.

26. Thousands of cattle were killed, stolen or raided by Hutu and so-called autochthonous militia through 1993. While the raids targeted a few large-scale Tutsi cattle owners, members of all communities were targeted, and their cows killed and looted.

27. Tegera 2009; Prunier 1995; Kimonyo 2008; Willame 1997; Malkki 1995; Lemarchand 1996.

28. Vlassenroot & Raeymaekers 2004a and 2009; Prunier 2009; Stearns 2010; Lemarchand 2009; Office of the United Nations High Commissioner for Human Rights 2010.

29. While this alliance triggered new Hutu groups and recruitment in Masisi, the AFDL quickly gained ground, marching towards Kisangani and conquering Zaire bit by bit. As Hutu were targeted by AFDL, RPF and their allies, a nascent coalition of ex-FAR and *interahamwe* with *combattants* and GACI (known as the Mongols) targeted Hunde, Tutsi and others.

30. The RCD tried to govern by mirroring the state administration. The *chefs de poste d'encadrement administratif* (heads of administrative supervision), a state office and title, fell into this category. It was only replaced by the *fonctionnaires délégués* (interim delegated officials) in 2016. The RCD administration had a lasting impact on land governance—especially in Masisi, Rutshuru and Kalehe, where ethnically laden land conflict was frequent—and also intervened in such conflict where state-leased estates expired or where occupants were unable to settle their debts. Facilitated by local elites such as Erasto Ntibaturana, the RCD named customary administrators, such as Muhima Kapenda (a nephew of Erasto) in 2000 for the Bashali—in violation of the custom, where the *bakungu* decide appointments—often leading to violent backlash.

31. Pottier 2006.

32. The wars are usually divided into three periods: the AFDL rebellion against Mobutu (1996–97); the Second Congo War, or 'Africa's World War', involving a dozen African countries and their proxies (1998–2003); and a low-intensity war later on. See Vogel & Stearns 2018.

33. Debos 2016; Richards 2005.

34. Based on the author's 2013 mapping exercise. See www.suluhu.org.

35. The CNDP was a result of fraught army integration and claims to defend Congolese Tutsi against the FDLR. Others saw in it a reincarnation of Rwandan-sponsored Tutsi rebellion, triggering new Hutu and Mai-Mai mobilisation. See Stearns 2012b; Vlassenroot & Raeymaekers 2009.

36. This led to rancour and later inspired the 2010 regimentation process to balance grievances, which caused new mobilisation by the Raia Mutomboki, in response to the deployment of Kinyarwanda-speaking officers into Shabunda, Kalehe and Walikale.
37. Based on the author's 2015 mapping exercise, in collaboration with Congo Research Group.
38. Based on the author's 2017 mapping exercise, in collaboration with Congo Research Group and Kivu Security Tracker.
39. Stearns et al. 2013a, 2013b and 2013c; Vlassenroot 2013.
40. Based on the author's 2020 mapping exercise, in collaboration with Congo Research Group and Kivu Security Tracker.
41. Congo Research Group 2016 and 2017.
42. Decree 13/027 of 13 June 2013 conferred the status of *ville* (city) and *commune* (municipality) to certain urban centres in the Kivus.
43. Verweijen et al. 2020 and 2021.
44. Congo Research Group 2020a; Sungura et al. 2021 and 2020b.
45. Congo Research Group 2021 and 2020b.
46. Sungura et al. 2020a; Sungura, van Soest & Kitonga 2019.

2. GENESIS OF A DIGITAL PARADIGM

1. Smith 2011; see also Barnes 2008.
2. Nest 2011.
3. Smith 2015; Nest 2011.
4. De Boeck 1998, p. 803.
5. Smith 2011, p. 32.
6. Jackson 2002; Smith 2011.
7. Ferguson 2006, p. 207.
8. Owenga Odinga 2014, pp. 179–82. See also Colle 1971; Kamuntu 1995.
9. For more detail, see Radley 2019, pp. 56–67.
10. A third and semi-industrial type, mainly through dredge operations, is applied in alluvial gold mining, e.g. in the Shabunda area (South Kivu).
11. Vwakyanakazi 1992.
12. For an ethnographic study of artisanal diamond mining, see de Boeck 1998.

13. Ferguson 2006, p. 9.

14. See Schouten 2016 for Kilo-Moto; see Radley 2019 for Banro.

15. Congo adopted a new mining law in 2018 (see République Démocratique du Congo 2017). To analyse the 'conflict minerals' story, its predecessor, decree 007/2002 of 11 July 2002 on the mining code (see République Démocratique du Congo 2002) and the decree 038/2003 of 26 March 2003 on the mining regulations (see République Démocratique du Congo 2003) are also highly relevant.

16. Hart 2008; Rubbers 2007.

17. Vogel, Musamba & Radley 2018.

18. Wai 2012; Mkandawire 2015.

19. Nest 2011.

20. Raeymaekers 2002; Cuvelier & Raeymaekers 2002.

21. Focusing more on gold, the Ugandan-backed RCD-K/ML did similarly in the Beni and Butembo regions. See Raeymaekers 2014; Sweet 2020.

22. Jackson 2002; Nest 2011; United Nations 2001.

23. Jourdan 2011; Hoffmann & Verweijen 2019; Schouten, Murairi & Kubuya 2017; Fairhead 1992.

24. Raeymaekers 2007, p. 31; see also Sweet 2020.

25. United Nations 2001, p. 29; Jackson 2002.

26. Luckham 2004, p. 489.

27. Vlassenroot & Raeymaekers 2004a, p. 23.

28. Nathan 2005; Cramer 2002; Korf 2006.

29. Militarisation is defined as a 'process of preparing, reshaping, and reorienting society in order to wage wars' (Bernazzoli & Flint 2009, p. 402). In Congo, where war and peace are not always spatio-temporally distinguishable, militarisation refers to the ways in which social and economic life is infiltrated by military networks and logics, and how, due to a lack of civilian infrastructure, regular and irregular military actors are compelled to invest significant resources in economic activities covering legal and illegal activities. See Verweijen 2015a.

30. Tull & Mehler 2005; Vlassenroot & Raeymaekers 2009.

31. Eriksson Baaz & Verweijen 2013; Vogel & Stearns 2018.

32. Raeymaekers 2007, p. 29.

33. Hoffmann, Vlassenroot & Marchais 2016.

34. Cuvelier & Raeymaekers 2002.

35. De Failly 2001; Pole Institute 2001.

36. Collier 2000, p. 91.

37. Tull & Mehler 2005; Eriksson Baaz & Verweijen 2013.

38. Mkandawire 2015, Wai 2012 and Dunn 2003 look at the historical roots and construction of such imageries from different angles.

39. Calain 2012, p. 3.

40. Raeymaekers 2010.

41. See, for example, an open letter signed by 72 Congolese and international stakeholders at www.suluhu.org/mining.

42. Jackson 2002, p. 517.

43. Ferguson 2006, p. 27.

44. Oakley & Proctor 2012; Mitchell 2016; Roberts 2016; Scott 1987 and 2009; Hazen 2010.

45. Callaghy, Kassimir & Latham 2001, p. 84.

46. Tsing 2004, p. 151.

47. Meagher, de Herdt & Titeca 2014, p. 3.

48. Mbembe 2001, p. 66–101.

49. Informal conversation with a long-standing Congolese coltan trader based in Goma.

50. Vogel et al. 2021.

51. Moore 1973.

52. Vlassenroot & Raeymaekers 2004a, p. 23.

53. Smith 2011, p. 29.

54. De Koning 2011, p. 8.

55. Lombard 2012, p. iv; see also Lombard 2016.

56. Abrams 1988.

57. Raeymaekers 2014, pp. 100–10; see also Kennes 2002.

58. Across eastern Congo, this term describes ways in which individuals and groups react to state weakness and embattled public authority. Similar to '*système D*' or '*article 15*'—the Congolese notions of muddling through—the idea of *autoprise en charge* involves a more security-related notion and is often invoked by armed actors and their civilian allies taking 'their destiny into their own hands'.

59. Raeymaekers 2014, p. 113–18; see also Sweet 2020.

60. Garrett, Sergiou & Vlassenroot 2009; United Nations 2010b.

61. Congo Research Group 2020a.

62. After Bisie, Matumo was a commander in two of South Kivu's gold hubs, Kamituga (2010–13) and Misisi (2013–17). His involvement in mining was backed by generals Etienne Bindu and Gabriel Amisi Kumba. See, for instance, United Nations 2017, 2011 and 2009.

63. See Vlassenroot & Raeymaekers 2005; Spittaels 2010; Observatoire Gouvernance et Paix 2010; Sematumba 2011; Zingg & Hilgert 2011; United Nations 2015a; Verweijen 2016; Vlassenroot, Mudinga & Hoffmann 2016.

64. Sanchez de la Sierra 2020.

65. Global Witness 2009.

66. Raeymaekers 2007, p. 27.

67. Callaghy, Kassimir & Latham 2001, p. 242.

68. Migdal & Schlichte 2005, p. 14.

69. Collier & Hoeffler 1998; Keen 1998; Collier 2000; Ross 2004.

70. Cramer 2002; Nathan 2005; Korf 2006.

71. Collier is strikingly self-referential, one of his articles having '16 references, eleven of which are to Collier himself' (Keen 2012, p. 765).

72. Keen 2012, pp. 758–61.

73. Keen 2012, p. 762; Cramer 2002; Nathan 2005; Stewart 2008.

74. A 2012 North Kivu inventory indicated 66 mines, of which 57 were under government control, seven under armed group control and two unclear.

75. In her research on civil-military interaction in eastern Congo, Verweijen 2015a impressively refutes simple binaries in that regard.

76. Congo's natural resource sector is subject to a UN sanctions regime, monitored by groups of experts tasked with investigating the fields of natural resources, arms trade and armed mobilisation. Although their recommendations do not have legal status, they have contributed to the establishment of sanctions lists of companies and individuals presumably involved in the illegal trade of minerals and arms. See https://www.un.org/securitycouncil/sanctions/1533/due-diligence-guidelines.

77. Raeymaekers 2002; Cuvelier & Raeymaekers 2002.

78. Shringarpure 2020; De Waal 2015.
79. Autesserre 2012.
80. That includes an often repeated, but erroneous, link between resources, militias and rape. Contrary to the claim that conflict minerals fuel sexual violence, there is no proven spatial correlation between mining and violence, or mining enclaves and particular kinds of violence.
81. Said 1979, p. 357.
82. Nordstrom 2004; Levi 1986.
83. For a theoretical argument beyond eastern Congo, see Lombard 2012.
84. Budabin & Richey 2021; Lewis 2021; Marijnen & Verweijen 2016; De Waal 2015.
85. While my research focuses less on gender (for this, see Bashwira 2017 instead) this resonates with research on the agency and victimisation of women and on 'sexurity' policies pushed by debates on gender-based violence. See Mertens & Pardy 2017; Eriksson Baaz & Stern 2013.

3. A CIVILISING MISSION 2.0?

1. Dunn 2003, p. 5.
2. Mbembe 2001.
3. See Hamilton 2012.
4. US Congress 2010, §1502.
5. Later, USAID commissioned this map to a consortium including IPIS, MONUSCO, and the BGR. This mapping is supposed to divide 'conflict-sensitive' from 'conflict-free' mining areas on the basis of international regulation, domestic Congolese legislation, and regional ICGLR protocols and templates with regard to mining and trading natural resources including 3T and gold. Today, IPIS spearheads these efforts by producing the most reliable maps.
6. United Nations 2010a.
7. See United Nations 2009b; Organisation for Economic Cooperation and Development 2016.
8. This happened by way of *note circulaire* (a type of ministerial instruction) 002/CAB.MIN/MINES/01/2011.
9. See Securities and Exchange Commission 2012.
10. See European Union 2017.

11. See Federal Office of Justice 2021a and 2021b.
12. Cuvelier, Vlassenroot & Olin 2014, p. 341.
13. Berdal & Malone 2000; Nathan 2005; Keen 2012; Cramer 2002.
14. Benda-Beckmann 2000 and 1981.
15. Cuvelier, Vlassenroot & Olin 2014, p. 341.
16. Radley & Vogel 2015.
17. Vogel et al. 2021.
18. Spittaels 2010, p. 7; Hoebeke, Chiza & Mukungilwa, 2022.
19. Vogel & Musamba 2016; Musamba, Vogel & Vlassenroot 2022.
20. Despite pilot testing of iTSCi, most practical initiatives only began to develop after the ban was lifted in March 2011. According to the official export statistics for South Kivu, for instance, cassiterite exports fell from 37,227,138 USD in 2009 to 9,218,850 USD in 2011, and coltan exports dropped from 2,646,333 USD to 233,916 USD.
21. Geenen 2012, p. 327. See also Sematumba 2011.
22. See Organisation for Economic Cooperation and Development 2013; US Congress 2010.
23. Gledhill 2009, p. 18; Ferguson 1990. See also Stearns 2010; Raeymaekers 2014.
24. Raeymaekers 2009, p. 583.
25. Cuvelier 2010, p. 67.
26. Cuvelier 2010; Spittaels 2010. See also Spivak 1988; Hall 1995.
27. Reimers 2014; Geenen 2012; Rasmussen & Lund 2018; Pereira 2015; Li 2014.
28. Benda-Beckmann 2000 and 1981.
29. For instance, the Kimberley Process; see Le Billon 2001.
30. Berndt 2013; Barnett et al. 2005.
31. Galtung 1969.
32. Rodney 1972, p. 10.
33. Tsing 2004; Li 2014; Kirsch 2014.
34. Ferguson 2006, p. 14.
35. Polanyi 2001.

INTERLUDE: GODFATHER'S TALES

1. This is an attempt at a poem based on and triangulated from leaked

internal iTSCi reports, civil society documents, multiple interviews by the author, and the testimony of one courageous individual. All documentation is on file with the author and Musemakweli can identify with this poem.

4. ETHICAL MONOPOLIES

1. International Peace Information Service 2019, p. 8.
2. Parts of this chapter draw from Vogel, Musamba & Radley 2018.
3. Luckham 2004, p. 482.
4. Iguma 2017.
5. Created in 2003, SAESSCAM (since 2018, SAEMAPE, the French version of the acronym) was intended to 'provide guidance and technical support to artisanal mining in order to lift it out of ungovernable informality [but] is simply yet another state representative without infrastructural power to fulfil its mandate, nevertheless translating its public authority mandate into a claim to legitimate taxation' (Schouten 2016, p. 8).
6. Ferguson 2006, p. 39.
7. The most detailed mappings are produced by the Antwerp-based International Peace Information Service. See www.ipisresearch.be.
8. However, local iTSCi/Pact staff spend most of their time in their offices, leaving the bulk of practical work to SAEMAPE.
9. Igoe & Brockington 2007, p. 440.
10. For some time, ITRI Ltd. (now ITA Ltd.) refused to share data with Kinshasa (Ministère des Mines 2013). Contradicting its own claims about transparency, this was a surprisingly secretive practice which has only been abolished after formal complaints.
11. See tonnage data at International Tin Supply Chain Initiative 2021.
12. International Peace Information Service 2019, pp. 37–38.
13. See Tantalum and Niobium International Study Centre 2017.
14. This data concerns the period 2014–16. However, given the complex and opaque character of supply chains it is both difficult and unreliable to extrapolate broader claims. This includes legal and illegal taxation along the upstream chain. World market prices and technical aspects, for instance contamination by other substances (e.g. arsenic) or the need for equipment such as water pumps, also shape local prices.

15. Cuvelier, Vlassenroot & Olin 2014.
16. United Nations 2015b and 2016a.
17. Neoliberal discourses of accountability can multiply opportunities for corruption. See Tidey 2013; Welker 2014, p. 118.
18. Bafilemba, Mueller & Lezhnev 2014.
19. Parker & Vadheim 2017; Stearns & Vogel 2015 and 2017.
20. See MONUSCO 2013; International Peace Information Service 2019; and regular reporting at www.kivusecurity.org.
21. Based on data from the International Peace Information Service (mines) and the Kivu Security Tracker (recorded killings and clashes 2017–21).
22. See, for example, Intel 2021.
23. Radley & Vogel 2015, p. 407. This 'labour migration' between mining and armed groups has long been known. The coltan boom, for instance, had 'people initially attracted into coltan by the possibility of dollars and then forced out by the crash swell militia ranks or "borrow" their cover' (Jackson 2003, p. 16). I collected various testimonies with interviewees 'navigating' between mining and militias.
24. Barnett et al. 2005.
25. Hilson 2016, p. 548; Hayes et al. 2010, p. 6. For Geenen & Radley, 'using the World Bank's methodology of allowing five dependents per artisanal miner, we can project that approximately 1–1.7 million people are dependent on ASM in the Kivu provinces' (2014, p. 59).
26. Abraham & van Schendel 2005.
27. Panella & Thomas 2015, p. 3.
28. See Intel 2021; Bafilemba, Mueller & Lezhnev 2014.
29. Rothenberg 2014.
30. Geenen 2011.
31. Panella & Thomas 2015, p. 5
32. Radley & Vogel 2015; Matthysen & Zaragoza 2013. Inspired by over 300 individual interviews and focus groups with multiple stakeholder groups stretching over four years and dozens of 3T mines in South Kivu, an exploratory survey in French and Swahili consisting of 30 items was developed. In three mining areas, 200 randomly sampled participants responded to this survey between 2016 and 2018 to control for the ethnographic data. The sample included miners, washers,

traders, cooperative agents, state agents, transporters, and others. These were randomly selected and provided informed consent. This means any individual could participate, and there was no targeting of respondents. In addition to three mines, two others served as control cases, and another 43 responded. Despite not being statistically representative, the survey converged with ethnographic findings. It convened a diverse set of respondents across geographic, gender, age, professional and educational strata. In total, 75 persons responded in Nzibira, 47 in Lemera, and 78 in Nyabibwe (plus 20 in Rubaya and 23 in Numbi). 64% were men, 32% women and 4% did not want to specify. 31% were 16–25 years of age, 27% 26–35, 15.5% 36–45, 9% 46–55, and 5% were 56 or older (12.5% did not indicate their age). Within the sample, 46.5% were miners, 31% were non-miners doing associated work, 8% were traders, 6% cooperative agents, and 4.5% state agents (4% did not specify their job). 40% attended secondary school, 19.5% left school during primary education, and 7.5% spent at least a year at a university. 15% had no formal education and 8% did not respond.

33. Blomley 2008; Taylor 1994.

34. Vigh 2008; Geenen & Radley 2014; Cuvelier 2010.

35. Guinier & Torres 2003, p. 11. While the miner's canary is a Western metaphor, it is illustrative of certain dynamics of eastern Congo's mining sector too. Seeing the economic well-being of artisanal miners as a canary indicates to policymakers (like the actual miner's canary indicated to miners) whether their livelihoods face existential threats hardly visible before they become irreversible.

36. Raeymaekers, Menkhaus & Vlassenroot 2008; Rubbers 2007; Lund 2006.

37. See Blomley 2008; Kirsch 2014; Rasmussen & Lund 2018; Scott 1998; Mitchell 2002.

38. Hilson 2016, p. 555.

39. Jackson 2002; Geenen 2012; Cuvelier, Vlassenroot & Olin 2014.

40. The similarity between the latter two is explicable through the fact these authorities usually operate together in the field.

41. This number declined between the two survey rounds as Abbas Kayonga, the notorious head of an anti-fraud office, was demoted and

later arrested after a shootout between his bodyguards and the army in Bukavu in November 2017.

42. 37.6% of all survey respondents reported increases in taxation, whereas 20.8% reported a decrease and 41.6% were unsure.

43. See Resolve 2021.

44. International Peace Information Service 2019, p. 55.

45. Monopoly means only one producer sells a product, whereas monopsony is the inverse (i.e. only one consumer buys a product).

46. Berndt 2013; Hall, Hirsch & Li 2011; Werner & Bair 2011.

47. Rothenberg & Radley 2014, p. 57.

48. Smith 2011.

49. Smith 2015.

50. See London Metal Exchange 2021.

51. Interview #85, 16 August 2014, Nyabibwe.

52. Interview #85, 16 August 2014, Nyabibwe; Interview #162, 10 September 2015, Rubaya; Interview #186, 24 September 2015, Lemera.

53. Interview #9, 28 May 2014, Nzibira. In addition, a range of taxes are reported to be lower in Rwanda than in Congo.

54. Spittaels, Matthysen & Bulzomi 2014; Cuvelier, Pöyhönen & Areskog 2010. See also Xiang 2012.

55. Maconachie & Hilson 2011, p. 301.

56. Mueller-Koné 2015.

57. Rothenberg & Radley, 2014, p. 21. SAESSCAM is the former name of SAEMAPE.

58. Interviews #130, 13 August 2015, Rubaya and #177, 18 September 2015, Bukavu. See also Global Witness 2013; United Nations 2016b.

59. Hilson 2016, p. 552.

60. Olivier de Sardan 2008a; Cleaver 2002.

61. Siegel & Veiga 2009; Diemel 2018; Salter & Mthembu-Salter 2017.

62. Scott 2009; Strange 1996; Dobler 2016; Dunn 2010; Roitman 1990; Ellis & MacGaffey 1996; Muhire 2017; Diemel & Cuvelier 2015; Benda-Beckmann 2000 and 1981; Griffiths 1986; Hilson 2011; De Haan & Geenen 2016; Babwine & Ruvunangiza 2016.

63. Mugangu 2008; Muchukiwa 2006.

64. Geenen 2012, p. 324.

65. Ribot 1998; Iguma 2018.

66. Moore 1973; Hoffmann & Kirk 2013; Lund 2016.

67. Radley 2016.

68. This is my own translation of a quote from a declaration of the Civil Society Thematic Group on Mining and Natural Resources.

69. Philipps 2011; Berndt 2013; Callaghy 1984.

70. Interview #177, 18 September 2015, Bukavu.

71. Research conducted by Ben Radley in 2013 found around a dozen combatants in a 50-strong Raia Mutomboki battalion who claimed to have joined the armed group after they lost employment either directly or indirectly dependent on mining.

72. Vlassenroot, Mudinga & Musamba 2020. See also Debos 2016 on the notion of occupation (*métier* in French).

73. Panella & Thomas 2015, p. 6; see also Raeymaekers 2014; Roitman 2005.

74. '*Cracas inafunga kazi kama inafunga ma colis.*' Interview #114, 2 February 2015, Rubaya.

75. '*Ma etiquette iko sawa prison.*' Interview #117, 3 February 2015, Rubaya.

76. Vogel et al. 2021; Stearns & Vogel 2017.

77. International Peace Information Service 2019, pp. 24–31.

78. Verweijen & Iguma 2015.

79. See Cole 2012.

80. Said 1979; De Certeau 1984.

81. Ferguson 2006, p. 8.

82. Li 2007; Tsing 2004.

5. BROKERS AND PATRONS

1. This chapter draws from Vogel & Musamba 2017 and Vogel 2021a.

2. Vigh 2008; Sahlins 1963; Themnér & Utas 2016.

3. Gupta & Ferguson 1997; Mitchell 1991; Abrams 1988.

4. Boissevain 1974, p. 148.

5. Raeymaekers 2014, p. 145.

6. Boissevain 1974, p. 154; Utas 2012; Sahlins 1963.

7. Scott 1972; Sahlins 1963.

8. Boissevain 1974.

9. Bierschenk, Chauveau & Olivier de Sardan 2002, p. 12.

10. This is analogous to 'the double opportunity of Nande businessmen' (Raeymaekers 2014, p. 65).

11. The 'Kinshasa bargain is an agreement between two or more parties that provides a return. ... Anyone in need of either a good or a service, or anyone who needs to resolve a problem, is invariably the "client" of one or more go-betweens' (Tréfon 2004, p. 20).

12. Adams 1970; Raeymaekers 2014; Utas 2012; Sahlins 1963.

13. Massey 1991, p. 27.

14. For a detailed overview of emic terminology and the set-up of local supply chains, see Musamba & Vogel 2016.

15. The two main government agencies in artisanal mining are SAEMAPE and the Centre d'Expertise, d'Evaluation, et Certification (CEEC).

16. Ribot & Peluso 2003, pp. 153–54 and 166.

17. See Sikor & Lund 2009; Hagmann & Péclard 2011; Englebert & Tull 2013.

18. Roitman 1990, p. 693. See also Raeymaekers 2002; Johnson 2013; Geenen 2011; Smith 2011.

19. Cuvelier 2010, p. 66. See also Iguma 2014; Landa 1981.

20. Koselleck & Richter 2006, p. 358.

21. Roitman 2016, p. 19.

22. Koselleck & Richter 2006, p. 372.

23. Koselleck & Richter 2006, p. 388.

24. Mbembe & Roitman 1995, p. 325.

25. Vigh 2008 and 2009.

26. Emirbayer & Mische 1998, p. 970.

27. Roitman 2016, p. 18.

28. Korf, Engeler & Hagmann 2010, p. 386, original emphasis.

29. Olivier de Sardan 2008a, p. 14; Watts 2003; Cramer 2002; Korf 2006; Nathan 2005.

30. Watts 2003; Korf, Engeler & Hagmann 2010, p. 389.

31. Boege et al. 2008, p. 6.

32. Roitman 1990, p. 695.

33. Rubbers 2007, p. 324; Hart 2008; Meagher 2009.

34. Mueller-Koné 2015; Jackson 2002.

35. Raeymaekers, Menkhaus & Vlassenroot 2008, p. 12.
36. Korf, Engeler & Hagmann 2010, p. 390.
37. Previously, artisanal mining existed clandestinely in Zaire, often at the margin of large-scale exploitation of gold and ferrous minerals by state-run corporations like Gécamines or SOMINKI. However, liberalisation motivated more people to seize the opportunities in and around parastatal concessions (Geenen 2011; Jackson 2002; Rubbers 2007; Ndaywel è Nziem 2009).
38. Hart 2008, p. 7.
39. De Villers 2016; Reno 1998.
40. Verweijen 2013, p. 70.
41. Due to famine, these tendencies preceded the wars in certain areas, including Walungu and Lubero; see Jackson 2002, p. 531.
42. United Nations 2001; Raeymaekers 2002; Johnson 2013.
43. Cuvelier, Vlassenroot & Olin 2014; Geenen 2011.
44. Moore 1973, p. 723.
45. Hayes et al. 2010, p. 86; Radley & Vogel 2015; Reimers 2014.
46. Hart 2008, p. 14.
47. Anderson 1983; Hobsbawm & Ranger 1983; Chatterjee 2004; Cramer 2006; Brabant 2016; Stearns 2014.
48. Smith 2011, p. 21; Ekeh 1975 (see below in this chapter for a more detailed discussion).
49. Interview #106, 23 December 2014, Bukavu.
50. Smith 2015, p. 3.
51. Geenen 2011.
52. Based on interview #126, 11 February 2015 (shortened), Goma.
53. 'Négociant anatoka na faranga, anafika mu terrain anapandisha écono-mie. Sa faranga haiko mu terrain ni problème, même manger c'est un dos-sier.' Interview #106, 23 December 2014, Bukavu.
54. Rubbers 2007; Meagher 2009.
55. Geenen 2011, p. 439.
56. Hayes et al. 2010, p. 70.
57. 'Creuseurs bakimufunga miye négociant sitakuwa na kitu. Kama niko na faranga nita bapatiya ile faranga ya deni ili akuwe libéré, kisha atakuya nilipa nyuma.' Interview #106, 23 December 2014, Bukavu.

58. Interview #26, 5 June 2014, Bukavu.

59. Interview #35, 16 July 2014, Lemera.

60. Based on interview #114, 2 February 2015 (shortened), Goma.

61. Stearns 2012b and 2013.

62. Büscher, Cuvelier & Mushobekwa 2014; Sungura et al. 2021.

63. '*Ile shida tuko nayo, ile ni juu ya ma etiquette.*' Interview #117, 3 February 2015, Rubaya.

64. '*Mbele ya ma cracas, batu yote balikuwa bien.*' Interview #51, 24 July 2014, Rubaya.

65. '*Oyebi, eza jeu de cartes omoni mundele.*' Interview #124, 11 February 2015, Goma.

66. Graph based on interviews #124 and #126, 11 February 2015, #127, 12 February 2015, and #199, 5 November 2015, all Goma.

67. '*Sur papier, SAEMAPE est un service d'assistance mais sur terrain il fonctionne comme service de taxation et de renseignement.*' Interview #149, 2 September 2015, Nzibira.

68. 'In Lubimbe II, you pay 2,000 Congolese Franc (CDF), in Kibandamangobo 2,000, in Mayimingi 1,000, in Isezya 1,000, in Nyalubemba 1,000' (controlled by the Raia Mutomboki in 2014; at the time, 925 CDF equalled 1 USD). Interview #106, 23 December 2014, Bukavu.

69. Interview #35, 16 July 2014, Goma.

70. Panella & Thomas 2015, p. 6.

71. '*Inabidii kwake nako kuwake mbabula.*' Interview #125, 11 February 2015, Nyabibwe.

72. Jackson 2002; Pottier 2006.

73. Verweijen 2016; Muchukiwa 2006; Hoffmann 2019; Jackson 2006; Dupriez 1987.

74. Verweijen 2013, p. 76.

75. Raeymaekers 2014, p. 90.

76. United Nations 2015b.

77. Based on interview #106, 23 December 2014 (shortened), Bukavu. Lemera has a history of militarised mineral exploitation (see below).

78. '*D'ailleurs, lorsqu'on renforce les mesures de controle, ça facilite la fraude davantage.*' Interview #125, 11 February 2015, Goma.

79. Jackson 2002.

80. Vlassenroot & Raeymaekers 2004, p. 23.
81. In connection to that, *négociants* have been infamous for investing their gains in extravagant lifestyles. This includes building luxurious houses in Goma and Bukavu, acquiring important stretches of land and cattle (i.e. in Masisi territory), and buying fancy cars and clothes.
82. Interview #6, 27 April 2014, Rubaya.
83. Mkandawire 2015; Wai 2012; Ekeh 1975.
84. Eisenstadt & Roniger 1980; Scott 1972; Lemarchand 1972; Chabal & Daloz 1999; Bayart 2000; Platteau 2004; De Waal 2009; Utas 2012.
85. Stearns, Verweijen & Eriksson Baaz 2013, p. 34.
86. Verweijen & van Bockhaven 2020; Hoffmann, Vlassenroot & Mudinga 2020.
87. Mbembe 2001.
88. Ekeh 1975.
89. Ekeh 1975, p. 107. See also Mkandawire 2015; Wai 2012.
90. Bayart 2000, p. 244.
91. Lemarchand 1972, p. 68.
92. Wolfe & Müller 2018, p. 3. See also Mkandawire 2015; Wai 2012.
93. Lemarchand 1972, p. 69.
94. Verweijen 2018, p. 631.
95. Eisenstadt & Roniger 1980, p. 50.
96. Kitschelt & Wilkinson 2007, p. 19.
97. Wolfe & Müller 2018, p. 7.
98. Bayart 2000, p. 267. See also Chabal & Daloz 1999; Bayart 2006.
99. Uberti 2016, p. 328; Kitschelt & Wilkinson 2007, p. 57.
100. MacKay 2006, p. 76.
101. Korf et al. 2018, p. 168. See also Lund 2006; Bierschenk & Olivier de Sardan 2014; Roitman 2005; Hagmann & Péclard 2011.
102. Hart 2008; Rubbers 2007.
103. De Waal 2009, p. 103.
104. Jessop, Brenner & Jones 2008; Bayart 2000; Deleuze & Guattari 1987.
105. Platteau, Somville & Wahhaj 2014, p. 227.
106. Actor-network theory (ANT) suggests 'to think in terms of nodes that have as many dimensions as they have connections' (Latour 1996, p. 4; see Lewis & Mosse 2006, pp. 14–16 for the potential of juxta-

posing ANT and anthropology). In this sense, in a rhizome, the 'engineering of pragmatic identity is the very heart of network production [and] networks are nested one within another' (Lee & Brown 1994, p. 784).

107. Inspired by Jessop, Brenner & Jones 2008.

108. Callon 1984, p. 204.

109. Jessop, Brenner & Jones 2008, p. 390; Allen 2009.

110. Hence, the network trumps physical spaces, both in state and non-state authority structures. See Latour 1996; MacKay 2006.

111. Lee & Brown 1994, p. 784.

112. De Waal 2009, p. 105; see also Granovetter 1985, p. 495.

113. Lund 2006a, p. 676; Vogel 2018.

114. Cartier-Bresson 1997, p. 469; Stys et al. 2020.

115. Granovetter 1985, p. 490.

116. Themnér & Utas 2016, p. 256; Tull & Mehler 2005.

117. Eriksson Baaz & Verweijen 2013.

118. Eisenstadt & Roniger 1980, p. 76.

119. Jackson 2007, p. 483; Dunn 2009; Bucyalimwe 1997.

120. Vogel & Raeymaekers 2016.

121. Based on interview #198, 4 November 2015; interview #200, 5 November 2015; interview #201, 5 November 2015, all Goma.

122. There was also army involvement, with escorts to facilitate nocturnal lake and border crossings. See United Nations 2015b.

123. See interview #184, 23 September 2015, Rubaya; interview #187, 24 September 2015, Rubaya; interview #105, 27 August 2014, Goma.

124. See interview #197, 2 November 2015, Goma.

125. Muchukiwa 2006. For instance, the 2014 Mutarule massacre illustrated how manipulations echo locally, with civilian populations on the losing end. The ethnically bifurcated village (a Bafuliiro and a Banyamulenge neighbourhood) in the Ruzizi Plain exemplifies how violence emerges from tit-for-tat logics, including cattle raids, especially since the death of *mwami* Ndabagoye. See Verweijen 2016.

126. The son's networks involved pro-government politicians, the Lemera *groupement* chief and Molière's militia. The half-brother garnered support from others, including opposition politicians, the Luvungi *groupement* chief and Mai-Mai.

127. Verweijen 2016, p. 37.

128. See interview #26, 5 June 2014, Lemera.

129. See interviews #89, 18 August 2014, Lemera, #168, 11 September 2015, Lemera. Meanwhile, the joint venture has begun paying the miners' registration fees with the state while the latter need to pay a tax for water to be supplied to the joint venture.

130. Muchukiwa 2006; Dupriez 1987; Bahati Bahalaokwibuye 2016.

131. The *kalinzi* lease system has a common history with customary land management in Rwanda, where it is called *karinzi* or *cikingi*. A Shi order also provides for rental agreements, which are referred to as *bugule*. I thank Loochi Muzaliwa for deep insights into this complex issue.

132. See interview #167, 11 September 2015, Bukavu.

133. Olivier de Sardan 2008a, p. 7.

134. Concession 5886 is a former SAKIMA property with 120 plots (*carrés*) (including Mushangi, Zola Zola, D23, Mahamba, Nyamugengula, Chembeke, Nzibira, Kihande, Katchuba, Chaminyago and Muhinga). The concession involving Chaminyago used to be held by Congo Eco Project, which used to cooperate with COMIDEA. However, the permit has expired, raising the chance to claim an artisanal exploitation zone.

135. Interview #163 & #165, 10 September 2015; interview #167, 11 September 2015; interview #171, 12 September 2015, all Bukavu. See also Bulongo 2016.

136. See interview #45, 18 July 2014, Bukavu; interview #82, 15 August 2014, Bukavu. This also speaks to Hoffmann, Vlassenroot & Mudinga 2020; Verweijen & van Bockhaven 2020.

137. Another cooperative-like entity is Générale des coopératives du Sud-Kivu, led by a pastor and cooperative leader. Representing cooperatives on paper, it is a tool of its powerful members, i.e. cooperative presidents. See de Haan & Geenen 2016, p. 827.

138. Similar observations can be made elsewhere (e.g. in Nyabibwe), where customary interests underpin rivalry between two cooperatives. While conflicts had been settled, tensions continued between and within the cooperatives. This is illustrated in the interference of leaders vying for

power within 'their' cooperative, such as in 2014 when the *mwami* of Buhavu tried to seize the presidency in 'his' cooperative.

139. Polanyi 2001; Ekeh 1975.
140. Cartier-Bresson 1997, p. 475.
141. Labonte 2011, p. 109.
142. Vlassenroot & Raeymaekers 2004a.
143. Bulongo 2016; Babwine & Ruvunangiza 2016; Iguma 2018; Musamba & Vogel 2016.
144. Greenhouse, Mertz & Warren 2002, p. 19.
145. Interview #85, 16 August 2014, Bukavu.
146. Granovetter 1985, p. 491. See also Granovetter 1973; Foucault 2004; Hansen & Stepp[u]tat 2006.
147. See also Blok 1974.

6. CONFLICTED CERTIFICATION

1. This chapter draws from Vogel 2018.
2. Lund 2006; Ribot & Peluso 2003; Moore 1973.
3. Allen 2009, p. 201.
4. Research in spaces of volatility, insecurity and 'informality' carries a number of caveats, making it difficult to generate conclusive answers (Ellis & MacGaffey 1996; Hann & Hart 2011; Raeymaekers 2014). It is therefore important to pay attention to spatial variation, comparing 'clean' and 'conflicted' mines through multisited ethnography, 'follow the thing' (Cook et al. 2004) exercises, and other methods.
5. Allen 2009, p. 201.
6. See Weber 1980. One might want to ask whether any state at any time in any policy field meets this scenario. The answer is probably no.
7. Tilly 1985.
8. Meagher, de Herdt & Titeca 2014; Hagmann & Péclard 2011.
9. See Smith 2011; Le Billon 2001. It is important to consider that the postcolonial Mobutist state and colonial rule were instrumental in cultivating a fertile soil out of which wars would shake eastern Congo, and which provided for key dynamics in mining governance (Jackson 2002).
10. Prunier 1995 and 2009; Lemarchand 2009; Stearns 2010 and 2012a; Vlassenroot & Raeymaekers 2004a; Vlassenroot 2013.

11. Radley & Vogel 2015; Jackson 2002.

12. Based on data by the International Peace Information Service (mines) and the 2020 mapping of armed groups by the author in collaboration with Kivu Security Tracker.

13. International Peace Information Service 2019; Kivu Security Tracker 2019.

14. Organisation for Economic Cooperation and Development 2015, p. 9.

15. South Kivu's provincial authorities inventoried over 900 mines alone. For North Kivu, estimations range between 500 and 1,000.

16. Nathan 2005; Cramer 2002; Keen 2012. In eastern Congo, these are minerals, charcoal, marijuana, timber, salt, soap, fuel, cocoa, coffee, etc. Most of these resources are ambivalent inasmuch as they are as important for local livelihoods and survival as conflict financing.

17. Vogel & Raeymaekers 2016; Garrett, Sergiou & Vlassenroot 2009; Nest 2011; United Nations 2001.

18. Cuvelier 2010; Hazen 2013. While some actors established tight militarised control over strategic mines, others were not able to do so. Their intermittent grasp of mines and trade routes heightened uncertainty, but also provided leverage. This resulted, amongst other things, in a higher price level and sometimes significant bargaining power for intermediary traders, up to the point where they could blackmail militiamen or the army, similar to Butembo's famous 'G8' and its ambiguous relation to Mbusa Nyamwisi's RCD-K/ML (Raeymaekers 2014).

19. Stearns & Vogel 2015; Vlassenroot & Raeymaekers 2009. I borrow the doll metaphor from exchanges with Stearns and Verweijen.

20. Cuvelier, Vlassenroot & Olin 2014; Vogel & Stearns 2018.

21. Lund 2006, p. 676.

22. Fortes & Evans-Pritchard 1950; Weber 1980; Gupta 1995; Taussig 1997; Migdal 1988; Aretxaga 2003; Das & Poole 2004.

23. Abrams 1988. These are manifold: uniforms, stamps, forms, documents, invented or real traditions, etc.

24. Even though I am interested in a spatially bounded case study—namely eastern Congo—the interactions it investigates span beyond it.

25. Mitchell 1991; Taussig 1997; Aretxaga 2003.

26. Allen 2009, p. 201.

27. Lund 2016, p. 1,200.
28. Allen 2009, p. 208, own emphasis.
29. Allen 2011; Olivier de Sardan 2008a; Hart 2008; Roitman 2005; Moore 1973; Hansen & Stepputat 2005.
30. Boege et al. 2008; Raeymaekers, Menkhaus & Vlassenroot 2008; Hagmann & Péclard 2011; Lund 2014a and 2014b.
31. Lund 2006, p. 686, own emphasis.
32. Ribot & Peluso 2003, p. 153, own emphasis.
33. Lund 2016, p. 1,204.
34. See Boone 2014; Vlassenroot & Raeymaekers 2004b. In Congo's 2002 mining code, concessions are primary over land titles. Whoever acquires a concession is entitled to dispossess, under condition of granting indemnity to landowners. A concession is thus hybrid: it combines traits of property and access. In practice, this is often problematic. First, it is often the case that a *concessionaire* is not a landowner; this results in shared authority within the same bounded space and a legitimacy dilemma between concession and land titles. In addition, land ownership is contested due to competing claims emanating from a duality of state-issued and customary titles or as a consequence of armed conflict and displacement.
35. Ribot & Peluso 2003, p. 154, original emphasis; Sikor & Lund 2009.
36. Strazzari & Kamphuis 2012; Roitman 1990; Moore 1973.
37. Interview #152, 3 September 2015, Lemera. 'Conflict-free' sourcing exists in eastern Congo, Rwanda and Burundi, including iTSCi.
38. Duffield 2001, p. 163.
39. 'Who will buy your minerals, if you do not pass via Jesus Christ [aka iTSCi]?' Interview #172, 12 September 2015, Rubaya.
40. Sikor & Lund 2009; Ribot & Peluso 2003, p. 163.
41. Cuvelier 2010, p. 72.
42. *Système D* refers to *se débrouiller*, 'muddling through' a socio-economically challenging environment by informal, sometimes illegal, means. It has become a widespread and (in)famous social phenomenon in Congo (Raeymaekers 2014, p. 111).
43. Cleaver 2002, p. 17.
44. Moore 1973, p. 723.

45. Allen 2009, p. 207. For instance, SAEMAPE staff 'invent' new taxes under iTSCi. Another illustration of this is an anti-fraud unit led by a former rebel politician that improvises new forms of taxation, threatens traders and arbitrarily seizes minerals.

46. Own field notes, 13 September 2015, Rubaya.

47. Cleaver 2002, p. 28.

48. There is a deliberate attempt to do so on the ground: 'iTSCi is an NGO that helps [sic]' (Interview #67, 8 August 2014, Numbi).

49. Interview #149, 2 September 2015, Lemera.

50. Several interlocutors described SAEMAPE—as an institution—'rather as a victim than an accomplice' of this situation.

51. Recently, this has led to criticism not only from Congolese but also Rwandan mining authorities.

52. In 2014, tin prices at the London Metal Exchange plummeted, but analysing local prices suggests even harsher price falls.

53. The Malaysia Smelting Corporation is one of the largest tin smelters worldwide. Despite the possibility of a *non-compromis d'achat*, room for manoeuvre is narrow as transactions must be pre-declared.

54. Philipps 2011.

55. Peluso & Lund 2011, p. 674.

56. The idea of a crumbling Congolese state taken hostage by iTSCi cuts across dozens of interviews, e.g. interview #66, 8 August 2014, Lemera.

57. For additional examples of violence and fraud not sanctioned, or openly abetted, by iTSCi, see Bulongo 2016.

58. Interview #88, 18 August 2014, Lemera. Not suspending operations, iTSCi abetted payments by its members to customary authorities and a local militia, members of which held positions in the mining administration and a cooperative. While numbers vary depending on sources, the commander roughly received 250 USD monthly and the militia-seconded interim head of the mining bureau 50 USD. iTSCi denied this.

59. See also Verweijen 2016 for a similar account.

60. Interview #89, 18 August 2014, Lemera. The militia in question has one commander responsible for 'mineshaft security'.

61. This also relates to the posture of iTSCi agents' 'filling in of docu-

ments and paper sheets', as one of their staff told me under condition of anonymity.

62. Interview #134, 18 August 2015, Nzibira. Customary, military and political leaders also claim influence in cooperatives and committees.

63. This affects academia too: via email, iTSCi asks scholars to register and provide details when visiting 'our sites [sic]', although iTSCi does not own concessions. This violates Congo's 2006 constitution (article 9) and specific laws on land and concessions.

64. While 'ministry' refers to the political branch, the 'division' is the ministry's technical branch.

65. Matthysen & Zaragoza 2013.

66. Interview #104, 26 August 2014, Isezya.

67. Vlassenroot, Mudinga & Hoffmann 2016; Verweijen 2013; Mampilly 2011.

68. Stearns et al. 2013a.

69. Hoffmann & Vlassenroot 2014.

70. Hoffmann, Vlassenroot & Marchais 2016; Hoffmann 2015; Hoffmann & Vlassenroot 2014.

71. These cards serve for identification, control of the professional categories, and a taxation technique.

72. Sisawa (killed in late 2014) and Maheshe (who surrendered) were attacked by other factions for 'over-taxing' civilian populations.

73. Hoffmann & Verweijen 2013.

74. Hoffmann & Vlassenroot 2014; Vogel 2014.

75. Congo Research Group 2021.

7. PEACE, ETHICS AND CONGO

1. See Cole 2012.

2. See Al Jazeera 2016.

3. See statistics at www.kivusecurity.org and the UN's human rights reporting in MONUSCO 2021.

4. See for instance Vogel 2021b.

5. Dunn 2003, p. 136.

6. Vogel & Stearns 2018.

7. Autesserre 2012.

8. For a critical discussion on celebrity humanitarianism in Congo and beyond, see Budabin & Richey 2021.

9. Vogel, Musamba & Radley 2018.

10. International Peace Information Service 2020.

11. See Stoinski 2017; Marijnen 2018; Marijnen & Verweijen 2018.

12. Meagher, de Herdt & Titeca 2014, p. 6. See also Titeca & de Herdt 2011; Raeymaekers 2013.

13. Schouten 2016, p. 15. See also Painter 2010; Mezzadra & Neilson 2013.

14. Strazzari & Kamphuis 2012, p. 69.

15. Ferguson 2006, p. 208.

16. Verweijen & van Meeteren 2015, p. 102.

17. Moore 1973.

18. Hansen & Stepputat 2006, p. 309.

19. Meagher, de Herdt & Titeca 2014, p. 3.

20. Ribot & Peluso 2003, p. 168.

21. Tsing 2004, p. 151; Peck & Theodore 2010, p. 171.

22. Schouten 2016, p. 16.

23. See De Waal 2015; Budabin & Richey 2021.

24. Themnér & Utas 2016, p. 256.

25. In the different context of the Western academy, but with examples relating to 'conflict minerals', I offer an embryonic proposition on how this could work in Vogel 2021b.

EPILOGUE

1. Haraway 1988; Thiong'o 1987.

2. Derrida 1967; Kuhn 1962; Feyerabend 1975.

3. Clifford & Marcus 1986, p. 6.

4. Mkandawire 2015, p. 602.

5. Keen 2012, p. 766.

BIBLIOGRAPHY

Abraham, Itty & van Schendel, Willem (2005), *Illicit Flows and Criminal Things: States, Borders, and the Other Side of Globalization*, Bloomington, IN: Indiana University Press.

Abrams, Philip (1988), 'Notes on the difficulty of studying the state (1977)', *Journal of Historical Sociology*, 1(1): 58–89.

Achebe, Chinua (1977), 'An image of Africa: Racism in Conrad's "Heart of Darkness"', *Massachusetts Review*, 18: 251–61.

Adams, Richard (1970), 'Brokers and career mobility systems in the structure of complex societies', *Southwestern Journal of Anthropology*, 26(4): 315–27.

Agnew, John (1994), 'The territorial trap: The geographical assumptions of international relations theory', *Review of International Political Economy*, 1(1): 53–80.

Al Jazeera (2016), 'Conflicted: The fight over Congo's minerals', *Al Jazeera*, 3 March. Available at: https://www.aljazeera.com/program/fault-lines/2016/3/3/conflicted-the-fight-over-congos-minerals/.

Allen, John (2011), 'Topological twists: Power's shifting geographies', *Dialogues in Human Geography*, 1(3): 283–98.

——— (2009), 'Three spaces of power: Territory, networks, plus a topological twist in the tale of domination and authority', *Journal of Power*, 2(2): 197–212.

Anderson, Benedict (1983), *Imagined Communities: Reflections on the Origin and Spread of Nationalism*, London: Verso.

BIBLIOGRAPHY

Arendt, Hannah (1963), *Eichmann in Jerusalem: A Report on the Banality of Evil*, London: Viking Press.

Aretxaga, Begoña (2003), 'Maddening states', *Annual Review of Anthropology*, 32: 393–4.

Autesserre, Séverine (2012), 'Dangerous tales: Dominant narratives on the Congo and their unintended consequences', *African Affairs*, 111(443): 1–21.

Babwine, Marline & Ruvunangiza, Philippe (2016), *Exploitants artisanaux & coopératives minières au Kivu. Enjeux et défis sur le chemin de formalisation* (Suluhu Working Paper no. 1). Available at: http://www.suluhu. org.

Bafilemba, Fidel, Mueller, Timo & Lezhnev, Sasha (2014), *The Impact of Dodd-Frank and Conflict Minerals Reforms on Eastern Congo's Conflict*, Washington, DC: Enough Project.

Bahati Bahalaokwibuye, Christian (2016), 'Le dilemme des coopératives minières de Walungu, entre ASBL et entreprise sociale', *Conjonctures Congolaises*, 2015: 299–325.

Ballentine, Karen & Sherman, Jake (2003), *The Political Economy of Armed Conflict: Beyond Greed and Grievance*, Boulder, CO: Lynne Rienner.

Barnes, Trevor (2008), 'Making space for the economy: Live performances, dead objects, and economic geography', *Geography Compass*, 2(5): 1,432–48.

Barnett, Clive, Cloke, Paul, Clarke, Nick and Malpass, Alice (2005), 'Consuming ethics: Articulating subjects and spaces of ethical consumption', *Antipode*, 37(1): 23–45.

Bashwira Nyenyezi, Marie-Rose (2017), 'Navigating obstacles, opportunities and reforms: Women's lives and livelihoods in artisanal mining communities in eastern DRC', PhD thesis, Wageningen University, Wageningen, the Netherlands.

Bayart, Jean-François (2006), *L'État en Afrique. La politique du ventre*, Paris: Fayard.

——— (2000), 'Africa in the world: A history of extraversion', *African Affairs*, 99(395): 217–67.

Benda-Beckmann, Franz von (2000), 'Legal pluralism and social justice in economic and political development', Proceedings of the IDS

BIBLIOGRAPHY

International Workshop on Rule of Law and Development, 1–3 June, Sussex.

Benda-Beckmann, Keebet von (1981), 'Forum shopping and shopping forums: Dispute settlement in a Minangkabau village in West Sumatra, Indonesia', *Journal of Legal Pluralism*, 19: 117–59.

Benton, Adia (2016), 'African expatriates and race in the anthropology of humanitarianism', *Critical African Studies*, 8(3): 266–77.

Berdal, Mats & Malone, David (2000), *Greed and Grievance: Economic Agendas in Civil Wars*, Boulder, CO: Lynne Rienner.

Bernazzoli, Richelle M. & Flint, Colin (2009), 'Power, place, and militarism: Toward a comparative geographic analysis of militarization', *Geography Compass*, 3(1): 393–411.

Berndt, Christian (2013), 'Assembling market b/orders: Violence, dispossession, and economic development in Ciudad Juárez, Mexico', *Environment and Planning A*, 45: 2,646–62.

Bex, Sean & Craps, Stef (2016), 'Humanitarianism, testimony and the white savior industrial complex: What is the what versus Kony 2012', *Cultural Critique*, 92: 32–56.

Bhabha, Homi (1994), *The Location of Culture*, London: Routledge.

Bierschenk, Thomas, Chauveau, Jean-Pierre & Olivier de Sardan, Jean-Pierre (2002), *Local Development Brokers in Africa: The Rise of a New Social Category*, Mainz: Johannes-Gutenberg University.

Bierschenk, Thomas & Olivier de Sardan, Jean-Pierre (eds) (2014), *States at Work: Dynamics of African Bureaucracies*, Leiden: Brill.

Blok, Anton (1974), *The Mafia of a Sicilian Village, 1860–1960: A Study of Violent Peasant Entrepreneurs*, London: Harper & Row.

Blomley, Nicholas (2008), 'Law, property, and the geography of violence: The frontier, the survey, and the grid', *Annals of the Association of American Geographers*, 93(1): 121–41.

Bøås, Morten & Dunn, Kevin (2014), 'Peeling the onion: Autochthony in North Kivu', *Peacebuilding*, 2(2): 141–56.

Boege Volker, et al. (2008), *On Hybrid Political Orders and Emerging States: State Formation in the Context of 'Fragility'*, Berlin: Berghof.

Boissevain, Jeremy (1974), *Friends of Friends: Networks, Manipulators and Coalitions*, Oxford: Basil Blackwell.

BIBLIOGRAPHY

Boone, Catherine (2014), *Property and Political Order in Africa: Land Rights and the Structure of Politics*, Cambridge: Cambridge University Press.

Borgatti, Stephen P. & Lopez-Kidwell, Virginie (2014), 'Network theory', in Scott & Carrington (eds), *SAGE Handbook of Social Network Analysis*, London: Sage, pp. 40–55.

Bourdieu, Pierre & Wacquant, Loic (1992), *An Invitation to Reflexive Sociology*, Cambridge: Polity Press.

Brabant, Justine (2016), *'Qu'on nous laisse combattre, et la guerre finira.' Avec les combattants du Kivu*, Paris: La Découverte.

Bucyalimwe Mararo, Stanislas (1997), 'Land, power, and ethnic conflict in Masisi (Congo-Kinshasa), 1940s–1994', *International Journal of African Historical Studies*, 30(3): 503–38.

Budabin, Alexandra Cosima & Richey, Lisa Ann (2021), *Batman Saves the Congo: How Celebrities Disrupt the Politics of Development*, Minneapolis, MN: University of Minnesota Press.

Büscher, Karen, Cuvelier, Jeroen & Mushobekwa, Franck (2014), 'La dimension politique de "l'urbanisation minière" dans un context fragile de conflit armé', *L'Afrique des Grands Lacs: Annuaire*, 2013–2014: 243–68.

Bulongo, Safanto (2016), *Evaluation de l'implementation du système de traçabilité dans la Province du Sud-Kivu*, Bukavu: Max Impact.

Burawoy, Michael (1998), 'The extended case method', *Sociological Theory*, 16(1): 4–33.

Calain, Philippe (2012), 'What is the relationship of medical humanitarian organisations with mining and other extractive industries?', *PLOS Medicine*, 9(8): 1–4.

Callaghy, Thomas (1984), *The State-Society Struggle: Zaire in Comparative Perspective*, New York: Columbia University Press.

Callaghy, Thomas, Kassimir, Ronald & Latham, Robert (eds) (2001), *Intervention and Transnationalism in Africa: Global–Local Networks of Power*, Cambridge: Cambridge University Press.

Callon, Michel (1984), 'Some elements of a sociology of translation: Domestication of the scallops and the fishermen of St Brieuc Bay', *Sociological Review*, 32(S1): 196–233.

BIBLIOGRAPHY

Campbell, Susanna (2017), 'Ethics of research in conflict environments', *Journal of Global Security Studies*, 2(1): 89–101.

Cartier-Bresson, Henri (1997), 'Corruption networks, transaction security and illegal social exchange', *Political Studies*, XLV: 463–76.

Césaire, Aimé (1972), *Discourse on Colonialism*, New York: Monthly Review Press.

Chabal, Patrick & Daloz, Jean-Pascal (1999), *Africa Works: Disorder as Political Instrument*, London: James Currey.

Chase, Seth (2019), 'We will win peace', YouTube, 13 February. Available at: https://www.youtube.com/watch?v=RFhb_1tzpgE.

Chatterjee, Partha (2004), *The Politics of the Governed: Reflections on Popular Politics in Most of the World*, New York: Columbia University Press.

Chrétien, Jean-Pierre (2006), *The Great Lakes of Africa: Two Thousand Years of History*, New York: Zone.

Cleaver, Frances (2002), 'Reinventing institutions: Bricolage and the social embeddedness of natural resource management', *European Journal of Development Research*, 14(2): 11–30.

Clifford, James & Marcus, George E. (1986), *Writing Culture: The Poetics and Politics of Ethnography*, Berkeley, CA: University of California Press.

Cole, Teju (2012), 'The white savior complex', *The Atlantic*, 21 March. Available at: https://www.theatlantic.com/international/archive/2012/03/the-white-savior-industrial-complex/254843/.

Colle, Pierre (1971), *Essai de monographie des Bashi*, Bukavu: Centre d'étude de langues africaines.

Collier, Paul (2000), *Economic Causes of Civil Conflict and their Implications for Policy*, Washington, DC: World Bank.

Collier, Paul & Hoeffler, Anke (2002), *Greed and Grievance in Civil War* (World Bank Policy Research Working Paper no. 2,355), Washington, DC: World Bank.

Collier, Paul & Hoeffler, Anke (1998), *On Economic Causes of Civil War*, Oxford: Oxford University Press.

Congo Research Group (2021), *Rebels, Doctors and Merchants of Violence: How the Fight Against Ebola Became Part of the Conflict in Eastern DRC*, New York: New York University.

——— (2020a), *For the Army, With the Army, Like the Army? The Rise of Guidon Shimiray and the NDC–Rénové in the Eastern Congo*, New York: New York University.

——— (2020b), *Ebola in the DRC: The Perverse Effects of a Parallel Health System*, New York: New York University.

——— (2017), *Mass Killings in Beni Territory: Political Violence, Cover Ups and Cooptation*, New York: New York University.

——— (2016), *Qui sont les tueurs de Beni?*, New York: New York University.

Cook, Ian, et al. (2004), 'Follow the thing: Papaya', *Antipode*, 36(4): 642–64.

Cramer, Christopher (2006), *Civil War is Not a Stupid Thing: Accounting for Violence in Developing Countries*, London: Hurst.

——— (2002), 'Homo economicus goes to war: Methodological individualism, rational choice and the political economy of war', *World Development*, 30(11): 1,845–64.

Cramer, Christopher, Hammond, Laura & Pottier, Jóhan (2011), *Researching Violence in Africa: Ethical and Methodological Challenges*, Leiden: Brill.

Cramer, Christopher, et al. (2016), 'Mistakes, crises, and research independence: The perils of fieldwork as a form of evidence', *African Affairs*, 115(458): 145–60.

Crenshaw, Kimberlé (1991), 'Mapping the margins: Intersectionality, identity politics and violence against women of colour', *Stanford Law Review*, 43(6): 1,241–99.

Cronin-Furman, Kate & Lake, Milli (2018), 'Ethics abroad: Fieldwork in fragile and violent contexts', *PS: Political Science and Politics*, 51(3): 607–14.

Cuvelier, Jeroen (2010), *The Complexity of Resource Governance in a Context of State Fragility: The Case of Eastern DRC*, Antwerp: International Peace Information Service.

Cuvelier, Jeroen, Pöyhönen, Päivi & Areskog Bjurling, Kristina (2010), *Voices from the Inside: Local Voices on Mining Reform in Eastern Congo*, Helsinki: Finnwatch.

Cuvelier, Jeroen & Raeymaekers, Timothy (2002), *European Companies and the Coltan Trade: Supporting the War Economy in the DRC*, Antwerp: International Peace Information Service.

Cuvelier, Jeroen, van Bockstael, Steven, Vlassenroot, Koen & Iguma, Claude (2014), *Analysing the Impact of the Dodd-Frank Act on Congolese Livelihoods*, New York: Social Science Research Council.

Cuvelier, Jeroen, Vlassenroot, Koen & Olin, Nathaniel (2014), 'Resources, conflict and governance: A critical review', *Extractive Industries and Society*, 1(2): 340–50.

Das, Veena & Poole, Deborah (eds) (2004), *Anthropology in the Margins of the State*, Santa Fe, NM: SAR Press.

De Boeck, Filip (1998), 'Domesticating diamonds and dollars: Identity, expenditure and sharing in southwestern Zaire (1984–1997)', *Development & Change*, 29: 777–810.

Debos, Marielle (2016), *Living by the Gun in Chad: Combatants, Impunity and State Formation*, London: Zed Books.

De Certeau, Michel (1984), *The Practice of Everyday Life*, Berkeley, CA: University of California Press.

De Failly, Didier (2001), 'Coltan, pour comprendre', *L'Afrique des Grands Lacs: Annuaire*, 2001: 279–306.

De Haan, Jorden & Geenen, Sara (2016), 'Mining cooperatives in Eastern DRC. The interplay between historical power relations and formal institutions', *Extractive Industries and Society*, 3(3): 823–31.

De Koning, Ruben (2011), *Conflict Minerals in the Democratic Republic of the Congo: Aligning Trade and Security Interventions* (Policy Paper 27), Stockholm: SIPRI.

Deleuze, Gilles & Guattari, Felix (1987), *A Thousand Plateaus: Capitalism and Schizophrenia*, London: Minnesota University Press.

Derrida, Jacques (1967), *De la grammatologie*, Paris: Editions de Minuit.

De Soto, Hernando (2000), *The Mystery of Capital: Why Capitalism Triumphs in the West and Fails Everywhere Else*, London: Black Swan.

De Sousa Santos, Boaventura (2007), *Another Knowledge is Possible: Beyond Northern Epistemologies*, London: Verso.

De Villers, Gauthier (2016), *Histoire du politique au Congo-Kinshasa: Les concepts à l'épreuve*, Louvain-la-Neuve: L'Harmattan.

De Waal, Alex (2015), *Advocacy in Conflict: Critical Perspectives on Transnational Activism*, London: Zed Books.

———— (2009), 'Mission without end? Peacekeeping in the African political marketplace', *International Affairs*, 85(1): 99–113.

Diemel, Jose (2018), 'Authority and access to the cassiterite and coltan trade in Bukama Territory (DRC)', *Extractive Industries and Society*, 5(1): 56–65.

Diemel, Jose & Cuvelier, Jeroen (2015), 'Explaining the uneven distribution of conflict mineral policy implementation in the Democratic Republic of the Congo: The role of the Katanga policy network', *Resources Policy*, 46: 151–60.

Dobler, Gregor (2016), 'The green, the grey and the blue: A typology of cross-border trade in Africa', *Journal of Modern African Studies*, 54(1): 145–69.

Doty, Roxanne Lyne (1996), *Imperial Encounters: The Politics of Representation in North-South Relations*, Minneapolis, MN: University of Minnesota Press.

Duffield, Mark (2001), *Global Governance and the New Wars: The Merging of Development and Security*, London: Zed Books.

Dunn, Kevin C. (2010), 'There is no such thing as the state: Discourse, effect and performativity', *Forum for Development Studies*, 37(1): 79–92.

———— (2009), '"Sons of the soil" and contemporary state making: Autochthony, uncertainty and political violence in Africa', *Third World Quarterly*, 30(1): 113–27.

———— (2003), *Imaging the Congo: The International Relations of Identity*, New York: Palgrave.

Dupriez, Hugues (1987), *Bushi, l'asphyxie d'un peuple*, Bukavu: ADI-Kivu.

Eisenstadt, S. N. & Roniger, Louis (1980), 'Patron–client relations as a model of structuring social exchange', *Comparative Studies in Society and History*, 22(1): 42–77.

Ekeh, Peter P. (1975), 'Colonialism and the two publics: A theoretical statement', *Comparative Studies in Society and History*, 17(1): 91–112.

Ellis, Stephen & MacGaffey, Janet (1996), 'Research on sub-Saharan Africa's unrecorded international trade: Some methodological and conceptual problems', *African Studies Review*, 39(2): 19–41.

Emirbayer, Mustafa & Mische, Ann (1998), 'What is agency?' *American Journal of Sociology*, 103(4): 962–1,023.

BIBLIOGRAPHY

Englebert, Pierre & Tull, Denis (2013), 'Contestation, negotiation et résistance: L'État Congolais au quotidien', *Politique Africaine*, 129: 5–22.

Enough Project (2011), 'Robin Wright in Congo', YouTube, 5 October. Available at: https://www.youtube.com/watch?v=k4o2lElFzM0.

———— (2009), 'Nicole Richie & John Prendergast—Congo's conflict minerals', YouTube, 20 May. Available at: https://www.youtube.com/watch?v=1alnuvr9bhM.

Eriksson Baaz, Maria & Stern, Maria (2013), *Sexual Violence as a Weapon of War? Perceptions, Prescriptions, Problems in the Congo and Beyond*, London: Zed Books.

Eriksson Baaz, Maria & Verweijen, Judith (2013), 'The volatility of a half-cooked bouillabaisse: Rebel-military integration and conflict dynamics in eastern DRC', *African Affairs*, 112(449): 563–82.

European Union (2017), 'Regulation (EU) 2017/821 of the European Parliament and of the Council of 17 May 2017 laying down supply chain due diligence obligations for Union importers of tin, tantalum and tungsten, their ores, and gold originating from conflict-affected and high-risk areas', Strasbourg: European Union. Available at: http://eur-lex.europa.eu/legal-content/EN/TXT/PDF/?uri=CELEX:32017R0821&from=EN.

Fairhead, James (1992), 'Paths of authority: Roads, the state and the market in Eastern Zaire', *European Journal of Development Research*, 4(2): 17–35.

Fanon, Frantz (1970), *Black Skin, White Masks*, New York: Grove.

Federal Office of Justice (Switzerland) (2021a), 'Volksinitiative "Für verantwortungsvolle Unternehmen"', Bern: Swiss Federal Office of Justice.

———— (2021b), 'Volksinitiative "Für verantwortungsvolle Unternehmen—zum Schutz von Mensch und Umwelt"', Bern: Swiss Federal Office of Justice.

Ferguson, James (2006), *Global Shadows: Africa in the Neoliberal World Order*, Durham, NC: Duke University Press.

———— (1990), *The Antipolitics Machine: Development, Depoliticization and Bureaucratic Power in Lesotho*, Cambridge: Cambridge University Press.

Ferguson, James & Gupta, Akhil (2002), 'Spatializing states: Toward an ethnography of neoliberal governmentality', *American Ethnologist*, 29(4): 981–1,002.

BIBLIOGRAPHY

Feyerabend, Paul (1975), *Against Method*, New York: New Left Books.

Fortes, Meyer & Evans-Pritchard, E. E. (1950), *African Political Systems*, Oxford: Oxford University Press.

Foucault, Michel (2004), *Sécurité, territoire, population*, Paris: Gallimard.

French, Howard W. (2021), *Born in Blackness: Africa, Africans, and the Making of the Modern World, 1471 to the Second World War*, New York: Liveright.

Galtung, Johan (1969), 'Violence, peace, and peace research', *Journal of Peace Research*, 6(3): 167–91.

Garrett Nicholas, Sergiou, Sylvia & Vlassenroot, Koen (2009), 'Negotiated peace for extortion: The case of Walikale territory in eastern DR Congo', *Journal of Eastern African Studies*, 3(1): 1–21.

Geenen, Sara (2012), 'A dangerous bet: The challenges of formalizing artisanal mining in the Democratic Republic of Congo', *Resources Policy*, 37(3): 322–30.

——— (2011), 'Relations and regulations in local gold trade networks in South Kivu, Democratic Republic of Congo', *Journal of Eastern African Studies*, 5(3): 427–46.

Geenen, Sara & Radley, Ben (2014), 'In the face of reform: What future for ASM in the eastern DRC?', *Futures*, 62: 58–66.

Geertz, Clifford (1973), *Thick Description: Toward an Interpretive Theory of Culture*, New York: Basic Books.

Gledhill, John (2009), 'Power in political anthropology', *Journal of Power*, 2(1): 9–34.

——— (2000a), 'Finding a new public face for anthropology', *Anthropology Today*, 16(6): 1–3.

——— (2000b), *Power and Its Disguises: Anthropological Perspectives on Politics*, London: Pluto Press.

Global Witness (2013), *Putting Principles into Practice: Risks and Opportunities for Conflict-Free Sourcing in Eastern Congo*, London: Global Witness. Available at: https://reliefweb.int/sites/reliefweb.int/files/resources/Putting%20principles%20into%20practice.pdf.

——— (2009), *'Faced with a Gun, What Can You Do?' War and the Militarisation of Mining in Eastern Congo*, London: Global Witness. Available at: https://www.globalwitness.org/documents/17817/report_en_final_0.pdf.

BIBLIOGRAPHY

Go, Julian (2020), 'Race, empire, and epistemic exclusion: Or the structures of sociological thought', *Sociological Theory*, 38(2): 79–100.

Gobbers, Erik (2016), 'Ethnic associations in Katanga province, the Democratic Republic of Congo: Multi-tier system, shifting identities and the relativity of autochthony', *Journal of Modern African Studies*, 54(2): 211–36.

Gondola, Christian Didier (2002), *The History of Congo*, Westport, CT: Greenwood Press.

Granovetter, Mark (1985), 'Economic action and social structure: The problem of embeddedness', *American Journal of Sociology*, 91(3): 481–510.

——— (1973), 'The strength of weak ties', *American Journal of Sociology*, 78(6): 1,360–80.

Greenhouse, Carol J., Mertz, Elisabeth & Warren, Kay B. (eds) (2002), *Ethnography in Unstable Places: Everyday Lives in Contexts of Dramatic Political Change*, Durham, NC: Duke University Press.

Griffiths, John (1986), 'What is legal pluralism?', *Journal of Legal Pluralism*, 24: 1–55.

Guinier, Lani & Torres, Gerald (2003), *The Miner's Canary: Enlisting Race, Resisting Power, Transforming Democracy*, Cambridge, MA: Harvard University Press.

Gupta, Akhil (2014), 'Authorship, research assistants and the ethnographic field', *Ethnography*, 15(3): 394–400.

——— (1995), 'Blurred boundaries: The discourse of corruption, the culture of politics, and the imagined state', *American Ethnologist*, 22(2): 375–402.

Gupta, Akhil & James Ferguson (1997), *Anthropological Locations: Boundaries and Grounds*, Berkeley: University of California Press.

Hagmann, Tobias & Péclard, Didier (eds) (2011), *Negotiating Statehood: Dynamics of Power and Domination in Africa*, Oxford: Wiley-Blackwell.

Hall, Derek, Hirsch, Philipp & Li, Tania Murray (2011), *Power of Exclusion: Land Dilemmas in Southeast Asia*, Honolulu, HI: University of Hawaii Press.

Hall, Stuart (1995), 'The whites of their eyes: Racist ideologies and the media', in Dines, Gail & Humez, Jean (eds), *Gender, Race and Class in Media*, London: Sage, pp. 18–22.

BIBLIOGRAPHY

Hamilton, Rebecca (2012), 'Special report: The wonks who sold Washington on South Sudan', *Reuters*, 11 July.

Hann, Chris & Hart, Keith (2011), *Economic Anthropology: History, Ethnography, Critique*, Cambridge: Polity.

Hansen, Thomas Blom & Stepputat, Finn (2006), 'Sovereignty revisited', *Annual Review of Anthropology*, 35: 295–315.

——— (2005), *Sovereign Bodies: Citizens, Migrants, and States in the Postcolonial World*, Princeton, NJ: Princeton University Press.

Haraway, Donna (1988), 'Situated knowledges: The science question in feminism and the privilege of partial perspective', *Feminist Studies*, 14(3): 575–99.

Hart, Keith (2008), *Between Bureaucracy and the People: A Political History of Informality* (DIIS Working Paper no. 27), Copenhagen: Danish Institute for International Studies.

Harvey, David (2006), *Spaces of Global Capitalism*, London: Verso.

Hayes, Karen, et al. (2010), *PROMINES Study: Artisanal Mining in the Democratic Republic of Congo*, Washington, DC: Pact Inc..

Hazen, Jennifer (2013), *What Rebels Want: Resources and Supply Networks in Wartime*, Ithaca, NY: Cornell University Press.

——— (2010), 'Understanding gangs as armed groups', *International Review of the Red Cross*, 92(878): 369–86.

Henriet, Benoit (2021), *Colonial Impotence: Virtue and Violence in a Congolese Concession (1911–1940)*, Leiden: De Gruyter.

Hilson, Gavin (2016), 'Farming, small-scale mining and rural livelihoods in Sub-Saharan Africa: A critical overview', *Extractive Industries and Society*, 3(2): 547–63.

——— (2011), 'Artisanal mining, smallholder farming and livelihood diversification in rural sub-Saharan Africa: An introduction', *Journal of International Development*, 23(8): 1,031–41.

Hobsbawm, Eric & Ranger, Terence (1983), *The Invention of Tradition*, Cambridge: Cambridge University Press.

Hochschild, Adam (1998), *King Leopold's Ghost: A Story of Greed, Terror and Heroism in Colonial Africa*, New York: Houghton Mifflin.

Hoffman, Danny (2003), 'Frontline anthropology: Research in a time of war', *Anthropology Today*, 19: 9–12.

BIBLIOGRAPHY

Hoebeke, Hans, Chiza, Christian & Mukungilwa, Bienvenu (2022), *The Old Is Dying and the New Cannot Be Born (Yet?). Security Sector Reform in the Democratic Republic of the Congo*, Ghent: Conflict Research Group.

Hoffman, Danny & Taravalley Jr., Mohamed (2014), 'Frontline collaborations: The research relationship in unstable places', *Ethnography*, 15(3): 291–310.

Hoffmann, Kasper (2019), 'Ethnogovernmentality: The making of ethnic territories and subjects in Eastern DR Congo', *Geoforum*, 119: 251–67.

——— (2015), 'Myths set in motion: The moral economy of Mai-Mai governance', in Arjona, Ana, Kasfir, Nelson & Mampilly, Zachariah (eds), *Rebel Governance in Civil Wars*, Cambridge: Cambridge University Press, pp. 158–80.

Hoffmann, Kasper & Kirk, Tom (2013), *Public Authority and the Provision of Public Goods in Conflict-Affected and Transitioning Regions*, London: London School of Economics.

Hoffmann, Kasper & Verweijen, Judith (2019), 'Rebel rule: A governmentality perspective', *African Affairs*, 118(471): 352–74.

——— (2013), 'The strategic reversibility of stateness: Contemporary Mai-Mai militias and processes of state (un)making in South Kivu, DR Congo', unpublished paper.

Hoffmann, Kasper & Vlassenroot, Koen (2014), 'Armed groups and the exercise of public authority: The cases of the Mayi-Mayi and Raya Mutomboki in Kalehe, South Kivu', *Peacebuilding*, 2(2): 202–20.

Hoffmann, Kasper, Vlassenroot, Koen & Marchais, Gauthier (2016), 'Taxation, stateness and armed groups: Public authority and resource extraction in eastern Congo', *Development & Change*, 47(6): 1,434–56.

Hoffmann, Kasper; Vlassenroot, Koen & Mudinga, Emery (2020), 'Courses au pouvoir': The struggle over customary capital in eastern Congo', *Journal of Eastern African Studies*, 14(1): 125–44.

Hunt, Nancy Rose (2015), *A Nervous State: Violence, Remedies, and Reverie in Colonial Congo*, Durham, NC: Duke University Press.

Igoe, Joe & Brockington, Dan (2007), 'Neoliberal conservation: A brief introduction', *Conservation & Society*, 5(4): 432–49.

Iguma, Claude Wakenge (2018), '"Referees become players": Accessing coltan mines in the Eastern Democratic Republic of Congo', *Extractive Industries and Society*, 5(1): 66–72.

BIBLIOGRAPHY

———— (2017), 'Stadium coltan: Artisanal mining, reforms and social change in Eastern Democratic Republic of Congo', PhD thesis, Wageningen University, Wageningen, the Netherlands.

———— (2014), 'Réguler un vieux jeu? Acteurs et défis à la réforme minière au Nord-Katanga (RDC)', *L'Afrique des Grand Lacs: Annuaire*, 2013–2014: 223–41.

Intel (2021), 'Conflict Minerals Policy'. Available at: http://www.intel.com/content/www/us/en/policy/policy-conflict-minerals.html.

International Peace Information Service (2020), *How Much Does a Miner Earn? Assessment of Miner's Revenue & Basic Needs Study in the DRC*, Antwerp: IPIS.

———— (2019), *Mapping Artisanal Mining Areas and Mineral Supply Chains in Eastern DR Congo*, Antwerp: IPIS.

International Tin Association (formerly ITRI Ltd.) (2014), *iTSCi Democratic Republic of Congo (DRC) Data Summary Q2 2011 to Q4 2013*, London: ITRI Ltd.

International Tin Supply Chain Initiative (2021), 'Mineral tonnage data'. Available at: https://www.itsci.org/mineral-tonnage-data/.

Invisible Children (2012), 'KONY 2012', YouTube, 5 March. Available at: https://www.youtube.com/watch?v=Y4MnpzG5Sqc.

Jackson, Stephen (2007), 'Of "doubtful nationality": Political manipulation of citizenship in the D. R. Congo', *Citizenship Studies*, 11(5): 481–500.

———— (2006), 'Sons of which soil? The language and politics of autochthony in eastern DR Congo', *African Studies Review*, 49(2): 95–123.

———— (2003), *Fortunes of War: The Coltan Trade in the Kivus* (HPG Background Paper), London: ODI.

———— (2002), 'Making a killing: Criminality & coping in the Kivu war economy', *Review of African Political Economy*, 29(93/94): 517–36.

Jamar, Astrid & Chappuis, Fairlie (2016), 'Conventions of silence: Emotions and knowledge production in war-affected research environments', *Parcours anthropologiques*, 11: 95–117.

JamboRDC.info. (2018), '"Le Congo est grand et demande de nous la grandeur", Flavien Zigashane (Lucha)'. Available at: https://jambordc.info/9538/.

Jessop, Bob, Brenner, Neil & Jones, Martin (2008), 'Theorizing socio-spatial relations', *Environment & Planning D*, 26: 389–401.

BIBLIOGRAPHY

Jewsiewicki, Bogumil (1977), 'The Great Depression and the making of the colonial economic system in the Belgian Congo', *African Economic History*, 4: 153–76.

Johnson, Dominic (2013), *No Kivu, No Conflict? The Misguided Struggle against 'Conflict Minerals' in the DRC*, Goma: POLE.

Jourdan, Luca (2011), 'Mayi-Mayi: Young rebels in Kivu, DRC', *African Development*, 36(3): 89–111.

Kagumire, Rosebell (2012), 'My response to KONY2012', YouTube, 7 March. Available at: https://www.youtube.com/watch?v=KLVY5j BnD-E.

Kalyvas, Stathis (2006), *The Logic of Violence in Civil War*, Cambridge: Cambridge University Press.

Kamuntu, K. (1995), *Luhwindja et ses transactions commerciales (1908–1982)*, Bukavu: ISP.

Katz-Lavigne, Sarah & Hönke, Jana (2018), 'Cobalt isn't a conflict mineral', *Africa Is a Country*. Available at: https://africasacountry.com/2018/09/cobalt-isnt-a-conflict-mineral/.

Keen, David (2012), 'Greed and grievance in civil war', *International Affairs*, 88(4): 757–77.

——— (1998), 'The economic functions of violence in civil wars', *Adelphi Papers*, 38(320): 1–88.

Kennes, Erik (2002), 'Footnotes to the mining story', *Review of African Political Economy*, 29(93–94): 601–06.

Kennes, Erik & Larmer, Miles (2016), *The Katangese Gendarmes and War in Central Africa*, Bloomington, IN: Indiana University Press.

Kimonyo, Jean-Paul (2008), *Rwanda. Un genocide populaire*, Paris: Karthala.

Kirsch, Stuart (2014), *Mining Capitalism: The Relationship between Corporations and their Critics*, Oakland, CA: University of California Press.

Kitschelt, Herbert & Wilkinson, Steven I. (eds) (2007), *Patrons, Clients, and Policies: Patterns of Democratic Accountability and Political Competition*, New York: Cambridge University Press.

Kivu Security Tracker (2019), *Congo, Forgotten: The Numbers behind Africa's Longest Humanitarian Crisis*, New York: Center on International Cooperation, New York University.

BIBLIOGRAPHY

Kopytoff, Igor (1987), *The African Frontier: The Reproduction of Traditional African Societies*, Bloomington, IN: Indiana University Press.

Korf, Benedikt (2011), 'Resources, violence and the telluric geographies of small wars', *Progress in Human Geography*, 35(6): 733–56.

———— (2006), 'Cargo cult science, armchair empiricism and the idea of violent conflict', *Third World Quarterly*, 27(3): 459–76.

Korf, Benedikt, Engeler, Michelle & Hagmann, Tobias (2010), 'The geography of warscapes', *Third World Quarterly*, 31(3): 385–99.

Korf, Benedikt & Raeymaekers, Timothy (eds) (2013), *Violence on the Margins: States, Conflict, and Borderlands*, New York: Palgrave Macmillan.

Korf, Benedikt, Raeymaekers, Timothy, Schetter, Conrad & Watts, Michael (2018), 'Geographies of limited statehood', in Risse, Thomas, et al. (eds), *Oxford Handbook of Governance and Limited Statehood*, Oxford: Oxford University Press, pp. 167–87.

Koselleck, Reinhart & Richter, Michaela (2006), 'Crisis', *Journal of the History of Ideas*, 67(2): 357–400.

Kovats–Bernat, J. C. (2002), 'Negotiating dangerous fields: Pragmatic strategies for fieldwork amid violence and terror', *American Anthropologist*, 104(1): 208–22.

Kristof, Nicholas (2008), 'The weapon of rape', *New York Times*, 15 June. Available at: https://www.nytimes.com/2008/06/15/opinion/15kristof.html.

Kuhn, Thomas S. (1962), *The Structure of Scientific Revolutions*, Chicago, IL: University of Chicago Press.

Labonte, Melissa T. (2011), 'From patronage to peacebuilding? Elite capture and governance from below in Sierra Leone', *African Affairs*, 111(442): 90–115.

Landa, Janet (1981), 'A theory of the ethnically homogeneous middleman group: An institutional alternative to contract law', *Journal of Legal Studies*, 10(2): 349–62.

Latour, Bruno (1996), 'On actor-network theory. A few clarifications plus more than a few complications', *Soziale Welt*, 47: 1–16.

Laumann, Edward O., Galaskiewicz, Joseph & Marsden, Peter V. (1978), 'Community structure as interorganizational linkages', *Annual Review of Sociology*, 4: 455–84.

BIBLIOGRAPHY

Le Billon, Philippe (2001), 'The political ecology of war: Natural resources and armed conflict', *Political Geography*, 20: 561–84.

Lee, Nick & Brown, Steve (1994), 'Otherness and the actor-network', *American Behavioral Scientist*, 37(6): 772–90.

Lemarchand, René (2009), *The Dynamics of Violence in Central Africa*, Philadelphia, PA: Philadelphia University Press.

——— (1996), *Burundi: Ethnic Conflict and Genocide*, Cambridge: Cambridge University Press.

——— (1972), 'Political clientelism and ethnicity in tropical Africa: Competing solidarities in nation-building', *American Political Science Review*, 66(1): 68–90.

Lentz, Carola (1998), 'The chief, the mine captain and the politician: Legitimating power in northern Ghana', *Africa*, 68: 46–67.

Levi, Primo (1986), *The Drowned and the Saved*, New York: Random House.

Lewis, Chloé (2021), 'The making and re-making of the "rape capital of the world": On colonial durabilities and the politics of sexual violence statistics in DRC', *Critical African Studies*, doi: 10.1080/21681392.20 21.1902831.

Lewis, David & Mosse, David (eds) (2006), *Development Brokers and Translators: The Ethnography of Aid and Agencies*, Boulder, CO: Kumarian Press.

Li, Tania (2014), *Land's End: Capitalist Relations on an Indigenous Frontier*, Durham, NC: Duke University Press.

Lombard, Louisa (2016), *State of Rebellion: Violence and Intervention in the Central African Republic*, London: Zed Books.

——— (2012), 'Raiding sovereignty in Central African borderlands', PhD thesis, Duke University, Durham, NC.

London Metal Exchange (2021), 'LME tin'. Available at: https://www. lme.com/en-gb/metals/non-ferrous/tin/.

Luckham, Robin (2004), 'The international community and state reconstruction in war-torn societies', *Conflict, Security & Development*, 4(3): 481–507.

Lund, Christian (2016), 'Rule and rupture: State formation through the production of property and citizenship', *Development & Change*, 47(6): 1,199–228.

———— (2014a), 'Of what is this a case? Analytical movements in qualitative social science research', *Human Organization*, 73(3): 224–34.

———— (2014b), 'The ethics of fruitful misunderstanding', *Journal of Research Practice*, 10(2): 1–5.

———— (2006), 'Twilight institutions: An introduction', *Development & Change*, 37(4): 673–84.

MacGaffey, Janet (1991), *The Real Economy of Zaire: The Contribution of Smuggling and Other Unofficial Activities to National Wealth*, Philadelphia, PA: University of Pennsylvania Press.

———— (1987), *Entrepreneurs and Parasites: The Struggle for Indigenous Capitalism in Zaire*, Cambridge: Cambridge University Press.

MacKay, Joseph (2006), 'State failure, actor-network theory, and the theorisation of sovereignty', *Brussels Journal of International Studies*, 3: 61–98.

Maconachie, Roy & Hilson, Gavin (2011), 'Safeguarding livelihoods or exacerbating poverty? Artisanal mining and formalization in West Africa', *Natural Resources Forum*, 35(4): 293–303.

Malkki, Lisa (1995), *Purity and Exile: Violence, Memory, and National Cosmology among Hutu Refugees in Tanzania*, Chicago, IL: University of Chicago Press.

Mamdani, Mahmood (2012), 'Kony: What Jason did not tell the Invisible Children', *Al Jazeera*, 13 March. Available at: https://www.aljazeera.com/opinions/2012/3/13/kony-what-jason-did-not-tell-the-invisible-children.

Mampilly, Zachariah Cherian (2011), *Rebel Rulers: Insurgent Governance and Civilian Life during War*, Ithaca, NY: Cornell University Press.

Marchal, Roland & Messiant, Christine (2002), 'De l'avidité des rebelles. L'analyse économique de la guerre civile selon Paul Collier', *Critique Internationale*, 16: 58–69.

Marcus, George E. (1995), 'Ethnography in/of the world system: The emergence of multi-sited ethnography', *Annual Review of Anthropology*, 24: 95–117.

Marijnen, Esther (2018), 'Public authority and conservation in areas of armed conflict: Virunga National Park as a "state within a state" in eastern Congo', *Development & Change*, 49(3): 790–814.

Marijnen, Esther & Verweijen, Judith (2018), 'Pluralizing political forests: Unpacking "the state" by tracing Virunga's charcoal chain', *Antipode*, 52(4): 996–1,017.

——— (2016), 'Selling green militarization: The discursive (re)production of militarized conservation in the Virunga National Park, Democratic Republic of the Congo', *Geoforum*, 75: 274–85.

Massey, Doreen (1991), 'A global sense of place', *Marxism Today*, 38: 24–29.

Mathys, Gillian (2017), 'Bringing history back in: Past, present, and conflict in Rwanda and the Eastern Democratic Republic of Congo', *Journal of African History*, 58(3): 465–87.

Matthysen, Ken & Zaragoza, Andrés (2013), *'Conflict Minerals' Initiatives in DR Congo: Perceptions of Local Mining Communities*, Antwerp: International Peace Information Service.

Mazur, Lucas (2021), 'The epistemic imperialism of science: Reinvigorating early critiques of scientism', *Frontiers in Psychology*, 11: 1–12.

Mbembe, Achille (2001), *On the Postcolony*, Berkeley, CA: University of California Press.

Mbembe, Achille & Roitman, Janet (1995), 'Figures of the subject in times of crisis', *Public Culture*, 7: 323–52.

Meagher, Kate (2009), *Culture, Agency and Power: Theoretical Reflections on Informal Economic Networks and Political Process*, Copenhagen: Danish Institute for International Studies.

Meagher, Kate, de Herdt, Tom & Titeca, Kristof (2014), *Unravelling Public Authority: Paths of Hybrid Governance in Africa* (JSRP Research Brief 10), London: London School of Economics.

Mengestu, Dinaw (2012), 'Not a click away: Joseph Kony in the real world', *Warscapes*, 12 March. Available at http://www.warscapes.com/reportage/not-click-away-joseph-kony-real-world.

Mertens, Charlotte & Pardy, Maree (2017), '"Sexurity" and its effects in eastern Democratic Republic of Congo', *Third World Quarterly*, 38(4): 956–79.

Mezzadra, Sandra & Neilson, Brett (2013), *Border as Method, or, the Multiplication of Labor*, Durham, NC: Duke University Press.

Migdal, Joel (1988), *Strong Societies and Weak States: State Relations and State Capabilities in the Third World*, Princeton, NJ: Princeton University Press.

Migdal, Joel & Schlichte, Klaus (2005), 'Rethinking the state', in Schlichte, Klaus (ed.), *The Dynamics of States: The Formation and Crises of State Domination*, London: Routledge, pp. 1–41.

Mignolo, Walter and Escobar, Arturo (2010), *Globalization and the Decolonial Option*, London: Routledge.

Mihai, Mihaela (2018), 'Epistemic marginalisation and the seductive power of art', *Contemporary Political Theory*, 17(4): 395–416.

Ministère des Mines (2013), *Rapport de la Réunion d'Evaluation des Activités du programme ITSCI en RDC du 19 au 21 Septembre 2013*, Kinshasa.

Mitchell, Katharyne (2016), 'Ungoverned space: Global security and the geopolitics of broken windows', *Political Geography*, 29(5): 289–97.

Mitchell, Timothy (2002), *Rule of Experts: Egypt, Techno-Politics, Modernity*, Berkeley, CA: University of California Press.

————— (1991), 'The limits of the state: Beyond statist approaches and their critics', *American Political Science Review*, 85(1): 77–96.

Mkandawire, Thandika (2015), 'Neopatrimonialism and the political economy of economic performance in Africa: Critical reflections', *World Politics*, 67(3): 563–612.

MONUSCO (2021), 'Human rights', United Nations Organization Stabilization Mission in the DR Congo. Available at: https://monusco.unmissions.org/en/human-rights.

————— (2013), 'Civil affairs section conflict database', unpublished document.

Moore, Sally Falk (2005), 'Comparisons: Possible and impossible', *Annual Review of Anthropology*, 34: 1–11.

————— (1973), 'Law and social change: The semi-autonomous social field as an appropriate subject of study', *Law & Society Review*, 7(4): 719–46.

Mosse, David (2015), 'Misunderstood, misrepresented, contested? Anthropological knowledge production in question', *Focaal—Journal of Global and Historical Anthropology*, 72: 128–37.

Muchukiwa, Bosco (2006), *Territoires ethniques et territoires étatiques: pou-*

voirs locaux et conflits interethniques au Sud-Kivu (RD Congo), Paris: L'Harmattan.

Mudimbe, V. Y. (1994), *The Idea of Africa*, London: James Currey.

―――― (1988), *The Invention of Africa: Gnosis, Philosophy and the Order of Knowledge*, London: James Currey.

Mueller-Koné, Marie (2015), 'Débrouillardise: certifying "conflict-free" minerals in a context of regulatory pluralism in South Kivu, DR Congo', *Journal of Modern African Studies*, 53(2): 145–68.

Mugangu, Séverin (2008), 'La crise foncière à l'est de la RDC', *L'Afrique des Grands Lacs: Annuaire*, 385–414.

Muhire, Blaise (2017), 'Legal pluralism, customary authority and conflict in Masisi, (Eastern) Democratic Republic of Congo', *Journal of Sociology and Development*, 1(1): 1–21.

Musamba, Josaphat, Vogel, Christoph, Vlassenroot, Koen et al. (2022), *It Takes (More Than) Two to Tango. Armed Politics, Combatant Agency and the Half-Life of DDR Programmes in the Congo*. Ghent: Conflict Research Group.

Musamba, Josaphat & Vogel, Christoph (2016), 'Rapprochements ethno-linguistiques aux zones minières artisanales à l'est de la RD Congo', *L'Afrique des Grands Lacs: Annuaire*, 207–31.

Naipaul, V. S. (1967), *The Mimic Men*, London: Penguin.

Nathan, Laurie (2005), '"The frightful inadequacy of most of the statistics": A critique of Collier and Hoeffler on causes of civil war', *Track Two*, 12(5): 5–36.

Ndaywel è Nziem, Isidore (2009), *Nouvelle histoire du Congo. Des origines à la République Démocratique*, Brussels: Le Cri.

Nest, Michael (2011), *Coltan*, Cambridge: Polity Press.

Newbury, David (2009), *The Land Beyond the Mists: Essays on Identity and Authority in Precolonial Congo and Rwanda*, Athens, OH: Ohio University Press.

―――― (1992), *Kings and Clans: A Social History of the Lake Kivu Rift Valley*, Madison, WI: University of Wisconsin Press.

Nordstrom, Carolyn (2004), *Shadows of War: Violence, Power, and International Profiteering in the Twenty-First Century*, Berkeley, CA: University of California Press.

Nordstrom, Carolyn & Robben, Antonius (1996), *Fieldwork Under Fire:*

Contemporary Studies of Violence and Culture, Berkeley, CA: University of California Press.

Nzongola-Ntalaja, Georges (2002), *The Congo from Leopold to Kabila: A People's History*, London: Zed Books.

Oakley, David & Proctor, Pat (2012), 'Ten years of GWOT, the failure of democratization and the fallacy of "ungoverned spaces"', *Journal of Strategic Security*, 5(1): 1–14.

Observatoire Gouvernance et Paix (2010), *La place des ressources minières dans l'organisation économique des groupes armés nationaux et étrangers*, Bukavu: OGP.

Office of the United Nations High Commissioner for Human Rights (2010), *Rapport du Projet Mapping concernant les violations les plus graves des droits de l'homme et du droit international humanitaire commises entre mars 1993 et juin 2003 en RDC*, Geneva: United Nations.

Olivier de Sardan, Jean-Pierre (2015), *Epistemology, Fieldwork and Anthropology*, New York: Palgrave.

———— (2008a), *Researching the Practical Norms of Real Governance in Africa* (Discussion Paper no. 5: Africa Power and Politics Research Programme), London ODI.

———— (2008b), *La rigeur du qualitatif: Les contraintes empiriques de l'interprétation socio-anthropologique*, Louvain-la-Neuve: Bruylant-Academia.

Organisation for Economic Cooperation and Development (2016), *OECD Due Diligence Guidance for Responsible Supply Chains of Minerals from Conflict-Affected and High-Risk Areas: Third Edition*, Paris: OECD Publishing. Available at: https://www.oecd.org/daf/inv/mne/OECD-Due-Diligence-Guidance-Minerals-Edition3.pdf.

———— (2015), *Mineral Supply Chains and Conflict Links in Eastern Democratic Republic of Congo: Five Years of Implementing Supply Chain Due Diligence*, Paris: OECD.

———— (2013), *Due Diligence Guidance for Responsible Supply Chains of Minerals from Conflict-Affected and High-Risk Areas* (2nd edition), Paris: OECD.

Owenga Odinga, E. L. (2014), *Droit minier, tome 1: régime minier général pour les mines et les carrières*. Kinshasa: Publications pour la promotion du droit congolais.

Painter, Joe (2010), 'Rethinking territory', *Antipode*, 42(5): 1,090–118.

Palestine Diary (2012), 'Edward Said on Orientalism', YouTube, 28 October. Available at: https://www.youtube.com/watch?v=fVC8EYd_Z_g.

Panella, Cristiana (2010), *Worlds of Debt: Interdisciplinary Perspectives on Gold Mining in West Africa*, Amsterdam: Rozenberg.

Panella, Cristiana & Thomas, Kedron (2015), 'Ethics, evaluation, and economies of value, amidst illegal practices', *Critique of Anthropology*, 35(1): 3–12.

Parker, Dominic & Vadheim, Bryan (2017), 'Resource cursed or policy cursed? US regulation of conflict minerals and violence in the Congo', *Association of Environmental and Resource Economists*, 4(1): 1–49.

Peck, Jamie & Theodore, Nic (2010), 'Mobilizing policy: Models, methods, mutations', *Geoforum*, 41: 169–74.

Peluso, Nancy & Lund, Christian (2011), 'New frontiers of land control: Introduction', *Journal of Peasant Studies*, 38(4): 667–81.

Pereira, Godofredo (2015), 'The underground frontier', *Continent*, 4(4): 4–11.

Peters, Krijn (2011), *War and the Crisis of Youth in Sierra Leone*, Cambridge: Cambridge University Press.

Philipps, Nicola (2011), 'Informality, global production networks and the dynamics of "adverse incorporation"', *Global Networks*, 11(3): 380–97.

Platteau, Jean-Philippe (2004), 'Monitoring elite capture in community-driven development', *Development & Change*, 35(2): 223–46.

Platteau, Jean-Philippe, Somville, Vincent & Wahhaj, Zaki (2014), 'Elite capture through information distortion: A theoretical essay', *Journal of Development Economics*, 106: 227–50.

Polanyi, Karl (2001), *The Great Transformation: The Political and Economic Origins of Our Time*, Boston, MA: Beacon.

Pole Institute (2001), *The Coltan Phenomenon*, Goma: POLE Institute.

Porter, Holly (2017), *After Rape: Violence, Justice, and Social Harmony in Uganda*, Cambridge: Cambridge University Press.

Pottier, Johan (2006), 'Roadblock ethnography: Negotiating humanitarian access in Ituri, Eastern DR Congo, 1999–2004', *Africa*, 76(2): 151–79.

Prunier, Gérard (2009), *From Genocide to Continental War*, London: Hurst.

BIBLIOGRAPHY

———— (1995), *The Rwanda Crisis: History of a Genocide*, Kampala: Fountain.

Rabinow, Paul & Sullivan, William (1988), *Interpretive Social Science: A Second Look*, Oakland, CA: University of California Press.

Radley, Ben (2019), 'Mining industrialisation in the African periphery: Disruption and dependency in South Kivu, DRC', PhD thesis, University of the Hague, the Netherlands.

———— (2016), 'The limits of mining sector corporate social responsibility and the possibilities for harnessing mining to reinstitute processes of state-led local development in the DRC', *L'Afrique des Grand Lacs: Annuaire*, 169–86.

Radley, Ben & Vogel, Christoph (2015), 'Fighting windmills in eastern Congo? The ambiguous impact of the "conflict minerals" movement', *Extractive Industries and Society*, 2(3): 406–10.

Raeymaekers, Timothy (2014), *Violent Capitalism and Hybrid Identity in the Eastern Congo: Power to the Margins*, Cambridge: Cambridge University Press.

———— (2013), 'Post-war conflict and the market for protection: The challenges to Congo's hybrid peace', *International Peacekeeping*, 20(5): 600–17.

———— (2012), 'Reshaping the state in its margins. The state, the market and the subaltern on a Central African frontier', *Critique of Anthropology*, 32(3): 334–50.

———— (2010), 'Protection for sale? War and the transformation of regulation on the Congo-Ugandan border', *Development and Change*, 41(4): 563–87.

———— (2009), 'The silent encroachment of the frontier: A politics of transborder trade in the Semliki Valley (Congo–Uganda)', *Political Geography*, 28(1): 55–65.

———— (2007), 'Sharing the spoils: The reinvigoration of Congo's political system', *Politorbis*, 42: 23–29.

———— (2002), *Network War: An Introduction to Congo's Privatised War Economy*, Antwerp: IPIS.

Raeymaekers, Timothy, Menkhaus, Ken & Vlassenroot, Koen (2008), 'State and non-state regulation in African protracted crises: Governance without government?', *Afrika Focus*, 21(2): 7–21.

Rasmussen, Matthias & Lund, Christian (2018), 'Reconfiguring frontier spaces: The territorialisation of resource control', *World Development*, 101: 388–99.

Reimers, Lucy (2014), 'Natural resource exploitation in the Democratic Republic of Congo. A genealogy of the narrative of illegality', MA thesis, IHEID, Geneva, Switzerland.

Reno, William (2006), 'Congo: From state collapse to "absolutism", to state failure', *Third World Quarterly*, 27(1): 43–56.

———— (1998), *Warlord Politics in African States*, Boulder, CO: Lynne Rienner.

République Démocratique du Congo (2017), 'Projet de loi modifiant et complétant le code minier de 2002'. Available at: https://congomines.org/reports/1411-projet-de-loi-modifiant-et-completant-le-code-minier-de-2002.

———— (2003), 'Reglement Minier RDC 2003'. Available at: http://congomines.org/reports/100-reglement-minier-rdc-2003.

———— (2002), 'Code Minier RDC 2002'. Available at: https://congomines.org/reports/101-code-minier-rdc-2002.

Resolve (2021), 'Conflict free tin initiative (CFTI)'. Available at: http://solutions-network.org/site-cfti/.

Reyntjens, Filip (2010), *The Great African War: Congo and Regional Geopolitics, 1996–2006*, Cambridge: Cambridge University Press.

Ribot, Jesse (1998), 'Theorizing access: Forest profits along Senegal's charcoal commodity chain', *Development & Change*, 29: 307–41.

Ribot, Jesse & Peluso, Nancy Lee (2003), 'A theory of access', *Rural Sociology*, 68(2): 153–81.

Richards, Paul (2005), *No Peace, No War: An Anthropology of Contemporary Armed Conflicts*, London: James Currey.

Roberts, Greg (2016), 'America's war on "ungoverned" space in Afghanistan', *SAIS Review of International Affairs*, 36(1): 97–107.

Rodney, Walter (1972), *How Europe Underdeveloped Africa*, Washington, DC: Howard University Press.

Roitman, Janet (2016), 'The stakes of crisis', in Kjaer, Poul F. & Olsen, Niklas (eds), *Critical Theories of Crisis in Europe*, London: Rowman & Littlefield, pp. 17–34.

———— (2005), *Fiscal Disobedience: An Anthropology of Economic Regulation in Central Africa*, Princeton, NJ: Princeton University Press.

———— (1990), 'The politics of informal markets in sub-Saharan Africa', *Journal of Modern African Studies*, 28(4): 671–96.

Rose, Gillian (1997), 'Situating knowledges: Positionality, reflexivities and other tactics', *Progress in Human Geography*, 21(3): 305–20.

Ross, Michael (2004), 'How do natural resources influence civil war? Evidence from thirteen cases', *International Organization*, 58(1): 35–67.

Rothenberg, Daniel (2014), *'Everything Is There in the Tunnels': Selected Oral Histories from the Artisanal Mining Industry in North and South Kivu*, Phoenix, AZ: Arizona State University.

Rothenberg, Daniel & Radley, Ben (2014), *The Lived Experience of Human Rights and Labor Violations in Select Artisanal Mining Sites in North and South Kivu*, Phoenix, AZ: Arizona State University.

Rubbers, Benjamin (2007), 'Retour sur le "secteur informel". L'économie du Katanga (Congo-Zaïre) face à la falsification de la loi', *Sociologie du travail*, 49: 316–29.

Sahlins, Marshall (1963), 'Poor man, rich man, big-man, chief: Political types in Melanesia and Polynesia', *Comparative Studies in Society and History*, 5(3): 285–303.

Said, Edward (1984), 'Permission to narrate', *London Review of Books*, 6(3). Available at: https://www.lrb.co.uk/the-paper/v06/n03/edward-said/permission-to-narrate.

———— (1979), *Orientalism*, London: Penguin.

Salter, Thomas & Mthembu-Salter, Gregory (2017), *A response to 'Terr(it) or(ies) of Peace? The Congolese Mining Frontier and the Fight against "Conflict Minerals"'* (Suluhu Working Paper no. 2). Available at: www.suluhu.org.

Sambanis, Nicholas (2004), 'Using case studies to expand economic models of civil war', *Perspectives on Politics*, 2(2): 259–79.

Sanchez de la Sierra, Raul (2020), 'On the origins of the state: Stationary bandits and taxation in eastern Congo', *Journal of Political Economy*, 128(1): 32–74.

Schatzberg, Michael (1988), *The Dialectics of Oppression in Zaire*, Bloomington, IN: Indiana University Press.

BIBLIOGRAPHY

Scheper-Hughes, Nancy (1995), 'The primacy of the ethical: Propositions for a militant anthropology', *Current Anthropology*, 36(3): 409–40 (including comment section of the issue).

Schiltz, Julie & Büscher, Karen (2018), 'Brokering research with war-affected people: The tense relationship between opportunities and ethics', *Ethnography*, 19(1): 124–46.

Schomerus, Mareike (2015), '"Make him famous": The single conflict narrative of Kony and Kony2012', in De Waal, Alex (ed.), *Advocacy in Conflict*, London, Zed Books, pp. 142–63.

Schouten, Peer (2016), *Extractive Orders: A Political Geography of Public Authority in Ituri, DR Congo* (Justice and Security Research Programme Paper 30), London: London School of Economics.

Schouten, Peer, Murairi, Janvier & Kubuya, Saidi (2017), *'Everything that Moves Will Be Taxed': The Political Economy of Roadblocks in North and South Kivu*, Antwerp: International Peace Information Service.

Scott, James (2009), *The Art of Not Being Governed: An Anarchist History of Upland Southeast Asia*, New Haven, CT: Yale University Press.

————— (1998), *Seeing Like a State: How Certain Schemes to Improve the Human Condition Have Failed*, New Haven, CT: Yale University Press.

————— (1987), *Weapons of the Weak: Everyday Forms of Peasant Resistance*, New Haven, CT: Yale University Press.

————— (1972), 'Patron-client politics and political change in southeast Asia', *American Political Science Review*, 66(1): 91–113.

Seay, Laura (2012), *What's Wrong with Dodd-Frank 1502? Conflict Minerals, Civilian Livelihoods, and the Unintended Consequences of Western Advocacy*, Washington, DC: Center for Global Development.

Securities and Exchange Commission (2012), 'Conflict minerals' (Release No. 34-67716; File No. S7-40-10), Washington, DC: Securities and Exchange Commission.

Sematumba, Onésphore (2011), *DRC: The Mineral Curse* (Regards Croisés no. 30 bis), Goma: POLE.

Shringarpure, Bhakti (2020), 'Africa and the digital savior complex', *Journal of African Cultural Studies*, 32(2): 178–94.

Siegel, Shefa & Veiga, Marcello (2009), 'Artisanal and small-scale mining as an extra-legal economy: De Soto and the redefinition of "formalization"', *Resources Policy*, 34(1/2): 51–56.

BIBLIOGRAPHY

Sikor, Thomas & Lund, Christian (2009), *The Politics of Possession: Property, Authority and Access to Natural Resources*, Oxford: Wiley-Blackwell.

Smith, James (2015), '"May it never end": Price wars, networks, and temporality in the "3Ts" mining trade of the Eastern DR Congo', *HAU: Journal of Ethnographic Theory*, 5(1): 1–34.

——— (2011), 'Tantalus in the digital age: Coltan ore, temporal dispossession, and "movement" in the Eastern Democratic Republic of the Congo', *American Ethnologist*, 38(1): 17–35.

Spittaels, Steven (2010), *The Complexity of Resource Governance in a Context of State Fragility: An Analysis of the Mining Sector in the Kivu Hinterlands*, Antwerp: International Peace Information Service.

Spittaels Steven, Matthysen, Ken & Bulzomi, Ann (2014), *Analysis of the Interactive Map of Artisanal Mining Areas in Eastern DR Congo: May 2014 Update*, Antwerp: International Peace Information Service.

Spivak, Gayatri Chakravorty (1988), 'Can the subaltern speak?' in Nelson, Cary & Grossberg, Lawrence (eds), *Marxism and the Interpretation of Culture*, Urbana & Chicago, IL: University of Illinois Press, pp. 271–313.

Stearns, Jason (2014), 'Causality and conflict: Tracing the origins of armed groups in the eastern Congo', *Peacebuilding*, 2(2): 157–71.

——— (2013), *PARECO: Land, Local Strongmen, and the Roots of Militia Politics in North Kivu*, London: Rift Valley Institute.

——— (2012a), *North Kivu: The Background to Conflict in North Kivu Province of Eastern Congo*, London: Rift Valley Institute.

——— (2012b), *From CNDP to M23: The Evolution of an Armed Movement in Eastern Congo*, London: Rift Valley Institute.

——— (2010), *Dancing in the Glory of Monsters: The Collapse of the Congo and the Great African War*, New York: Public Affairs.

Stearns, Jason & Hege, Steve (2010), *Independent Oversight for Mining in the Eastern Congo? A Proposal for a Third-Party Monitoring & Enforcement Mechanism*, New York: New York University.

Stearns, Jason, Verweijen, Judith & Eriksson Baaz, Maria (2013), *The National Army and Armed Groups in the Eastern Congo: Untangling the Gordian Knot of Insecurity*, London: Rift Valley Institute.

BIBLIOGRAPHY

Stearns, Jason & Vogel, Christoph (2017), *The Landscape of Armed Groups in the Eastern Congo: Fragmented, Politicized Networks*, New York: Congo Research Group & Kivu Security Tracker.

——— (2015), *The Landscape of Armed Groups in the Eastern Congo*, New York: Congo Research Group, New York University.

Stearns, Jason, et al. (2013a), *Raia Mutomboki: The Flawed Peace Process in the DRC and the Birth of an Armed Franchise*, London: Rift Valley Institute.

——— (2013b), *Banyamulenge: Insurgency and Exclusion in the Mountains of South Kivu*, London: Rift Valley Institute.

——— (2013c), *Mai-Mai Yakutumba: Resistance and Racketeering in Fizi, South Kivu*, London: Rift Valley Institute.

Stewart, Frances (2008), *Horizontal Inequalities and Conflict: Understanding Group Violence in Multi-Ethnic Societies*, New York: Palgrave Macmillan.

Stoinski, Tara (2017), 'Mining for conflict minerals is driving gorillas to extinction', *Gorilla Fund*, 2 May. Available at: https://gorillafund.org/mining-conflict-minerals-driving-gorillas-extinction/.

Strange, Susan (1996), *The Retreat of the State: The Diffusion of Power in the World Economy*, Cambridge: Cambridge University Press.

Strazzari, Francesco & Kamphuis, Bertine (2012), 'Hybrid economies and statebuilding: On the resilience of the extra-legal', *Global Governance*, 18: 57–72.

Stys, Patricja, et al. (2020), 'Brokering between (not so) overt and (not so) covert networks in conflict zones', *Global Crime*, 21(1): 74–110.

Sungura, Amir, Kitonga, Limbo, van Soest, Bernard & Ndakasi, Ndeze (2020a), *Violence and Instability in Ituri: Djugu's Mystic Crisis and the Camouflage of Ethnic Conflict*, Ghent: Conflict Research Group.

Sungura, Amir, Mbamba, Murenzi & Kitonga, Limbo (2020b), *Proxy Wars and the Dawn of Godfathers: Reshaping Violent Orders in Bashali and Bwito (North Kivu)*, Ghent: Conflict Research Group.

Sungura, Amir, van Soest, Bernard & Kitonga, Limbo (2019), *Reigniting Ituri? Towards a Preliminary Reading of the 2018 Djugu Violence*, Utrecht: Pax for Peace.

Sungura, Amir, et al. (2021), *The Past is the Present: Change and Continuity in the Politics of Conflict in Nord-Kivu*, Ghent: Conflict Research Group.

Sweet, Rachel (2020), 'Bureaucrats at war: The resilient state in the Congo', *African Affairs*, 119(475): 224–50.

Swyngedouw, Eric (1997), 'Neither global nor local—"glocalization" and the politics of scale', in Cox, Kevin (ed.), *Spaces of Globalization: Reasserting the Power of the Local*, New York: The Guilford Press, pp. 136–67.

Tamm, Henning (2019), 'Status competition in Africa: Explaining the Rwandan–Ugandan clashes in the Democratic Republic of Congo', *African Affairs*, 118(472): 509–30.

Tantalum and Niobium International Study Centre (2017), 'iTSCi in focus: lifting the lid on finances', *TIC Bulletin*, 170.

Taussig, Michael (1997), *The Magic of the State*, New York: Routledge.

———— (1980), *The Devil and Commodity Fetishism in South America*, Chapel Hill, NC: University of North Carolina Press.

Taylor, Peter T. (1994), 'The state as container: territoriality in the modern world-system', *Progress in Human Geography*, 18(2): 151–62.

Tegera, Aloys (2009), 'Les Banyarwanda du Nord-Kivu (RDC) au 20ième siècle. Analyse historique et socio-politique d'un groupe transfrontalier (1885–2006)', PhD thesis, Université Panthéon-Sorbonne Paris, Paris, France.

Themnér, Anders & Utas, Mats (2016), 'Governance through brokerage: Informal governance in post-civil war societies', *Civil Wars*, 18(3): 255–80.

Thiong'o, Ngũgĩ wa (1987), 'Decolonizing the mind (short version)', *Diogenes*, 184(46): 101–05.

Tidey, Sylvia (2013), 'Corruption and adherence to rules in the construction sector: Reading the "bidding books"', *American Anthropologist*, 115: 188–202.

Tilly, Charles (1985), 'War making and state making as organized crime', in Evans, Peter, Rueschemeyer, Dietrich & Skocpol, Theda (eds), *Bringing the State Back In*, Cambridge: Cambridge University Press, pp. 169–91.

Titeca, Kristof & de Herdt, Tom (2011), 'Real governance beyond the "failed state": Negotiating education in the Democratic Republic of the Congo', *African Affairs*, 110(439): 213–31.

Tréfon, Théodore (2004), *Reinventing Order in the Congo: How People Respond to State Failure in Kinshasa*, London: Zed Books.

BIBLIOGRAPHY

Tsing, Anna Lowenhaupt (2004), *Friction: An Ethnography of Global Connection*, Princeton, NJ: Princeton University Press.

Tull, Denis & Mehler, Andreas (2005), 'The hidden costs of power-sharing: Reproducing insurgent violence in Africa', *African Affairs*, 104(416): 375–98.

Turner, Thomas & Young, Crawford (1985), *The Rise and Decline of the Zairian State*, Madison, WI: University of Wisconsin Press.

Uberti, Luca J. (2016), 'Can institutional reforms reduce corruption? Economic theory and patron–client politics in developing countries', *Development & Change*, 47(2): 317–45.

United Nations (2017), *Final Report of the Group of Experts on the Democratic Republic of the Congo (S/2017/672.Rev1)*, New York: United Nations.

———— (2016a), *Final Report of the Group of Experts on the Democratic Republic of the Congo (S/2016/466)*, New York: United Nations.

———— (2016b), *Midterm Report of the Group of Experts on the Democratic Republic of the Congo (S/2016/1102)*, New York: United Nations.

———— (2015a), *Final Report of the Group of Experts on the Democratic Republic of the Congo (S/2015/19)*, New York: United Nations.

———— (2015b), *Midterm Report of the Group of Experts on the Democratic Republic of the Congo (S/2015/797)*, New York: United Nations.

———— (2011), *Final Report of the Group of Experts on the Democratic Republic of the Congo (S/2011/738)*, New York: United Nations.

———— (2010a), *Due Diligence Guidelines of the UN Group of Experts on the Democratic Republic of the Congo*, New York: United Nations.

———— (2010b), *Final Report of the Group of Experts on the Democratic Republic of the Congo (S/2010/596)*, New York: United Nations.

———— (2009a), *Final Report of the Group of Experts on the Democratic Republic of the Congo (S/2009/603)*, New York: United Nations.

———— (2009b), *Due Diligence Guidelines for the Responsible Supply Chain of Minerals from Red Flag Locations to Mitigate the Risk of Providing Direct or Indirect Support for Conflict in the Eastern Part of the Democratic Republic of the Congo*, New York: United Nations. Available at: https://www.un.org/securitycouncil/sites/www.un.org.securitycouncil/files/due_diligence_guidelines.pdf.

———— (2001), *Final Report of the Panel of Experts on Illegal Exploitation of Natural Resources and Other Forms of Wealth of the Democratic Republic of Congo (S/2001/357)*, New York: United Nations.

US Congress (2010), *Dodd-Frank Wall Street Reform and Consumer Protection Act* (Public Law 111–203), Washington, DC: United States Congress.

Utas, Mats (ed.) (2012), *African Conflicts and Informal Power: Big Men and Networks*, London: Zed Books.

Vansina, Jan (1990), *Paths in the Rainforests*, Madison, WI: University of Wisconsin Press.

———— (1966), *Kingdoms of the Savanna*, Madison, WI: University of Wisconsin Press.

Verbruggen, Didier, Francq, Evie & Cuvelier, Jeroen (2011), *Guide to Current Mining Reform Initiatives in Eastern DRC*, Antwerp: International Peace Information Service.

Verhaegen, Benoit (1969), *Rebellions au Congo. Tome 2*, Brussels: CRISP.

———— (1966), *Rebellions au Congo. Tome 1*, Brussels: CRISP.

Verweijen, Judith (2018), 'Soldiers without an army? Patronage networks and cohesion in the armed forces of the DR Congo', *Armed Forces & Society*, 44(4): 626–46.

———— (2016), *A Microcosm of Militarization: Conflict, Governance, and Armed Mobilization in Uvira, South Kivu*, London: Rift Valley Institute.

———— (2015a), 'The ambiguity of militarization: The complex interaction between the Congolese armed forces and civilians in the Kivu Provinces, Eastern DR Congo', PhD thesis, Utrecht University, Utrecht, the Netherlands.

———— (2015b), 'Coping with the barbarian syndrome: Studying everyday civilian-military interaction from below in eastern DR Congo', in Nakray, Keerty, Alston, Margaret & Whittenbury, Kerri (eds), *Social Science Research Ethics for a Globalizing World*, New York: Routledge, pp. 243–58.

———— (2013), 'Military business and the business of the military in the Kivus', *Review of African Political Economy*, 40(135): 67–82.

Verweijen, Judith, Dunia, Oscar, Twaibu, Juvénal & Ndisanze, Alexis (2020), *The Ruzizi Plain: A Crossroads of Violence and Conflict*, Ghent: Conflict Research Group.

BIBLIOGRAPHY

Verweijen, Judith & Iguma, Claude Wakenge (2015), *Understanding Armed Group Proliferation in the Eastern Congo*, London: Rift Valley Institute.

Verweijen, Judith & van Bockhaven, Vicky (2020), 'Revisiting colonial legacies in knowledge production on customary authority in Central and East Africa', *Journal of Eastern African Studies*, 14(1): 1–23.

Verweijen, Judith & van Meeteren, Michiel (2015), 'Security alliances and the territorialisation of state authority in the post-Cold War Great Lakes Region', *Territory, Politics, Governance*, 3(1): 97–111.

Verweijen, Judith, et al. (2021), *Mayhem in the Mountains: How Violent Conflict on the Hauts Plateaux of South Kivu Escalated*, Ghent: Conflict Research Group.

Vigh, Henrik (2009), 'Motion squared: A second look at the concept of social navigation', *Anthropological Theory*, 9(4): 419–38.

——— (2008), 'Crisis and chronicity: Anthropological perspectives on continuous conflict and decline', *Ethnos*, 73(1): 5–24.

Vlassenroot, Koen (2013), *South Kivu: Identity, Territory, and Power in the Eastern Congo*, London: Rift Valley Institute.

——— (2006), 'War and social research: The limits of empirical methodologies in war-torn environments', *Civilisations*, 54: 191–98.

Vlassenroot, Koen, Mudinga, Emery & Hoffmann, Kasper (2016), *Contesting Authority: Armed Rebellion and Military Fragmentation in Walikale and Kalehe, North and South Kivu*, London: Rift Valley Institute.

Vlassenroot, Koen, Mudinga, Emery & Musamba, Josaphat (2020), 'Navigating social spaces: Armed mobilization and circular return in eastern DR Congo', *Journal of Refugee Studies*, 33(4): 832–52.

Vlassenroot, Koen & Raeymaekers, Timothy (2009), 'Kivu's intractable security conundrum', *African Affairs*, 108(432): 475–84.

——— (2005), '"Divisez par deux": Conflict and artisanal mining in Kamituga (South Kivu)', *L'Afrique des Grands Lacs: Annuaire*, 2004/2005: 200–34.

——— (2004a), *Conflict and Social Transformation in Eastern DR Congo*, Ghent: Academia Press.

——— (2004b), 'The politics of rebellion and intervention in Ituri: The emergence of a new political complex?' *African Affairs*, 103(412): 385–412.

Vogel, Christoph (2021a), 'The politics of "*incontournables*": Entrenching patronage networks in eastern Congo's changing mineral markets', *Review of African Political Economy*, 48(168): 178–95.

———— (2021b), 'Colonial frameworks: Networks of political and economic order', *The Elephant*, 15 May. Available at: https://www.theelephant.info/ideas/2021/05/15/colonial-frameworks-networks-of-political-and-economic-order/.

———— (2018), 'Between tags & guns: Fragmentations of public authority in eastern DRC's 3T mines', *Political Geography*, 63: 94–103.

———— (2014), 'Contested statehood, security dilemmas and militia politics: The rise and transformation of Raia Mutomboki in eastern DRC', *L'Afrique des Grand Lacs: Annuaire*, 2013–2014: 307–32.

———— (2013), 'The heart of brightness', christophvogel.net. Available at: https://suluhu.org/2013/06/15/the-heart-of-brightness/.

———— (2012), *Operational Stalemate or Politically Induced Failure? On the Dynamics Influencing Humanitarian Aid in the Democratic Republic of the Congo*, Marburg: Tectum.

Vogel, Christoph & Musamba, Josaphat (2022), 'Towards a politics of collaborative worldmaking: ethics, epistemologies and mutual positionalities in conflict research', *Ethnography*, doi: 10.1177/14661381221090895.

———— (2017), 'Brokers of crisis: The everyday uncertainty of eastern Congo's mineral *négociants*', *Journal of Modern African Studies*, 55(4): 567–92.

———— (2016), *Recycling Rebels? Demobilization in the Congo*, London: Rift Valley Institute.

Vogel, Christoph, Musamba, Josaphat & Radley, Ben (2018), 'A miner's canary: Formalisation of artisanal 3T mining and precarious livelihoods in South Kivu', *Extractive Industries and Society*, 5(1): 73–80.

Vogel, Christoph & Raeymaekers, Timothy (2016), 'Terr(it)or(ies) of peace: The Congolese mining frontier and the fight against "conflict minerals"', *Antipode*, 48(4): 1,102–21.

Vogel, Christoph & Stearns, Jason (2018), 'Kivu's intractable security conundrum, revisited', *African Affairs*, 117(469): 695–707.

Vogel, Christoph, et al. (2021), *The Landscape of Armed Groups in Eastern*

BIBLIOGRAPHY

Congo: Missed Opportunities, Protracted Insecurity and Self-Fulfilling Prophecies, New York: Kivu Security Tracker.

Vwakyanakazi, Mukoya (1992), 'Creuseurs d'or et crise socio-économique au Nord-Kivu en République du Zaire', *Africa: Rivista trimestrale di studi e documentazione dell'IsIAO*, 47(3): 375–91.

Wacquant, Loïc (2012), 'Three steps to a historical anthropology of actually existing neoliberalism', *Social Anthropology*, 20(1): 66–79.

Wai, Zubairu (2012), 'Neo-patrimonialism and the discourse of state failure in Africa', *Review of African Political Economy*, 39(131): 27–43.

Watts, Michael (2003), 'Development & governmentality', *Singapore Journal of Tropical Geography*, 24(1): 6–34.

Weber, Max (1980 [1922]), *Wirtschaft und Gesellschaft. Grundriss der verstehenden Soziologie*, Tübingen: Mohr.

Welker, Marine (2014), *Enacting the Corporation: An American Mining Firm in Post-Authoritarian Indonesia*, Berkeley, CA: University of California Press.

Wendt, Alexander (1999), *Social Theory of International Relations*, New York: Cambridge University Press.

Werner, Marion & Bair, Jennifer (2011), 'Commodity chains and the uneven geographies of global capitalism: A disarticulations perspective', *Environment and Planning A*, 43(5): 988–97.

Willame, Jean-Claude (1997), *Banyarwanda et Banyamulenge. Violences ethniques et gestion de l'identitaire au Kivu* (Cahiers Africains 25), Paris: L'Harmattan.

Wolfe, Sven & Müller, Martin (2018), 'Crisis neopatrimonialism: Russia's new political economy and the 2018 World Cup', *Problems of Post-Communism*, 65(2): 101–14.

Wood, Elizabeth (2006), 'The ethical challenges of field research in conflict zones', *Qualitative Sociology*, 29: 373–86.

Xiang, Biao (2012), 'Predatory princes and princely peddlers: The state and international labour migration intermediaries in China', *Pacific Affairs*, 85(1): 47–68.

Young, Crawford (1967), *Politics in Congo: Decolonization and Independence*, Princeton, NJ: Princeton University Press.

Yu, Chunhua (2020), 'Rising scholar: An examination of the institutionally oppressive white savior complex in Uganda through Western documentaries', *International Social Science Review*, 97(2): 1–28.

Zingg, Sarah & Hilgert, Filip (2011), *Bisie: A One-Year Snapshot of the DRC's Principal Cassiterite Mine*, Antwerp: International Peace Information Service.

INDEX

INDEX

INDEX

INDEX

INDEX

INDEX

INDEX

INDEX

INDEX

INDEX

Development (USAID), 94–5, 227*n*5
US Securities and Exchange Commission (SEC), 93, 96–7
Uvira, 21, 64, 192

Validation, 99
Verweijen, Judith, 155
Vietnam, 69
Vigh, Henrik, 137–8
Virunga National Park, 89–90, 204–5

Walikale, 54, 64, 101, 195
Wall Street Reform and Consumer Protection Act. *See* Dodd–Frank Act (Section 1502)
Walungu territory, 166
'war economy', 138, 140
Watts, Michael, 138
Weber, Max, 12–13
Weberian ideal-types, 15
West African wars (1990), 3
Western 'conflict minerals' advocacy, 184
Western campaigning, 19

Western consumer ethics, 11
Western consumers, 1–2, 21, 89, 110, 210–11
Western governments, 155
white saviourism, 11, 16–18, 104
'white saviours', 1–2
wolfram ($_{74}$W), 69
wolframite ore, 69
World Bank, 87, 208
World Health Organization (WHO), 197
World War II, 5, 24
Wright, Robin, 16

xenophobia, 55

Yakotumba, Amuri, 55
Yira community, 83
YouTube, 201
Yumbi violence (2018), 64

Zaire. *See* Democratic Republic of the Congo
Zairianisation policies (1973), 139
ZEAs. *See* dedicated artisanal mining areas (ZEAs)